Essentials

of WJ III® Tests of Achievement Assessment

Nancy Mather, Barbara J. Wendling, and Richard W. Woodcock

 John Wiley & Sons, Inc.

NEW YORK • CHICHESTER • WEINHEIM • BRISBANE • SINGAPORE • TORONTO

Library of Congress Cataloging-in-Publication Data:
Mather, Nancy.
    Essentials of WJ III tests of achievement assessment / Nancy Mather, Barbara J. Wendling, Richard W. Woodcock.
        p. cm. — (Essentials of psychological assessment series)
    Includes bibliographical references and index.
    ISBN 0-471-33059-0 (cloth : alk. paper)
        1. Woodcock-Johnson Psycho-Educational Battery.   I. Title: Essentials of WJ 3 tests of achievement assessment.   II. Title: Essentials of WJ three tests of achievement assessment.   III. Wendling, Barbara J.   IV. Woodcock, Richard W.   V. Title.   VI. Series.

LB1131.75.W66 M37 2001
153.9'3—dc21
                                                                        2001026192

Printed in the United States of America.

CONTENTS

SERIES PREFACE

I n the *Essentials of Psychological Assessment* series, we have attempted to provide the reader with books that will deliver key practical information in the most efficient and accessible style. The series features instruments in a variety of domains, such as cognition, personality, education, and neuropsychology. For the experienced clinician, books in the series will offer a concise yet thorough way to master utilization of the continuously evolving supply of new and revised instruments as well as a convenient method for keeping up to date on the tried-and-true measures. The novice will find here a prioritized assembly of all the information and techniques that must be at one's fingertips to begin the complicated process of individual psychological diagnosis.

Wherever feasible, visual shortcuts to highlight key points are utilized alongside systematic, step-by-step guidelines. Chapters are focused and succinct. Topics are targeted for an easy understanding of the essentials of administration, scoring, interpretation, and clinical application. Theory and research are continually woven into the fabric of each book, but always to enhance clinical inference, never to sidetrack or overwhelm. We have long been advocates of "intelligent" testing—the notion that a profile of test scores is meaningless unless it is brought to life by the clinical observations and astute detective work of knowledgeable examiners. Test profiles must be used to make a difference in the child's or adult's life, or why bother to test? We want this series to help our readers become the best intelligent testers they can be.

The *Essentials of WJ III® Tests of Achievement Assessment* is designed to be a helpful reference to all examiners, whether they are experienced with the WJ-R or just learning the WJ III. The authors have incorporated fine points of administration, scoring, and interpretation to assist examiners in building their competency with the WJ III ACH. The authors weave expert guidance throughout to help the reader avoid common examiner errors. The Appendix includes answers to frequently asked questions.

Too often, the focus of testing is on getting a score or establishing a numeric discrepancy. Much more information can be derived from an achievement test than just a score. In this book, the authors have attempted to provide access to the rich, interpretive information available when using the WJ III ACH.

Alan S. Kaufman, PhD, and Nadeen L. Kaufman, EdD, Series Editors
Yale University School of Medicine

One

OVERVIEW

Although many standardized instruments exist for measuring academic performance, the Woodcock-Johnson Tests of Achievement (WJ ACH) is often cited as one of the most widely used and respected individual achievement tests since its original publication in 1977 (Gregory, 1996). The latest revision, the Woodcock-Johnson III® Tests of Achievement (WJ III ACH) (Woodcock, McGrew, & Mather, 2001b), provides examiners with an even more comprehensive and useful instrument. The WJ III ACH is a companion instrument to the Woodcock-Johnson III Tests of Cognitive Abilities (WJ III COG). These two instruments form the Woodcock-Johnson III (WJ III), a comprehensive battery of individually administered tests designed to measure general intellectual ability, specific cognitive abilities, oral language abilities, and achievement. Depending on the purpose of the assessment, these instruments may be used independently, in conjunction with each other, or with other assessment instruments.

The *Essentials of WJ III® Tests of Achievement Assessment* provides an easy-to-use guide and reference for professionals and practitioners who wish to learn the key features of this instrument. This guide is appropriate for a wide array of professionals, whether their goal is to learn how to administer the test or simply to increase familiarity with the instrument. The topics covered include administration, scoring, interpretation, and application of the WJ III ACH. All chapters include "Rapid Reference," "Caution," and "Don't Forget" boxes that highlight important points. At the end of each chapter is a "Test Yourself" section designed to help examiners review and reinforce the key information presented. These features make the guide an ideal resource for both in-service and graduate training in the application and interpretation of the WJ III ACH. Examiners may wish to read the book from cover to cover or turn to individual chapters to find specific information.

≡Rapid Reference 1.1

Woodcock-Johnson III Tests of Achievement

Authors: Richard W. Woodcock, Kevin S. McGrew, and Nancy Mather

Publication Date: 2001

What the Test Measures: oral language, reading, written language, mathematics, and academic knowledge

Age Range: 2 to 95+ years

Grade Range: K.0 through 18.0

Administration Time: Standard Battery–60 to 75 minutes; with Extended Battery approximately 90 minutes; selective testing–5 to 10 minutes per test

Qualifications of Examiners: Undergraduate, graduate, or professional-level training and background in test administration and interpretation

Publisher: The Riverside Publishing Company
425 Spring Lake Drive
Itasca, IL 60143
Customer Service: 800.323.9540
Fax: 630.467.7192
www.riversidepublishing.com

Prices: WJ III ACH complete test price without case $425.00
(as of January 2001)

A companion book in this series, *Essentials of WJ III® Tests of Cognitive Abilities* (Schrank, Flanagan, Woodcock, & Mascolo, 2001) is available for practitioners wishing to learn more about the use and interpretation of the WJ III COG. Rapid Reference 1.1 provides basic information on the WJ III ACH and its publisher.

HISTORY AND DEVELOPMENT

The original Woodcock-Johnson Tests of Achievement was published in 1977 as part of the Woodcock-Johnson Psycho-Educational Battery (WJ) (Woodcock & Johnson, 1977). The WJ provided the first comprehensive, co-normed battery of cognitive abilities, achievement, and interests. The battery of tests measured a continuum of human abilities across a wide age range and provided common norms for interpretation. The Tests of Achievement consisted of 10 tests organized into four areas: reading, mathematics, written language, and knowledge.

The Woodcock-Johnson-Revised (WJ-R®) (Woodcock & Johnson, 1989) was designed to expand and increase the diagnostic capabilities of the WJ. The tests were divided into two main batteries, the Tests of Cognitive Ability (WJ-R COG) and the Tests of Achievement (WJ-R ACH). The WJ-R COG and WJ-R ACH each had two easel test books, the Standard Battery and the Supplemental Battery. The WJ-R Tests of Achievement consisted of 14 tests organized into four curricular areas: reading, mathematics, written language, and knowledge. Several new tests were added to the reading and written language areas. To facilitate pre- and posttesting, parallel, alternate forms of the Tests of Achievement, Forms A and B, were published.

Like its predecessor, the Woodcock-Johnson III (published in 2001) has two distinct batteries, the Tests of Cognitive Abilities and the Tests of Achievement. Together these batteries comprise a comprehensive system for measuring general intellectual ability (g), specific cognitive abilities, predicted achievement, oral language, and achievement across a wide age range. As with the original WJ, one of the most important features of the WJ III system is that norms for the WJ III COG and WJ III ACH are based on data from the same sample of individuals. This co-norming provides greater accuracy and validity when making comparisons among and between an individual's obtained scores.

ORGANIZATION OF THE WJ III ACH

As noted, the WJ III ACH is a revised and expanded version of the WJ-R Tests of Achievement (Woodcock & Johnson, 1989). The WJ III ACH has 22 tests that are organized into five areas: reading, mathematics, written language, knowledge, and oral language. These tests are contained in two easel test books, the Standard Battery and the Extended Battery. The organization of the WJ III ACH is shown in Table 1.1 and applies to both Forms A and B.

Although many of the basic features have been retained, the extensive renorming and addition of new tests and interpretive procedures improve and increase the diagnostic capabilities of the WJ III ACH. The areas of reading, mathematics, and written language each include measures of basic skills, fluency or automaticity, and application or higher-level skills. The oral language

Table 1.1 Organization of the WJ III Tests of Achievement (Forms A and B)

	Standard Battery Tests	Extended Battery Tests
Reading		
Basic Reading Skills	Letter-Word Identification	Word Attack
Reading Fluency	Reading Fluency	
Reading Comprehension	Passage Comprehension	Reading Vocabulary
Mathematics		
Math Calculation Skills	Calculation	
Math Fluency	Math Fluency	
Math Reasoning	Applied Problems	Quantitative Concepts
Written Language		
Basic Writing Skill	Spelling	Editing
Writing Fluency	Writing Fluency	
Written Expression	Writing Samples	
Oral Language		
Oral Expression	Story Recall	Picture Vocabulary
Listening Comprehension	Understanding Directions	Oral Comprehension
Knowledge		Academic Knowledge
Supplemental Tests	Story Recall-Delayed	Spelling of Sounds
	Handwriting Legibility Scale	Sound Awareness
	Writing Evaluation Scale	Punctuation/Capitalization

area includes measures of expressive and receptive language. The Academic Knowledge test samples biological and physical sciences, history, geography, government, economics, art, music, and literature. Table 1.2 provides an overview of the content and task demands for each of the 22 achievement tests. Figure 1.1 illustrates item types for each of the achievement tests. The sample items shown are not actual test items.

Table 1.2 Content and Task Demands of the 22 WJ III Achievement Tests

Area	Test Name	Description	Task Demands
Reading	Test 1: Letter-Word Identification	Measures an aspect of reading decoding.	Requires identifying and pronouncing isolated letters and words.
	Test 2: Reading Fluency	Measures reading speed.	Requires reading and comprehending simple sentences and then deciding if the statement was true or false by marking yes or no. (3-minute time limit)
	Test 9: Passage Comprehension	Measures reading comprehension of contextual information.	Requires reading a short passage and supplying a key missing word.
	Test 13: Word Attack	Measures aspects of phonological and orthographic coding.	Requires applying phonic and structural analysis skills in pronouncing phonically regular nonsense words.
	Test 17: Reading Vocabulary	Measures reading vocabulary and comprehension.	Requires reading and providing synonyms or antonyms, or solving analogies.
	Test 21: Sound Awareness	Measures four aspects of phonological awareness: rhyming, deletion, substitution, and reversal.	Requires analyzing and manipulating phonemes.
Math	Test 5: Calculation	Measures the ability to perform mathematical computations.	Requires calculation of simple to complex mathematical facts and equations.
	Test 6: Math Fluency	Measures aspects of number facility and math achievement.	Requires rapid calculation of single-digit addition, subtraction, and multiplication facts. (3-minute time limit)

(continued)

Table 1.2 (Continued)

Area	Test Name	Description	Task Demands
	Test 10: Applied Problems	Measures the ability to analyze and solve practical math problems, mathematical reasoning.	Requires comprehending the nature of the problem, identifying relevant information, performing calculations, and stating solutions.
	Test 18: Quantitative Concepts	Measures aspects of quantitative reasoning and math knowledge.	Requires pointing to or stating answers to questions on number identification, sequencing, shapes, symbols, terms, and formulas.
Written Language	Test 7: Spelling	Measures the ability to spell dictated words.	Requires writing the correct spelling of words presented orally.
	Test 8: Writing Fluency	Measures aspects of automaticity with syntactic components of written expression.	Requires formulating and writing simple sentences rapidly. (7-minute time limit)
	Test 11: Writing Samples	Measures quality of meaningful written expression and ability to convey ideas.	Requires writing sentences in response to a series of demands that increase in difficulty.
	Test 16: Editing	Measures the ability to identify and correct errors in spelling, usage, punctuation, and capitalization.	Requires identifying errors in short written passages and correcting them orally.
	Test 20: Spelling of Sounds	Measures aspects of phonological/orthographic coding.	Requires spelling nonsense words that conform to conventional English spelling rules.

Area	Test Name	Description	Task Demands
	Test 22: Punctuation and Capitalization	Measures knowledge of punctuation and capitalization rules.	Requires inserting punctuation and capitals into written words.
	(WES) Writing Evaluation Scale	Measures writing skills by informal, analytic evaluation of longer, more complex passages.	Requires writing an essay or composition.
	(H) Handwriting	Measures writing legibility.	Requires producing legible handwriting.
Oral Language	Test 3: Story Recall	Measures aspects of language development, listening ability, and meaningful memory.	Requires listening to passages and recalling story elements.
	Test 4: Understanding Directions	Measures aspects of language development and listening ability.	Requires pointing to objects in pictures after listening to instructions of increasing linguistic complexity.
	Test 14: Picture Vocabulary	Measures aspects of word knowledge.	Requires naming familiar to less familiar pictured objects.
	Test 15: Oral Comprehension	Measures aspects of listening ability and language development.	Requires listening to a short passage and providing the missing final word.
	Test 12: Story Recall-Delayed	Measures aspects of meaningful memory.	Requires recalling elements of stories presented earlier in Test 3.
Academic Knowledge	Test 19: Academic Knowledge	Measures acquired knowledge in content areas of science, social studies, and humanities.	Requires providing an oral response to orally presented questions. Many items provide visual stimuli.

Standard Battery

Test 1: Letter-Word Identification

The task requires identifying and pronouncing isolated letters and words

g   r   cat   palm   officiate

Test 2: Reading Fluency (timed)

The task requires rapidly reading and comprehending simple sentences.

The sky is green.	YES	(NO)
You can sit on a chair.	(YES)	NO
A bird has four wings.	YES	(NO)

Test 3: Story Recall (taped)

The task requires listening to passages of gradually increasing length and complexity and then recalling the story elements.

> Martha went to the store to buy groceries. When she got there, she discovered that she had forgotten her shopping list. She bought milk, eggs, and flour. When she got home she discovered that she had remembered to buy everything except the butter.

Test 4: Understanding Directions

The task requires pointing to objects in a picture after listening to instructions that increase in linguistic complexity.

Point to the man on the bike. Go.
Point to car in the intersection after you point to one of the flying birds. Go.
Before you point to the tallest building, point to the tree closest to a corner. Go.

Test 5: Calculation

The task includes mathematical computations from simple addition facts to complex equations.

$$2 + 4 =$$
$$3x + 3y = 15, 2x - y = 1, \quad x =$$
$$y =$$

Test 6: Math Fluency (timed)

The task requires rapid calculation of simple, single-digit addition, subtraction, and multiplication facts.

Test 7: Spelling

The task involves written spellings of words presented orally.

> Spell the word "horn." She played the horn in the band. Horn.

Test 8: Writing Fluency (timed)

The task requires formulating and writing simple sentences quickly when given three words and a picture.

books _____
reads
likes _____

Test 9: Passage Comprehension

The task requires reading a short passage silently and then supplying a key missing word.

> The boy _____ off his bike. (Correct: fell, jumped, etc.)

> The book is one of a series of over eighty volumes. Each volume is designed to provide convenient _____ to a wide range of carefully selected articles. (Correct: access)

Test 10: Applied Problems

The task involves analyzing and solving practical mathematical problems.

> Bill had $7.00. He bought a ball for $3.95 and a comb for $1.20. How much money did he have left?

Test 11: Writing Samples

The task requires writing sentences in response to a variety of demands that are then evaluated based on the quality of expression.

> Write a good sentence to describe the picture.

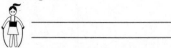

Figure 1.1 WJ III ACH-Like Sample Items

Extended Battery

Test 12: Story Recall-Delayed

The task requires the subject to recall, after a 30-minute to 8-day delay, the story elements presented in the Story Recall test.

> Yesterday you heard some short stories. I am going to read a few words from the story and I want you to tell me what you remember about the rest of the story.
>
> Martha went to the store ...

Test 13: Word Attack

The task requires pronouncing nonwords that conform to English spelling rules.

> flib
> bungicality

Test 14: Picture Vocabulary

> The task requires naming common to less familiar pictured objects.
>
> What is this person holding? (Correct: Gavel)

Test 15: Oral Comprehension (taped)

The task requires listening to short passages and then supplying the missing final word.

> Without a doubt, his novels are more complex than the novels of many other contemporary _____.
>
> (Correct: writers, novelists, authors)

Test 16: Editing

The task requires identifying and correcting mistakes in spelling, punctuation, capitalization, or word usage in written passages.

> Bobby's face was so sunburned, it looked like he had fell into a bucket of red paint. (Correct: fallen)

Task 17: Reading Vocabulary

The test involves reading stimulus words for three different tasks: providing synonyms, providing antonyms, and completing analogies.

Figure 1.1 (Continued)

Test 18: Quantitative Concepts

The task requires applying mathematical concepts and analyzing numerical relationships.

> How many ducks in this picture?
>
> What number belongs in this series:
> 126 _____ 120

Test 19: Academic Knowledge:

The task involves answering questions about curricular knowledge in various areas of the biological and physical sciences, history, geography, government, economics, art, music, and literature.

> On a musical scale, how many notes are in an octave?

Test 20: Spelling of Sounds

The task requires spelling nonwords that conform to English spelling rules.

> barches
> smuff

Test 21: Sound Awareness

The task includes four measures of phonological awareness (rhyming, deletion, substitution, and reversal).

> Tell me a word that rhymes with goat. (rhyming)
>
> Say the word "cat" without the /k/ sound. (deletion)
>
> Change the /s/ in sack to /b/. (substitution)
>
> Say the sounds in the word "tire" backward. (reversal)

Test 22: Punctuation and Capitalization

The task requires the use of correct punctuation and capitalization in orally dictated words and phrases.

> Write the month "September." (Scored for capitalization.)
>
> Write the city and state "Chicago, Illinois." (Scored for comma.)

Item content was selected to provide a broad sampling of achievement rather than an in-depth assessment of any one area. Each broad area was designed to measure a hierarchy of abilities ranging from lower-order, less complex tasks to higher-level, more complex tasks. Broad measurement of these important achievement areas assists examiners in identifying present performance levels and instructional needs. Table 1.3 shows the clusters available in the WJ III ACH.

Changes from the WJ-R ACH to WJ III ACH

Examiners familiar with the WJ-R ACH will find it easy to learn the overall structure and organization of the WJ III ACH. There are seven new tests and eight new clusters (see Rapid Reference 1.2). Five of the new tests and three of the new clusters are in the oral language domain. Other changes include the renaming and reformatting of several tests that were in the WJ-R: Editing (formerly Proofing), Spelling (formerly Dictation), Punctuation and Capitalization (formerly derived from Dictation and Proofing), and Academic Knowledge (formerly comprised of Science, Social Studies, and Humanities).

Important new diagnostic and interpretive options are now available to examiners using the achievement battery. For example, the addition of the

---

≡ Rapid Reference 1.2

Quick Overview of the New WJ III ACH Tests & Clusters

7 New Tests
- Reading Fluency
- Story Recall
- Story Recall-Delayed
- Understanding Directions
- Math Fluency
- Spelling of Sounds
- Sound Awareness

8 New Clusters
- Oral Language
- Listening Comprehension
- Oral Expression
- Academic Fluency
- Academic Skills
- Academic Applications
- Total Achievement
- Phoneme/Grapheme Knowledge

Table 1.3 Content and Uses of the WJ III Achievement Clusters

Cluster	Tests Required	Uses
Reading		
Broad Reading	ACH Tests 1, 2, 9 (Letter-Word Identification, Reading Fluency, Passage Comprehension)	Provides a broad measure of reading achievement.
Basic Reading Skills	ACH Tests 1, 13 (Letter-Word Identification, Word Attack)	Provides a measure of both sight and phonic skills.
Reading Comprehension	ACH Tests 9, 17 (Passage Comprehension, Reading Vocabulary)	Provides a measure of reading comprehension skills ranging from words in isolation to short passages.
Mathematics		
Broad Mathematics	ACH Tests 5, 6, 10 (Calculation, Math Fluency, Applied Problems)	Provides a broad measure of math achievement.
Math Calculation Skills	ACH Tests 5, 6 (Calculation, Math Fluency)	Provides a measure of basic mathematical skills.
Mathematics Reasoning	ACH Tests 10, 18 (Applied Problems, Quantitative Concepts)	Provides a measure of mathematical knowledge and quantitative reasoning.
Written Language		
Broad Written Language	ACH Tests 7, 8, 11 (Spelling, Writing Fluency, Writing Samples)	Provides a broad measure of written language.

(continued)

Table 1.3 (Continued)

Cluster	Tests Required	Uses
Basic Writing Skills	ACH Tests 7, 16 (Spelling, Editing)	Provides a measure of basic writing skills including spelling and correcting errors.
Written Expression	ACH Tests 8, 11 (Writing Fluency, Writing Samples)	Provides a measure of written expression skills including producing simple to complex sentences.
Oral Language		
Standard	ACH Tests 3, 4 (Story Recall, Understanding Directions)	Provides a broad measure of oral language.
Extended	ACH Tests 3, 4, 14, 15 (Story Recall, Understanding Directions, Picture Vocabulary, Oral Comprehension)	Provides a more comprehensive measure of oral language.
Oral Expression	ACH Tests 3, 14 (Story Recall, Picture Vocabulary)	Provides a measure of expressive language ability.
Listening Comprehension	ACH Tests 4, 15 (Understanding Directions, Oral Comprehension)	Provides a measure of receptive language (listening comprehension).

Cluster	Tests Required	Uses
Phoneme/Grapheme Knowledge	ACH Tests 13, 20 (Word Attack, Spelling of Sounds)	Provides a measure of proficiency with phonic and orthographic patterns, decoding and encoding.
Academic Skills	ACH Tests 1, 5, 7 (Letter-Word Identification, Calculation, Spelling)	Provides an overall basic achievement skills measure.
Academic Fluency	ACH Tests 2, 6, 8 (Reading Fluency, Math Fluency, Writing Fluency)	Provides an overall score of academic fluency.
Academic Applications	ACH Tests 9, 10, 11 (Passage Comprehension, Applied Problems, Writing Samples)	Provides an overall measure of application of academic skills.
Academic Knowledge	ACH Test 19 (Academic Knowledge)	Provides a measure of information in curricular areas, including science, social studies, and humanities.
Total Achievement	ACH Tests 1, 2, 5, 6, 7, 8, 9, 10, 11	Provides an overall score of achievement.

≡ *Rapid Reference 1.3*

WJ III ACH Major Changes

- Provides updated norms and content.
- Includes a computerized scoring and profiling program that eliminates hand scoring.
- Expands broad achievement clusters by including a fluency test with the basic skill and application tests.
- Increases interpretive options by adding seven new tests and eight new clusters.
- Adds five oral language tests, including one delayed recall measure.
- Provides ability/achievement discrepancy evaluation using oral language as a predictor.
- Includes oral language in the procedure for evaluating intra-achievement discrepancies.
- Designed to be more useful at early reading levels by measuring phonological awareness.
- Expands Reading Vocabulary to include analogy items.
- Measures fluency in reading and math as well as writing.
- Includes new diagnostic spelling measure (spelling of pseudowords).
- Combines three knowledge tests (Science, Social Studies, and Humanities) into one test of Academic Knowledge.

oral language tests to the WJ III ACH allows examiners to (a) calculate ability/achievement discrepancies, (b) use oral language in intra-achievement discrepancies, and (c) obtain cluster scores for receptive and expressive language. Rapid Reference 1.3 provides a summary of the major changes in the WJ III ACH.

Early Development Tests

In the WJ-R, early development tests (EDev) were clearly identified in the Selective Testing Table. That is not the case with WJ III. This does not mean that tests in the WJ III are inappropriate for use at the preschool level. In fact, the

WJ III has many more tests with content and norms appropriate for use at the 2, 3, 4, and 5-year levels. These tests are not limited for use with preschool age children. The early items on these tests are also appropriate for individuals of any age who have severe developmental delays.

The *WJ III Examiner Manual* (page 16) identifies 12 tests that are most usable with preschool children. The clinician should use judgment in selecting which tests to administer to

> # DON'T FORGET
> ....
> ## Reminders to Examiners
>
> - The oral language tests are now included in the WJ III ACH.
> - Oral language may be used as an ability to predict achievement.
> - Important additional diagnostic information can be obtained by using the co-normed WJ III COG.
> - It is not necessary to administer all of the tests in the WJ III ACH.

an individual and should consider the examinee's opportunity to acquire the skills and knowledge that are measured by these tests. Table 1.4 lists all 22 tests and indicates the lowest age at which reliability is reported in the *WJ III Technical Manual* (Appendix A-2 (McGrew & Woodcock, 2001)). The 12 listed first are the ones identified in the *Examiner's Manual* as most usable with preschoolers.

THEORETICAL FOUNDATION OF THE WJ III

The WJ III is based on current theory and research on the structure of human cognitive abilities. The theoretical foundation is derived from the Cattell-Horn-Carroll theory of cognitive abilities (CHC theory). Although this is most commonly discussed in relation to the WJ III Tests of Cognitive Abilities, applying the CHC theory to the WJ III Tests of Achievement provides a common framework for describing performance and interpreting results. This creates a powerful tool for measuring human performance across the continuum of cognitive abilities and achievement.

CHC theory is a combination of two research-based theories: *Gf-Gc* theory based on the work of Raymond Cattell and John Horn, and the three-stratum theory based on the work of John Carroll. Both bodies of work focus on multiple broad abilities, each of which subsumes several narrow cognitive abilities. For more information about these theories, consult the *WJ III Technical Manual*

Table 1.4 WJ III ACH Early Development Tests and Age at Which Reliability is First Reported

Test Name/Number	2	3	4	5	6	7
1: Letter-Word Identification	X					
3: Story Recall	X					
4: Understanding Directions	X					
7: Spelling	X					
9: Passage Comprehension	X					
10: Applied Problems	X					
12: Story Recall-Delayed		X				
13: Word Attack			X			
14: Picture Vocabulary	X					
15: Oral Comprehension	X					
19: Academic Knowledge	X					
21: Sound Awareness			X			
2: Reading Fluency					X	
5: Calculation				X		
6: Math Fluency						X
8: Writing Fluency						X
11: Writing Samples				X		
16: Editing					X	
17: Reading Vocabulary				X		
18: Quantitative Concepts	X					
20: Spelling of Sounds					X	
22: Punctuation and Capitalization					X	

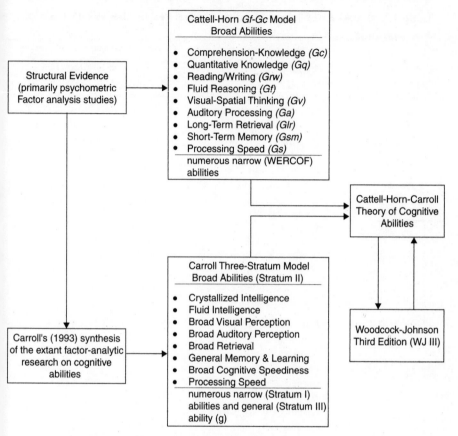

Figure 1.2 Relationship of the WJ III to CHC Theory

Source: From the WJ III Tests of Achievement, by R. W. Woodcock, K. S. McGrew, and N. Mather, 2001, Itasca, IL: Riverside Publishing. Copyright © 2001 by The Riverside Publishing Company. Adapted with permission.

(McGrew & Woodcock, 2001). Figure 1.2 illustrates the relationship between the WJ III and CHC theory.

The WJ III measures nine broad abilities: comprehension-knowledge *(Gc)*, fluid reasoning *(Gf)* visual-spatial thinking *(Gv)*, short-term memory *(Gsm)*, long-term retrieval *(Glr)*, processing speed *(Gs)*, auditory processing *(Ga)*, reading/writing *(Grw)*, and quantitative knowledge *(Gq)*. (See Rapid Reference 4.5 in Chapter 4 for definitions of these abilities.) The WJ III ACH includes measures of five of these broad abilities. Table 1.5 shows the broad and narrow abilities that are measured by each of the 22 tests in the WJ III ACH.

Table 1.5 Broad and Narrow Abilities Measured by the WJ III Tests of Achievement

Broad CHC Ability	Standard Battery Test (Primary Narrow Abilities)	Extended Battery Test (Primary Narrow Abilities)
Reading-Writing *(Grw)*	1: Letter-Word Identification (Reading decoding) 2: Reading Fluency (Reading speed) 9: Passage Comprehension (Reading comprehension, verbal (printed) language comprehension) 7: Spelling (Spelling ability) 8: Writing Fluency (Writing speed) 11: Writing Samples (Writing ability)	13: Word Attack (Reading decoding, phonetic coding: analysis/synthesis) 17: Reading Vocabulary (Verbal (printed) language comprehension, lexical knowledge) 16: Editing (Language development/ English usage) 22: Punctuation/Capitalization (English usage)
Mathematics *(Gq)*	5: Calculation (Math achievement) 6: Math Fluency (Math achievement, numerical facility) 10: Applied Problems (Quantitative reasoning, math achievement, math knowledge)	18: Quantitative Concepts (Math knowledge, quantitative reasoning)
Comprehension-Knowledge *(Gc)*	3: Story Recall (Language development, listening ability) 4: Understanding Directions (Listening ability, language development)	14: Picture Vocabulary (Language development, lexical knowledge) 15: Oral Comprehension (Listening ability) 19: Academic Knowledge (General information, science information, cultural information, geography achievement)
Auditory Processing *(Ga)*		13: Word Attack (Reading decoding, phonetic coding: analysis/synthesis)

Table 1.5 (Continued)

Broad CHC Ability	Standard Battery Test (Primary Narrow Abilities)	Extended Battery Test (Primary Narrow Abilities)
		20: Spelling of Sounds (Spelling ability, phonetic coding: analysis) 21: Sound Awareness (Phonetic coding: analysis/ synthesis)
Long-Term Retrieval *(Glr)*	12: Story Recall-Delayed (Meaningful memory)	

STANDARDIZATION AND PSYCHOMETRIC PROPERTIES OF THE WJ III ACH

Intended to be broadly applicable from the preschool to the geriatric levels for either comprehensive or focused assessment, the WJ III was developed with a special emphasis on technical quality. Normative data were based on a single sample that was administered the cognitive and achievement tests. The national standardization included 8,818 individuals between the ages of 24 months and 95+ years, as well as college and university undergraduate and graduate students from over 100 geographically diverse U.S. communities. The sample was selected to be representative of the United States population from age 24 months to age 95 years and older. The preschool sample (2 to 5 years of age and not enrolled in kindergarten) was composed of 1,143 individuals. The kindergarten to 12th grade sample was composed of 4,783 individuals. The college/university sample was composed of 1,165 individuals. The adult non-school sample (14 to 95+ years of age and not enrolled in secondary school or college) was composed of 1,843 individuals. Individuals were randomly selected with a stratified sampling design that controlled for 10 specific community and subject variables: census region, community size, sex, race, Hispanic origin, funding of college/university, type of college/university, education of adults, occupational status of adults, and occupation of adults in the labor force. In addition to region and size, 13 socioeconomic status (SES) variables were considered in the selection of communities in order to avoid a bias toward any specific type of community. The 13 SES variables are (a) three levels of education in the adult population, (b) four levels of household income, (c) three categories of labor force characteristics, and (d) three types of occupation.

For the school-age sample, the continuous-year procedure was used to gather data rather than gathering data at one or two points in the year, such as fall and spring. This produces continuous-year norms that meet the reporting requirements for educational programs such as Title I. The grade norms are

≡Rapid Reference 1.4

WJ III ACH Test Reliabilities

WJ III ACH Cluster	Median Reliability Across Age
Letter-Word Identification	.94
Reading Fluency	.90
Story Recall	.87
Understanding Directions	.83
Calculation	.86
Math Fluency	.90
Spelling	.90
Writing Fluency	.88
Passage Comprehension	.88
Applied Problems	.93
Writing Samples	.87
Story Recall-Delayed	.81
Word Attack	.87
Picture Vocabulary	.81
Oral Comprehension	.85
Editing	.90
Reading Vocabulary	.90
Quantitative Concepts	.91
Spelling of Sounds	.76
Sound Awareness	.81
Punctuation and Capitalization	.79

reported for each tenth of a year from grades K.0 through 18.0. The age norms are reported for each month from ages 2-0 through 18-11 and then by one-year intervals from 19 through 95+ years of age.

Complete technical information can be found in the *WJ III Technical Manual* (McGrew & Woodcock, 2001). The number of items and average item density in each test were set so that a reliability of .80 or higher would usually be obtained. The goal for cluster score reliabilities was set at .90 or higher. The median split-half reliabilities for the tests and composite reliabilities for the clusters are provided in Rapid Reference 1.4 and 1.5, respectively.

≡ Rapid Reference 1.5

WJ III ACH Cluster Reliabilities

WJ III ACH Cluster	Median Reliability Across Age
Oral Language-Standard	.87
Oral Language-Extended	.92
Oral Expression	.85
Listening Comprehension	.89
Broad Reading	.94
Basic Reading Skills	.95
Reading Comprehension	.92
Broad Mathematics	.95
Math Calculation Skills	.91
Mathematics Reasoning	.95
Broad Written Language	.94
Basic Writing Skills	.94
Written Expression	.91
Phoneme/Grapheme Knowledge	.90
Academic Skills	.96
Academic Fluency	.93
Academic Applications	.95
Academic Knowledge	.90
Total Achievement	.98

PURPOSES

Because it is a comprehensive instrument, the WJ III ACH can be used with confidence in a variety of settings and for multiple purposes. The wide age range and breadth of coverage allow the tests to be used for educational, clinical, or research purposes from the preschool to the geriatric level. Uses of the WJ III ACH include (a) establishing an individual's present performance levels in achievement, (b) determining an individual's academic strengths and weaknesses, (c) comparing an individual's level of attainment to his or her peers, (d) exploring eligibility for special programs, (e) monitoring educational progress across the school years, (f) investigating the effectiveness of curricula, and (g) assisting with recommendations for specific curricular adaptations.

The fact that the WJ III ACH is co-normed with the WJ III COG provides a "best-practice" scenario for identifying an individual's unique strengths and weaknesses as well as for obtaining information for instructional planning and programming. The combined and co-normed information provided by the WJ III COG and WJ III ACH is especially appropriate for documenting the nature of, and differentiating intra-ability and ability/achievement discrepancies.

Intra-ability (intra-cognitive, intra-achievement, intra-individual) discrepancies are useful for understanding an individual's strengths and weaknesses, diagnosing and documenting the existence of specific disabilities, and acquiring the most relevant information for educational and vocational planning. The intra-achievement discrepancy is available when using only the WJ III ACH, whereas the other two intra-ability discrepancies also require the WJ III COG.

Ability/achievement (predicted

DON'T FORGET

Purposes and Uses of the Test

- Describe individual strengths and weaknesses
- Determine present performance levels
- Assist with diagnosis of disabilities
- Determine ability/achievement and intra-achievement discrepancies
- Assist with program planning
- Assess growth
- Evaluate programs
- Conduct research

achievement or intellectual ability/achievement, oral language ability/achievement) discrepancies are typically used as part of the selection criteria for learning disability programs. The oral language ability/achievement discrepancy is available when using only the WJ III ACH, but the remaining two ability/achievement discrepancy procedures require the WJ III COG as well. Readers should see Chapter 4 for further discussion about discrepancies.

CAUTION

Possible Kinds of Test Misuse

- Using a test for an inappropriate purpose
- Being unfamiliar with the content and organization of the test
- Not completing proper training or study for test use
- Not understanding the applications and limitations of scores and discrepancy procedures

COMPREHENSIVE REFERENCES ON TEST

The *WJ III Tests of Achievement Examiner's Manual* (Mather & Woodcock, 2001), the *WJ III Technical Manual* (McGrew & Woodcock, 2001), and the *Examiner Training Workbook* (Wendling & Mather, 2001) currently provide the most detailed information about the WJ III. The *Examiner's Manual* presents the basic principles of individual clinical assessment, specific information regarding use of the test, and suggested procedures for learning to administer, score, and complete the interpretative portions of the WJ III. The development, standardization, and technical characteristics of the tests are described in the separate *Technical Manual*. The *Workbook* covers important aspects of administration and scoring, and it includes practice exercises and reproducible checklists to aid examiners in building and evaluating their competency.

🦅 TEST YOURSELF 🦅

1. **What are the five major curricular areas included in the WJ III ACH?**
2. **For what age range is the WJ III ACH appropriate?**
3. **What grade range is available in the WJ III ACH norms?**
4. **Which of the following tests is new to the WJ III ACH?**
   (a) Letter-Word Identification
   (b) Writing Fluency
   (c) Sound Awareness
   (d) Applied Problems
5. **Which of the following clusters is new to the WJ III ACH?**
   (a) Reading Comprehension
   (b) Phoneme/Grapheme Knowledge
   (c) Math Reasoning
   (d) Written Expression
6. **Which of the following tests is an oral language measure?**
   (a) Letter-Word Identification
   (b) Applied Problems
   (c) Picture Vocabulary
   (d) Word Attack
7. **The WJ III ACH contains a procedure for calculating an ability/achievement discrepancy.** True or False?
8. **The WJ III ACH does not share common norms with the WJ III Tests of Cognitive Abilities.** True or False?
9. **Parallel, alternate forms of the WJ III ACH are available.** True or False?
10. **All tests in the WJ III ACH are appropriate for use with individuals functioning at a 24-month level.** True or False?

Answers: 1. reading, mathematics, written language, oral language, academic knowledge; 2. 2 to 95+ years; 3. K. 0 to 18.0; 4. c; 5. b; 6. c; 7. True; 8. False; 9. True; 10. False

Two

HOW TO ADMINISTER THE WJ III ACH

Proper administration of the WJ III ACH requires training. Although individuals in a wide range of professions can learn the actual procedures for administering the WJ III ACH, a higher degree of skill is required to interpret results or to test individuals who have special problems. Some examiners can adequately administer a test but may lack the expertise to interpret the results. Only properly trained individuals should administer, score, and interpret standardized tests, especially in high-stakes situations such as making eligibility decisions.

Standards applicable to testing have been developed through a collaborative effort of three professional organizations: the American Educational Research Association (AERA), the American Psychological Association (APA), and the National Council on Measurement in Education (NCME). These standards are published in a document titled *Standards for Educational and Psychological Testing* (1999). Standards referenced in this chapter are from that source.

Based on the principle of selective testing, it is seldom necessary to

CAUTION

Examiner Qualifications

Standard 11.3: Responsibility for test use should be assumed by or delegated only to those individuals who have the training, professional credentials, and experience necessary to handle this responsibility (AERA, APA, & NCME, 1999, p. 114).

Standard 12.8: Professionals should ensure that persons under their supervision, who administer and score tests, are adequately trained in the settings in which the testing occurs and with the professional ethics requirements (AERA, APA, & NCME, 1999).

administer all of the WJ III ACH tests or complete all of the interpretive options for a single person. For example, if an individual were referred for a reading evaluation, the examiner may only want to administer the tests that are related to reading performance. A selective testing table (see Figure 2.1), included in each Test Book and Manual, depicts which tests need to be administered to obtain various cluster scores.

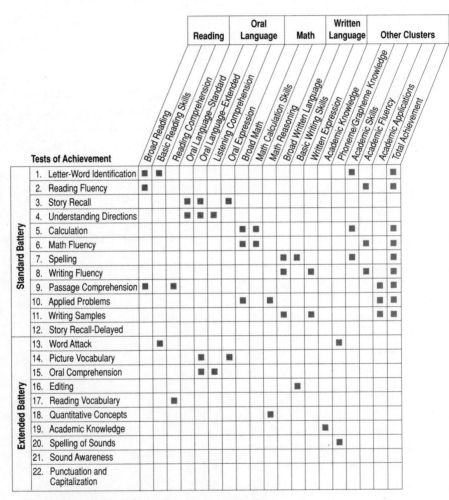

Figure 2.1 WJ III ACH Selective Testing Table

Source: From the *WJ III Tests of Achievement*, by R. W. Woodcock, K. S. McGrew, and N. Mather, 2001, Itasca, IL: Riverside Publishing. Copyright © 2001 by The Riverside Publishing Company. Adapted with permission.

CAUTION

Possible Problems in Test Administration

- Failing to follow the standardized administration procedures
- Being too lenient or stringent on scoring responses
- Administering all tests to all examinees

APPROPRIATE TESTING CONDITIONS

Testing Environment

The examiner should select a testing room that is quiet, comfortable, and has adequate ventilation and lighting. Ideally, only the examiner and the examinee should be in the room. The room should have a table or desk and two chairs, one of which is an appropriate size for the examinee. The seating arrangement must allow the examiner to view both sides of the easel book, point to all parts on the examinee's test page in the Test Book and in the response booklet, and record responses out of view. The examinee should be able to view only the examinee pages.

The best seating arrangement is one in which the examiner sits diagonally across from the examinee at the corner of a table. Another possible arrangement is for the examiner to sit directly across the table. With this arrangement, the table must be narrow and low enough so that the examiner can see over the upright Test Book to point to the examinee's test page when necessary.

Testing Materials

The basic materials necessary for administering the WJ III ACH are the Test Books, a Test Record, a Subject Response Booklet (SRB), tape player, the test audio recording, at least two sharpened pencils with erasers, and a stopwatch or watch with a second hand. The test kit does not include the audio player, pencils, or a stopwatch.

The easel format of the Test Book provides easy access to all administration directions. When positioned properly, the Test Book provides a screen so that the examiner can record responses on the Test Record out of the examinee's view and shield the correct answers that are printed on the Test Record.

Getting Ready to Test

Prior to beginning the test, the examiner should fill in the examinee's name and date of birth. The examiner should check if the individual should be wearing glasses or a hearing aid. Spaces are provided on the Test Record to record the number of years an individual has been retained or skipped in school. Some examiners prefer to complete this information with the examinee during the rapport-setting time.

When testing a school-age individual, the software that accompanies the test will automatically calculate the exact tenth-of-a-year grade placement for the standard school year once the examiner enters the grade level. If the individual is tested during the summer months, the examiner should record the grade that has just been completed. For example, the grade placement for a student evaluated in July who had just completed eighth grade would be 8.9.

If an individual is not attending school (i.e., kindergarten through college), it is not necessary to record a grade placement unless it would be useful to compare the individual's performance with the average performance of students at some specified grade placement. If an individual is enrolled in some type of nongraded program, then the normal grade placement for students of this individual's age at the time of testing may provide the most appropriate reference group for test interpretation.

In cases where the individual is attending a year-round school, the WJ III software program will calculate the exact grade placement. The clinician should select Program Options from the menu bar, click on the Interface Options tab, select "year-round" school, and click "OK." A calculator icon appears next to the data entry box for Grade. The clinician should click on the "calculator" and enter the total number of instructional days in the school year and the number of days completed at the time of testing to obtain the exact grade placement.

Establishing and Maintaining Rapport with Examinee

In most instances, the examiner will have little difficulty establishing a good relationship with the examinee. However, the clinician should not begin testing unless the person seems relatively at ease. If he or she does not feel well or does not respond appropriately, the examiner should not attempt testing. Often, examiners begin the testing session with a short period of conversation, perhaps while completing the examinee information portion of the Test Record. It is not necessary to provide a lengthy explanation of the test. A suggested statement is provided in the introductory section, labeled "Introducing the Test," of each Test Book.

Throughout the testing session, the examiner should let the examinee know that he or she is doing a good job, using such comments as "fine" and "good" and should encourage a response even when items are difficult. It is fine to say, "Would you like to take a guess on that one?" Clinicians should be careful, however, that their comments do not reveal whether answers are correct or incorrect. For example, they should not say "good" only after correct responses or pause longer after incorrect responses waiting for the examinee to change a response. During the test, the examiner should make sure the examinee feels that the experience is enjoyable.

TESTING INDIVIDUALS WITH SPECIAL NEEDS

DON'T FORGET

Keys for Preparing to Administer Test

- Have all necessary testing materials prior to beginning testing.
- Select an appropriate location for the testing session.
- Complete the examinee identification section on the Test Record prior to beginning the test.
- Calculate the exact grade placement using the software that accompanies test.
- *Standard 5.4:* The testing environment should furnish reasonable comfort with minimal distractions (AERA, APA, & NCME, 1999, p. 63).

CAUTION

Appropriate Examiner/Examinee Interactions

- Be careful not to reveal item answers.
- Do not indicate if responses are correct or incorrect.
- Provide encouragement throughout the administration, not just when the examinee has difficulty or has made an error.

At times the standard test procedures may need to be modified in order to accommodate an individual's special limitations. Because modifications may have a compromising effect on the validity of the test results, examiners must

CAUTION

Modifying Standardized Procedures

- may invalidate the normative interpretation of test results.
- should be noted on the Test Record and report.
- requires professional judgment on a case by case basis.

Standard 5.1: Test administrators should follow carefully the standardized procedures for administration and scoring specified by the test developer, unless the situation or a test taker's disability dictates that an exception should be made. "Note also that accommodations are not needed or appropriate under a variety of circumstances. First the disability may, in fact, be directly relevant to the focal construct" (AERA, APA, & NCME, 1999, p. 63).

Standard 10.1: In testing individuals with disabilities, test developers, test administrators, and test users should take steps to ensure that the test score inferences accurately reflect the intended construct rather than any disabilities and their associated characteristics extraneous to the intent of the measurement. Regular norms are appropriate when the purpose involves the test taker's functioning relative to the general population. (AERA, APA, & NCME, 1999, p. 106)

determine whether the procedures have been altered to the extent that caution must be used when interpreting the results. When test procedures are modified, the clinician should note and describe these modifications on the Test Record and in the test report.

Three broad classes of individuals who often require accommodations in the assessment process are preschoolers, English Language Learners (ELL), and individuals with disabilities.

Preschool Examinees

Some young children are uncomfortable with unfamiliar adults and may perform better if a parent is nearby. If a parent will be present during the testing session, before actual testing begins the clinician should briefly explain the testing process, including the establishment of test ceilings and the importance of not assisting the child on any item. After testing, an examiner may invite the parent to try certain items with the child to see if there are significant differences in performance.

Initially, some children may be shy and refuse to speak to a stranger. If after several rapport-building activities, such as interacting with a puppet, the child still refuses to speak, the examiner should discontinue testing and try again at a later date.

Some tests are more useful than others with preschool children. See Table 1.4 in Chapter 1 for a listing of tests that have developmentally appropriate content.

English Language Learners (ELL)

Before using the WJ III ACH (or any English test) with an ELL it is important to determine the individual's proficiency with English and language dominance. If the individual is English-dominant, the examiner can use the WJ III ACH. If conducting a bilingual assessment, the examiner can use the WJ III ACH as the English achievement measure.

The vocabulary and syntax used in the test instructions may be too complex for some individuals who are just learning English. Although the test instructions are controlled for complexity, the examiner may need to further explain the task. This modification of the standardized testing procedures requires documentation and the norms may not be used for interpretation of the individual's performance.

Individuals with Disabilities

In modifying test procedures and interpreting test results for individuals with disabilities, the examiner should be sensitive to the limitations different im-

DON'T FORGET
....

Possible Modifications When Testing Preschool Children

- Allow a parent to remain in the room but not directly in view of the child.
- Allow the child to sit on a parent's lap if separation is not possible.
- Provide breaks between tests.
- Vary the activity level of tasks (e.g., fine-motor activity, oral activity).
- Provide reinforcements (e.g., stickers, snacks).
- Sit on the floor with the child when administering the test.
- Maintain a fun, interesting, and fast pace.

DON'T FORGET

Possible Modifications When Testing English Language Learners

- Use English words that may be more familiar to the individual when presenting directions.
- Provide supplemental practice or review test directions to enhance understanding.
- Do not modify standardized procedures when measuring some aspect of an individual's English language ability (i.e., reading, writing, listening, or speaking skills).
- Do not translate test items. When available, use a test in the individual's primary language. For example, use Batería Woodcock-Muñoz Pruebas de aprovechamiento—Revisado (1996) if Spanish is the primary language.

CAUTION

Standards to Consider When Testing English Language Learners

Standard 9.3: When testing an examinee proficient in two or more languages for which the test is available, the examiner's relative language proficiencies should be determined. The test generally should be administered in the test taker's most proficient language, unless proficiency in the less proficient language is part of the assessment (AERA, APA, & NCME, 1999).

"It is important to consider language background in developing, selecting, and administering tests and in interpreting test performance ... test norms based on native speakers of English either should not be used with individuals whose first language is not English or such individuals' test results should be interpreted as reflecting in part current level of English proficiency rather than ability, potential, aptitude or personality characteristics or symptomatology" (AERA, APA, & NCME, 1999, p. 91).

pairments may impose on an individual's abilities and behavior. Some tests cannot be administered to individuals with profound impairments. The most appropriate tests to use will need to be determined on a case by case basis. Table 2.1 presents considerations and possible modifications for individuals with sensory or physical impairments.

Table 2.1 Considerations and Possible Modifications When Testing Individuals with Sensory or Physical Impairments

Hearing Impairments	Visual Impairments	Physical Impairments
Be sure hearing aid is worn and functioning	Place yellow acetate over test pages to reduce glare.	Provide rest periods or breaks during testing session.
Use examinee's mode of communication, e.g., American Sign Language, Signed English, written responses	Make environmental modifications, e.g., positioning lamp to provide additional light or dimmed illumination.	Modify response mode when necessary (e.g., allow oral responses when individual is unable to write).
Use interpreter if examiner is not proficient in examinee's mode of communication	Allow examinee to hold test pages closer or alter position of Test Book.	When appropriate, allow use of special equipment (e.g., keyboard for writing responses).
	Enlarge test materials.	
	If available, use Braille version of test when necessary.	

Learning Disabilities and Reading Disabilities

Accommodations are usually not provided on standardized tests for students who struggle with learning or reading. Although an accommodation may improve performance, the resulting score may not be an accurate reflection of a person's capabilities. In most instances, the purpose of the assessment is to document the severity of the impairment in learning or reading. Clearly, it would not be appropriate to read the reading tests to an individual with reading difficulties, as the main purpose of the evaluation is to determine the extent and severity of the reading impairment, not to measure oral language comprehension. The goal of the evaluation is to determine an individual's unique pattern of strengths and weaknesses and then to use this assessment data to suggest appropriate classroom accommodations and to recommend possible teaching strategies and interventions.

For some children with severe perceptual impairments, it may be necessary to use a card or piece of paper to highlight or draw attention to specific items. Individuals with poor fine-motor control may need to keyboard responses rather than write in the Subject Response Booklet. Individuals who are easily frustrated by tasks that become too difficult may respond better to several short testing sessions, rather than one lengthy session.

Behavioral Disorders/Attention-deficit Hyperactivity Disorder

Clinical expertise is needed to assess children with severe behavior or attention difficulties. Specific behavioral management techniques often can be implemented that will increase the likelihood of compliance. It is a good idea for examiners to become familiar with the typical classroom behavior of individuals who exhibit severe attention or behavior challenges prior to conducting the assessment. One of roles of the evaluator is to determine whether the test results provide a valid representation of the individual's present performance level. When evaluating individuals with challenging behaviors, it is important to attempt to ascertain the effects of the problem behaviors on the assessment process and to determine how the behaviors affect performance. In some situations, the problem behaviors produce test results that are not representative of the individual's true performance or capabilities.

Confidentiality of Test Materials and Content

Test security is the responsibility of test users and has two aspects, careful storing of the materials and protection of test content. Examiners should keep tests such as the WJ III in locked cabinets, if stored in an area accessible to people with a nonprofessional interest in the tests. The test should not be left unattended where examinees or others may see the materials and look at the test items.

During a discussion of the test results, the nature of items included in a test may be described but examiners should avoid actual review of specific test content. Examples similar to test items can be used without revealing actual items.

The issue of test confidentiality is also important. Test content or results should not be shared with curious nonprofessionals nor should materials be available for public inspection. During testing or after testing has been completed, examiners should not inform examinees of the correct answers to any of the questions. Disclosing specific test content invalidates future administrations. As noted on the copyright pages of the WJ III test materials, the WJ

III is not to be used in programs that require disclosure of questions or answers.

ADMINISTRATION CONSIDERATIONS

The goal of standardized testing is to see how well a person can respond when given instructions identical to those presented to individuals in the norm sample. If an examiner is learning to administer the tests of the WJ III ACH, he or she should study the contents of the Test Book, paying particular attention to the information after the tabbed page, the specific instructions on the test pages, and the boxes with special instructions. The clinician should then administer several practice tests, treating them as actual administrations and striving for exact and brisk administrations.

Order of Administration

In most cases, examiners follow the order of tests as they are presented in the easel Test Books. The tests have been ordered so that tasks alternate between different formats (e.g., timed versus untimed) and achievement areas (e.g., writing versus math). However, examiners may administer the tests in any order. As a general rule, clinicians should not administer two timed

---

CAUTION

Responsibility for Test Security

Standard 5.7: Test users have the responsibility of protecting the security of test materials at all times (AERA, APA, & NCME, 1999, p. 64).

Standard 12.11: Professionals and others who have access to test materials and test results should ensure the confidentiality of the test results and testing materials consistent with legal and professional standards (AERA, APA, & NCME, 1999, pp. 132–133).

DON'T FORGET

Exact Administration

Bold, blue type in Test Book presents the directions the examiner reads to examinee.

Directions to the examiner, such as when to point, are printed in black in Test Book.

Special instructions are presented in boxes in the Test Book.

Brisk Administration

Proceed to next item as soon as the examinee completes a response.

Do not stop and "visit" during the testing session.

Keep testing brisk to enhance rapport and help maintain attention.

CAUTION

Common Errors in Administration

- Not following standardized administration procedures
- Not testing by complete pages when stimuli are visible on examinee's page
- Not establishing basals or ceilings
- Not following cutoff or continuation instructions
- Not querying when indicated
- Not following directions in the Error or No Response boxes
- Not adhering to time limits on timed tests

tests, two listening tests, or two tests involving sustained writing (such as the Writing Samples and Writing Fluency tests) in a row. Testing may be discontinued between the administration of any two tests.

Suggested Starting Points

Using the Suggested Starting Points with basal and ceiling levels helps to reduce testing time. The Suggested Starting Points are located in the Test Book following the tabbed title page for each test. The clinician should select a starting point based on an estimate of the examinee's *achievement level* rather than by the age or grade placement. For example, individuals who are low-functioning may need to begin with a lower item than indicated by their present grade placement.

Time Requirements

As a general rule, experienced examiners require about 60 to 70 minutes to administer the tests in the Standard Battery. The Writing Samples test requires 15 to 20 minutes to administer, whereas the other tests require from 5 to 10 minutes each. The tests in the Extended Battery require an additional 5 to 10 minutes each.

The amount of time varies depending upon an examinee's characteristics. Clinicians should allow a reasonable time for a person to respond and then suggest moving on to the next item. If requested, more time may be given on a specific item, provided that the test directions allow for additional time.

Basal and Ceiling Rules

The purpose of basal and ceiling rules is to limit the span of items administered but still be able to estimate, with high probability, the score that would have been obtained if all items were administered. Test items span a wide range of difficulty, with the easiest item presented first and the most difficult item last. Consequently, a number of items in the test will be beyond a given individual's operating range (the set of items between the basal and ceiling levels). The basal level is the point below which a person has essentially a 100% chance of responding correctly to all items. The ceiling level is the point above which he or she essentially has a 0% chance of responding correctly to any items.

Criteria for basal and ceiling levels are included at the beginning of each test in the Test Book and are stated briefly at the top of the recording area for each test in the Test Record. Examiners should review the starting and stopping points of each test before testing.

The majority of the achievement tests indicate that the basal level is established after six consecutive correct responses. Testing begins with the Suggested Starting Point. If an examinee responds correctly to the first six or more consecutive items, testing continues until the ceiling criterion is met. If the basal is not obtained when the first six items are administered, the examiner should test backward page by complete page until six consecutive items are correct or until the page with Item 1 has been administered. Then he or she should return to the point at which testing was interrupted and continue testing from there until the ceiling criterion of failing the six highest-numbered consecutive items is met, or until the page with the last test item has been administered.

The best practice is to test by complete pages when stimulus material appears on the examinee's side of the easel. Because examinees do not see any of the pages that fall below the basal level or above the ceiling level, they are essentially unaware of the other test questions in the Test Book. If an individual reaches a ceiling in the middle of a test page and there is no material on the examinee's side, the examiner discontinues testing.

If a basal has not been established, then Item 1 serves as the basal. When a ceiling is not reached, the last item serves as the ceiling. In cases where there appears to be two basals, the clinician should use the six lowest-numbered consecutive correct responses as the true basal. Conversely, when there appears to be two ceilings, the clinician should use the six highest-numbered consecutive incorrect responses as the true ceiling. The best procedure for estimating a person's true score is to take into account all items passed and all items missed. The basal and ceiling rules are simply guides to minimize testing time.

Figure 2.2 illustrates how a basal and a ceiling were determined on Test 1:

Test 1 Letter-Word Identification

Basal: 6 lowest correct
Ceiling: 6 highest incorrect

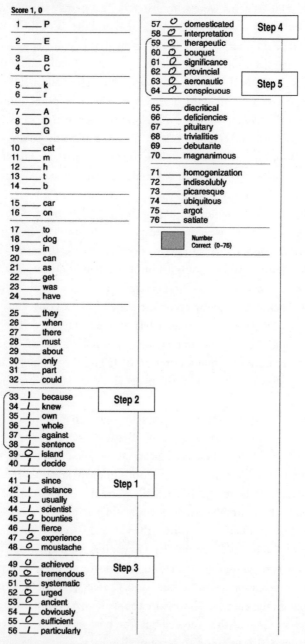

Score 1, 0

1 ____ P	
2 ____ E	
3 ____ B	
4 ____ C	
5 ____ k	
6 ____ r	
7 ____ A	
8 ____ D	
9 ____ G	
10 ____ cat	
11 ____ m	
12 ____ h	
13 ____ t	
14 ____ b	
15 ____ car	
16 ____ on	
17 ____ to	
18 ____ dog	
19 ____ in	
20 ____ can	
21 ____ as	
22 ____ get	
23 ____ was	
24 ____ have	
25 ____ they	
26 ____ when	
27 ____ there	
28 ____ must	
29 ____ about	
30 ____ only	
31 ____ part	
32 ____ could	

33 _1_ because
34 _1_ knew   **Step 2**
35 _1_ own
36 _1_ whole
37 _1_ against
38 _1_ sentence
39 _O_ island
40 _1_ decide

41 _1_ since
42 _1_ distance   **Step 1**
43 _1_ usually
44 _1_ scientist
45 _O_ bounties
46 _1_ fierce
47 _O_ experience
48 _O_ moustache

49 _O_ achieved
50 _O_ tremendous **Step 3**
51 _O_ systematic
52 _O_ urged
53 _O_ ancient
54 _1_ obviously
55 _O_ sufficient
56 _1_ particularly

57 _O_ domesticated   **Step 4**
58 _O_ interpretation
59 _O_ therapeutic
60 _O_ bouquet
61 _O_ significance
62 _O_ provincial
63 _O_ aeronautic   **Step 5**
64 _O_ conspicuous

65 ____ diacritical
66 ____ deficiencies
67 ____ pituitary
68 ____ trivialities
69 ____ debutante
70 ____ magnanimous

71 ____ homogenization
72 ____ indissolubly
73 ____ picaresque
74 ____ ubiquitous
75 ____ argot
76 ____ satiate

> **Number
> Correct (0–76)**

Figure 2.2 Determination of Basal and Ceiling Levels for Crystal, an Eighth Grader, on Test 1: Letter-Word Identification

Source: From the *WJ III Tests of Achievement*, by R. W. Woodcock, K. S. McGrew, and N. Mather, 2001, Itasca, IL: Riverside Publishing. Copyright © 2001 by The Riverside Publishing Company. Adapted with permission.

Letter-Word Identification for an 8th-grade girl, Crystal, who was referred for reading difficulties.

Step 1. The examiner estimated Crystal's reading level at Grade 5 to 6. The Suggested Starting Points table indicates testing should begin with Item 41. Crystal answered Items 41 to 44 correctly, but missed Item 45. Although she missed Item 45, the examiner administered the rest of the page, following the complete page rule. Crystal answered Item 46 correctly but missed Items 47 and 48. No basal was established.

Step 2. The examiner then flipped back one page and presented Items 33 to 40. Although Crystal missed Item 39, a basal level has been established. She correctly answered the six consecutive lowest-numbered items (33–38).

Step 3. The examiner returned to the point at which testing was interrupted and resumed testing with Item 49. Crystal missed Items 49 to 52. Although Crystal had now missed six consecutive items (47–52) the examiner completed the page because there was stimulus material visible on the examinee's side of the Test Book. In the process of completing the page, Crystal missed Items 53 and 55 but answered Items 54 and 56 correctly. Therefore, a ceiling was not established (six consecutive highest-numbered items administered incorrect) and testing continued.

Step 4. The examiner administered all the items on the next page (57–64) and obtained a ceiling when Crystal mispronounced them all. Although Crystal had missed six items (57–62), the page had to be completed.

Step 5. The examiner stopped testing with Item 64 because the ceiling level had been reached and the page had been completed.

Requests for Information by the Examinee

Occasionally individuals will request information. Generally, it will be easy to recognize whether it is appropriate to supply the requested information. The examiner should never tell the person whether specific answers are correct or incorrect. If the examiner cannot supply the requested information, he or she should respond with a comment such as "I'm not supposed to help you with that."

DON'T FORGET

Basal/Ceiling Rules

Tests with Basal of Six Consecutive Correct and Ceiling of Six Consecutive Incorrect

Letter-Word Identification, Calculation, Spelling, Passage Comprehension, Applied Problems, Word Attack, Picture Vocabulary, Oral Comprehension, Editing, Punctuation and Capitalization

Timed Tests

3-minute limit: Reading Fluency, Math Fluency

7-minute limit: Writing Fluency

Tests with Sets or Blocks of Items

Story Recall, Understanding Directions, Writing Samples, Story Recall-Delayed

Tests with Multiple Parts and Variable Basal/Ceiling Rules

Reading Vocabulary (4/4 for each part), Quantitative Concepts (4/4 for part A, 3/3 for part B), Academic Knowledge (3/3 for each part), Sound Awareness (4/4 for parts A and B, 3/3 for parts C and D), Spelling of Sounds (4/4)

Tests Requiring the Subject Response Booklet

The WJ III ACH SRB is needed when administering any of the following tests: Test 2 (Reading Fluency), Test 5 (Calculation), Test 6 (Math Fluency), Test 7 (Spelling), Test 8 (Writing Fluency), Test 11 (Writing Samples), Test 20 (Spelling of Sounds), and Test 22 (Punctuation and Capitalization). In addition, the SRB also contains a worksheet to use with Test 10 (Applied Problems) and Test 18 (Quantitative Concepts). The examiner gives the examinee the SRB and a pencil when directed to do so by instructions in the Test Book.

Timed Tests

Test 2 (Reading Fluency), Test 6 (Math Fluency), and Test 8 (Writing Fluency) are timed tests. The time limit is 3 minutes each for Reading Fluency and Math Fluency and 7 minutes for Writing Fluency. The time limits are noted on the test page as well as on the Test Record. Depending on the examinee's performance, testing may be discontinued prior to the time limit. The guidelines for stopping early on the three timed tests are:

Reading Fluency   2 or less correct on Samples C through F
Math Fluency   3 or less correct after 1 minute
Writing Fluency   0 on Samples B through D or 3 or fewer correct after
                      2 minutes

If possible, the examiner administers these tests using a stopwatch. If a stopwatch is not available, a watch or clock with a second hand may be used. The clinician should write down the exact starting and stopping times in minutes and seconds in the spaces provided in the Test Record rather than depend on memory. The times are entered into the WJ III Compuscore and Profiles Program (Schrank & Woodcock, 2001) to generate the scores for these tests. Bonus points are awarded to individuals who finish before the time limit expires. Limited adjustments are also made if an examiner accidentally allows the individual to work a few seconds past the time limit.

Audio-Recorded Tests

Several tests in the WJ III ACH are presented using the standardized test audio recording: Test 3 (Story Recall), Test 4 (Understanding Directions), Test 15 (Oral Comprehension), Test 20 (Spelling of Sounds), and Test 21 (Sound Awareness). As a general procedure when administering a recorded test, the examiner should look away from the examinee when a test item is presented. Immediately after the beep, he or she should look at the examinee to encourage a response.

On Test 3 (Story Recall) the examiner must pause or stop the recording after each story. On Test 4 (Understanding Directions) the examiner must pause or stop the recording between each picture administered to allow time for the examinee to review the new picture. On the other tests, there is adequate time between items for most people to respond. However, the pause or stop function may be used on any recorded WJ III ACH test if additional time is needed.

When administering these tests, examiners should use high-quality audio equipment and, if available, headphones. Audio equipment with a digital counter facilitates use of the recording in testing by readily locating starting points. Spaces to note starting points are provided in the introductory section of each recorded test in the Test Book. Although several of the tests may be presented using live voice, use of the test audio recording is expected and

DON'T FORGET

The test audio recording is required in the administration of the following tests:

- Story Recall
- Understanding Directions
- Oral Comprehension
- Spelling of Sounds
- Sound Awareness

DON'T FORGET

Keys to Competent Administration

- Know correct pronunciation of test items.
- Be fluent in administration.
- Understand basal/ceiling rules.
- If examinee gives more than one response to an item, score the last response given.
- Do not penalize for errors due to articulation or for regional, or dialectical speech differences.
- Test by complete pages when items are visible on examinee's test page.

headphones are recommended unless the person being tested resists wearing headphones or has difficulty attending to a recorded presentation.

Behavioral Observations

Because testing is a 1:1 situation, it provides an opportunity for careful observation of behavior. This information is an extremely important aspect of the evaluation process. Noting the examinee's reaction to the tests and the response style, as well as how he or she responds to items as they increase in difficulty, provides valuable insights for interpreting results or making recommendations. The WJ III facilitates this process by including a Test Session Observations Checklist on the first page of each Test Record. This checklist is a brief, seven-category behavior rating scale intended to systematize and document a number of salient examiner observations. The categories include levels of conversational proficiency, cooperation, level of activity, attention and concentration, self-confidence, care in responding, and response to difficult tasks. A range of possible responses is provided for each category in order to help identify whether the behavior is typical or atypical for the age or grade of the individual being assessed. The clinician may enter the information from the Test Session Observations Checklist into the software program for inclusion in the narrative report.

TEST BY TEST RULES OF ADMINISTRATION

Although the WJ III ACH *Examiner's Manual* and Test Books provide detailed rules for test by test administration, this section presents important reminders about the test. Whether the reader is familiar with the WJ-R Tests of Achievement or just learning the test, this section will serve as a guide or a good refresher. The information presented applies to Forms A and B. While studying the following descriptions of test administration procedures, it is recommended that the reader also follow the material in the Test Book and Test Record.

> ### DON'T FORGET
>
> #### Qualitative Information
>
> - Observe behavior during testing. Note reactions to the various tests, response style, level of effort, attention, persistence, level of cooperation, and conversational proficiency.
> - Use the Test Session Observations Checklist included in each WJ III Test Record to facilitate the collection of observational data.
> - Record errors for further analysis after testing is completed. Error analysis often provides important information for instructional planning.

HOW TO ADMINISTER THE STANDARD BATTERY, FORM A AND FORM B

Test 1: Letter-Word Identification

Administration

Select an appropriate starting point by consulting the Suggested Starting Points table located on the page after the tab in the Test Book. Establish a basal by testing by complete pages until the six consecutive lowest-numbered items are correct or until Item 1 has been administered. Continue testing by complete pages until the examinee misses the six highest-numbered items administered or until you have administered the page with the last item.

Know the correct pronunciation of each item. Pronunciation guides are provided in the test but you may consult a standard dictionary. Do not tell or help the examinee with any letters or words during this test. Do not read items to examinees.

If the examinee sounds out the word first and then says the correct word fluently, score it as correct. This is not a test of automaticity. Many readers need to employ decoding strategies to read words and should not be penalized for this. For example, if the examinee reads the stimulus word "island" as "is-land" and then says, "Oh, that's island" (pronouncing the stimulus correctly), score the item as correct. However, if the examinee reads "island" as "is-land" and never blends it together to pronounce the word correctly, score the item as incorrect. If the examinee's last response to an item is read phoneme by phoneme or syllable by syllable, score that item 0 and then suggest that the examinee "first read the word silently and then say the word smoothly." Give this reminder only once during the test.

When you are unsure of or did not hear the examinee's response to a specific item, do not ask him or her to repeat that item. Instead, have the examinee repeat all items on that page. Score only the item in question; do not re-score the other items.

Record incorrect responses for later error analysis. This analysis can provide valuable insights into the examinee's knowledge of grapheme/phoneme relationships as well as decoding skills and strategies. Rapid Reference 2.1 lists the key administration points for Letter-Word Identification.

≡Rapid Reference 2.1

Key Administration Points for Test 1: Letter-Word Identification

- *Materials needed:* Standard Battery Test Book and Test Record.
- Use Suggested Starting Points.
- Follow basal/ceiling rules: six consecutive correct/six consecutive incorrect.
- Know the exact pronunciation of each word.
- Do not tell the examinee any words or letters.
- Do not ask the examinee to repeat a specific word.
- Only accept correct responses that are pronounced as a complete word.
- Remember to complete the page, even after ceiling has been reached. If the examinee gives any correct responses in the process of completing the page, continue testing to reach a new ceiling.
- Record errors for analysis after testing is completed.
- Do not penalize for articulation errors or regional/dialectical speech differences.

Item Scoring

Score each correct response 1 and each incorrect response 0. Do not penalize an examinee for mispronunciations resulting from articulation errors, dialects, or regional speech patterns.

Common Examiner Errors

Common examiner errors include (a) having the examinee repeat a specific word, (b) failing to complete a page, (c) accepting responses that are sounded out but not blended back together, and (d) telling the examinee letters or words on the test.

Test 2: Reading Fluency

Administration

All examinees begin this test with the sample items. If the examinee has less than three correct answers on Practice Exercises C through F, discontinue testing and record a score of 0 in the Reading Fluency "Number Correct" box in the Test Record.

When ready to begin the test, give the examinee a sharpened pencil and the SRB. The 3-minute time limit begins with the administration of Item 1. Be sure to record the exact starting time in minutes and seconds if you are not using a stopwatch. During the test, if the examinee appears to be answering items without reading the sentences, remind him or her to read each sentence. If the examinee stops at the bottom of a page, remind him or her to continue to the top of the next column or on to the next page. Due to the way this test is scored, it is important that the examinee work in numeric sequence, only skipping the items that are unknown. If the examinee stops to erase an answer, encourage him or her to just quickly cross out the incorrect one. Because this is a timed test, it is important that the examinee not spend valuable time erasing.

Discontinue testing after *exactly 3 minutes* and collect the pencil and response booklet. If the examinee finishes in less than 3 minutes or the examiner accidentally exceeds 3 minutes, record the exact finishing time in minutes and seconds on the Test Record. Rapid Reference 2.2 lists the key administration points for Reading Fluency.

≡Rapid Reference 2.2

Key Administration Points for Test 2: Reading Fluency

- *Materials needed:* Standard Battery Test Book, Test Record, SRB, two pencils, and stopwatch or watch with second hand.
- Administer sample items to all examinees.
- Do not administer test if the examinee has less than three correct on Practice Exercises C through F.
- Begin with Item 1 for all examinees.
- Observe the 3-minute time limit.
- When not using a stopwatch, record exact starting time in minutes and seconds.
- Remind examinees to try to read the sentences if it appears they are simply circling answers randomly.
- Do not help the examinee with any words on this test.
- Remind examinees to continue working if they stop at the bottom of a page.
- Remind examinees to work in numeric sequence if it appears they are skipping around. It is acceptable to skip items that are not known.
- Remind examinees to quickly cross out (rather than erase) responses they wish to change.

Item Scoring

Score each correct response 1 and each incorrect response 0. A scoring guide overlay is provided for convenience and accuracy.

Common Examiner Errors

Common examiner errors include (a) failing to record exact starting or finishing times in minutes and seconds when not using a stopwatch, (b) failing to provide appropriate guidance during the test, and (c) providing help on words or sentences.

Test 3: Story Recall

Administration

Use the examinee's present level of oral comprehension skill as an estimate of where to begin testing. Consult the table in the Test Book to choose the appropriate starting point. Before administering the test, note the date and the time on the Test Record if you plan to administer Test 12: Story Recall-Delayed. Do not inform the examinee that he or she is going to be asked to recall the stories at a later time. If Test 12: Story Recall-Delayed will be administered within the same testing session, administer Test 3: Story Recall near the beginning of the testing session to allow for the greatest interval between administrations. The minimum interval is 30 minutes.

Administer this test using the audio recording. After playing each story, pause or stop the audio recording and look at the examinee to elicit a response. If the examinee does not respond, say, "Tell me the story." In rare cases, the examiner may present the items orally. Attempt to say the item in the same manner that it is presented on the audio recording. Rapid Reference 2.3 lists the key administration points for Story Recall.

≡ Rapid Reference 2.3

Key Administration Points for Test 3: Story Recall

- *Materials needed:* Standard Battery Test Book, Test Record, audio recording, and audio equipment.
- Use the examinee's current level of oral language comprehension to estimate starting point.
- Select the appropriate starting point from the table in the Test Book.
- Use audio recording to administer each story.
- Pause or stop the recording after each story to allow the examinee to recall elements.
- Do not repeat or replay any stories.
- The examinee must recall elements in bold type exactly (except for examples previously noted).
- Accept synonyms or paraphrased responses if elements are not in bold.
- In the Test Record, place a check mark over each element the examinee correctly recalled.
- Elements may be recalled in any order.
- Follow the continuation rules to determine when to administer additional stories or when to discontinue testing.
- Do not penalize for mispronunciations resulting from articulation errors, dialect variations, or regional speech patterns.
- Do not tell examinee if you intend to administer Test 12: Story Recall-Delayed.

Item Scoring

On the Test Record, slashes (/) separate the story elements. When scoring the test, place a check mark over each element recalled correctly. The elements may be recalled in any order. When words are in bold type, the examinee must recall the specific information exactly. For example, if the words *blowing bubbles* are in bold and the examinee says, "popping bubbles," do not give credit for the element. Two exceptions to this rule apply:

1. If the examinee gives a derivation of the bold word, allow credit for the element (e.g., "blew" for "blowing").
2. If the examinee uses a synonym very close in meaning (e.g., "afraid" for "scared"), allow credit for the element.

In addition, do not penalize for mispronunciations resulting from articulation errors, dialects, or regional speech patterns (e.g., "browing" for "blowing").

Elements that are not bold indicate that the examinee just needs to recall the general information or concept presented in the element. Examinees may use synonyms, such as "large" for "big" or paraphrase the information in any way that preserves meaning.

Continuation rules are presented after each set of two stories. These rules provide direction to the examiner regarding whether additional stories should be administered or testing should be discontinued. Follow these rules to ensure that the score is based on the best estimate of the examinee's recall ability.

Common Examiner Errors

Common examiner errors include (a) not using the audio recording, (b) not scoring the elements correctly, (c) not reading the story as it sounds on the tape (when administering the test orally), and (d) not following the continuation rules.

Test 4: Understanding Directions

Administration

Select a starting point based on an estimate of the examinee's present level of oral language skill. Consult the Suggested Starting Points table located in the Test Book to determine which picture or set of pictures to administer first. The three Suggested Starting Points are Picture 1 (preschool), Pictures 2 and 3 (kindergarten through grade 4), or Pictures 4 and 5 (grade 5 through adult). Administer all items for each picture in the suggested set. Follow the rules shown at the end of each set of pictures to determine when to discontinue testing or what additional pictures to administer. Continue testing until you reach the discontinue criterion for a particular set of pictures.

Before administering each picture, allow the examinee to review the picture for about 10 seconds. Do not repeat or replay an item unless the examinee did not hear it because of some type of noise, such as a school bell ringing. In this case, finish the picture and then rewind the tape and re-administer the specific item. In rare cases, you may present the items orally. Attempt to say the item in the same manner that it is presented on the audio recording. Rapid Reference 2.4 lists key administration points for Understanding Directions.

≡Rapid Reference 2.4

Key Administration Points for Test 4: Understanding Directions

- *Materials needed:* Standard Battery Test Book, Test Record, audio recording, and audio equipment.
- Use examinee's current level of oral language comprehension to estimate starting point.
- Use the audio recording to administer this test.
- Allow examinee to review the picture for 10 seconds before administering items for that picture.
- Do not allow the examinee to begin pointing until the word "go" is stated for each item.
- Complete all questions for each picture administered.
- The examinee must complete all steps to receive credit on an item.
- The examinee must recall steps in order unless order is not specified.
- Follow the rules shown after each set of pictures to determine when to discontinue or what additional pictures to administer.
- Do not repeat any items unless an obvious noise prevents the examinee from hearing the item.
- Know the pictures and items in order to facilitate scoring the examinee's pointing responses.

Item Scoring

Score each correct response 1 and each incorrect response 0. For the item to be scored as correct, the examinee must complete all of the steps of the direction. Many of the items require the examinee to point to certain objects before pointing to other objects. If the direction does not specify the sequence, the examinee may point in any order.

Common Examiner Errors

Common examiner errors include (a) not using the audio recording, (b) not scoring the items correctly, (c) not allowing the examinee to review the picture for 10 seconds before administering the items, and (d) not reading the directions as presented on the tape if administering the test orally.

Test 5: Calculation

Administration

Using the Suggested Starting Points located in the Test Book, select an appropriate starting point based on the examinee's present estimated level of math skills. When prompted, give the examinee a pencil with an eraser and the SRB. If the examinee misses both sample items, you may discontinue testing and score the test a 0. Administer the test following the basal and ceiling rules: six consecutive lowest-numbered items correct, six consecutive highest-numbered items failed. Rapid Reference 2.5 lists key administration points for Calculation.

Rapid Reference 2.5

Key Administration Points for Test 5: Calculation

- *Materials needed:* Standard Battery Test Book, Test Record, SRB, and two pencils.
- Select a starting point based on examinee's present estimated math skill level.
- Follow basal/ceiling rules: six consecutive correct/six consecutive incorrect.
- Discontinue testing and record a score of 0 if both sample items are missed.
- Complete all appropriate queries.
- Do not provide additional guidance, such as pointing out the signs.
- Score skipped items 0.
- Do not penalize for poorly formed numbers or reversals.
- Score transposed numbers 0.

Item Scoring

Score each correct calculation 1 and each incorrect response 0. Any items the examinee skipped before the last completed item should be scored 0. Do not penalize for poorly formed or reversed numbers on this test. Score a transposition of numbers (e.g., 13 for 31) as incorrect.

Common Examiner Errors

Common examiner errors include (a) failing to complete queries, (b) failing to establish a basal or ceiling, and (c) providing inappropriate guidance, such as alerting the examinee to pay attention to the signs.

Test 6: Math Fluency

Administration

All examinees begin this test with Item 1. When prompted, give the examinee a sharpened pencil and the SRB. If the examinee has three or less correct after 1 minute, discontinue testing and record a time of 1 minute in the Test Record. For all others, discontinue testing after exactly 3 minutes and collect the pencil and SRB. Once testing has started, do not point to the signs or remind the examinee to pay attention to the signs.

If the examinee finishes in less than 3 minutes or the examiner inadvertently exceeds the 3-minute time, record the exact finishing time in minutes and seconds on the Test Record. Rapid Reference 2.6 lists the key administration points for Math Fluency.

≡ Rapid Reference 2.6

Key Administration Points for Test 6: Math Fluency

- *Materials needed:* Standard Battery Test Book, Test Record, SRB, two pencils, and stopwatch or watch with second hand.
- When not using a stopwatch, record the exact starting time in minutes and seconds.
- Begin with Item 1 for all examinees.
- Observe the 3-minute time limit.
- Discontinue testing if the examinee has three or less correct after 1 minute. Record 1 minute.
- Do not point out the signs.
- Score all skipped items 0.

Item Scoring

Score each correct response 1 and each incorrect response 0. Score any items skipped prior to the last item the examinee completed as incorrect. Do not penalize for poorly formed or reversed numbers. A scoring guide overlay is provided to facilitate scoring.

Common Examiner Errors

A common examiner error is providing inappropriate guidance during the test, such as pointing out the signs.

Test 7: Spelling

Administration

Before administering this test, be sure to know the pronunciation of all test items. Using the table in the Test Book, select a starting point based on an estimate of the examinee's present level of spelling skill. When prompted, give the examinee a sharpened pencil with an eraser and the SRB. Printed responses are requested, but cursive responses are acceptable. Administer the test following the basal and ceiling rules: either six consecutive lowest-numbered items correct or Item 1; either six consecutive highest-numbered items failed or last item. Rapid Reference 2.7 lists key administration points for Spelling.

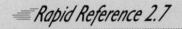

Rapid Reference 2.7

Key Administration Points for Test 7: Spelling

- *Materials needed:* Standard Battery Test Book, Test Record, SRB, and two pencils.
- Know the pronunciation of all test items.
- Use Suggested Starting Points.
- Follow basal/ceiling rules: six consecutive correct/six consecutive incorrect.
- Request printed responses but accept cursive writing.
- Do not penalize for poor handwriting or reversals, unless the reversal becomes a new letter.
- Accept upper- or lowercase responses unless case is specified.

Item Scoring

Score each correct response 1 and each incorrect response 0. Do not penalize for reversed letters as long as the letter does not become a new letter. For example, a reversed lowercase "c" would not be penalized, whereas a reversed lowercase letter "b" would be penalized because it becomes a new letter "d."

Common Examiner Errors

Common examiner errors include: mispronouncing items, scoring items incorrectly, or penalizing for reversed letters that do not become new letters.

Test 8: Writing Fluency

Administration

Complete the sample items and then begin with Item 1 for all examinees. If the examinee receives a zero on Samples B through D, discontinue testing and record a score of 0 for the test. If the examinee has three or fewer correct within the first 2 minutes, testing may be discontinued. Record a time of 2 minutes and enter the number correct (0–3). For all other examinees, discontinue testing after exactly 7 minutes and collect the pencil and response booklet. If the examinee finishes before the 7-minute time period has elapsed, or if the examiner inadvertently exceeds 7 minutes, record the actual finishing time in minutes and seconds on the Test Record.

In this test, you may read any of the stimulus words when requested by the examinee. This test may be administered to a small group of two or three individuals at one time if, in the examiner's judgment, this procedure will not affect any examinee's performance. Rapid Reference 2.8 lists key administration points for Writing Fluency.

Item Scoring

Score each correct response 1 and each incorrect response 0. Score any items skipped prior to the last item the examinee completed as incorrect. Do not penalize for errors in spelling, punctuation, or capitalization or for poor handwriting, unless the writing on an item is illegible.

Sometimes it may not be immediately apparent whether to score an item as correct or incorrect. To receive credit for an item the writer must (a) use the three stimulus words in a complete sentence, (b) not change the stimulus words in any way, and (c) provide a response that is a reasonable sentence. Awkward sentences (if the meaning is clear) and sentences with the understood subject "you" are scored as correct. Sentences that use alternate characters such as an ampersand (&) or plus sign (+) for the word "and" or an abbreviation like "w/"

≡Rapid Reference 2.8

Key Administration Points for Test 8: Writing Fluency

- *Materials needed:* Standard Battery Test Book, Test Record, SRB, two pencils, and stopwatch or watch with second hand.
- Test may be administered to a small group of two to three individuals.
- Complete sample items with all examinees.
- Discontinue testing if examinee has a 0 on Samples B through D.
- Begin test with Item 1 for all examinees.
- Observe the 7-minute time limit.
- Testing may be discontinued if examinee has three or fewer correct in first 2 minutes.
- Read any word requested by the examinee.
- To receive credit the examinee must use three stimulus words and may not change them.
- Do not penalize for poor writing or errors in capitalization, punctuation, or spelling as long as the response is legible.
- Score all skipped items 0.

instead of the full word "with" are scored as correct if the response meets all other criteria. If the examinee omits a word that is critical to the sentence meaning, score the response as incorrect. Do not penalize for an accidental omission of a less meaningful word ("a," "the," "an") in a sentence.

If, after reviewing these guidelines, it is still unclear how to score one or more items, balance the scores given to these responses. For example, if two items are unclear, score one item 1 and the other 0. Do not always give the examinee the benefit of the doubt when scoring questionable responses.

Common Examiner Errors

Examiner errors include being too lenient or too stringent on scoring the sentences and failing to note that the examinee has changed or not included a stimulus word.

Test 9: Passage Comprehension

Administration

Using the table in the Test Book, select a starting point based on an estimate of the examinee's present level of reading skill. Begin with the Introduction for examinees believed to be functioning at preschool or kindergarten level. Test by complete pages until examinee correctly answers the six lowest-numbered items administered or until you have administered the page with Item 1. Continue testing by complete pages until the examinee misses the six highest-numbered items administered or until you have administered the page with the last item.

The passages should be read silently. Some individuals, especially younger ones, will often read aloud. When this happens remind the examinee to read silently. If the examinee continues to read aloud, do not insist on silent reading. Do not help the examinee with any words on this test. The examinee needs only to identify the specific word that goes into the blank. If the examinee reads the sentence aloud with the correct answer say, "Tell me the one word that should go in the blank." If the examinee cannot provide the word, score the response as incorrect. Rapid Reference 2.9 lists the key administration points for Passage Comprehension.

Item Scoring

Score each correct response 1 and each incorrect response 0. Unless noted, only one-word responses are acceptable. If a person gives a two-word or longer response, ask for a one-word answer. Responses are correct when they

≡Rapid Reference 2.9

Key Administration Points for Test 9:
Passage Comprehension

- *Materials needed:* Standard Battery Test Book and Test Record.
- Use Suggested Starting Points.
- Follow basal/ceiling rules: six consecutive correct/six consecutive incorrect.
- Test by complete pages.
- When necessary, remind examinee to read silently.
- If the examinee reads a passage aloud, the word that belongs in the blank must be identified separately.
- Do not provide help with any words on this test.
- Do not penalize for responses that differ in tense or number.
- Score responses that substitute a different part of speech as incorrect.
- Do not penalize for articulation errors or regional, dialectical speech differences.

differ from the correct response only in verb tense or number (singular/plural). A response is incorrect if the examinee substitutes a different part of speech, such as a noun for a verb. Do not penalize for mispronunciations resulting from articulation errors, dialects, or regional speech patterns.

Common Examiner Errors

Common examiner errors include (a) providing help with words, (b) not completing queries, (c) penalizing for responses that differ only in verb tense or number, and (d) accepting responses that substitute a different part of speech.

Test 10: Applied Problems

Administration

Using the table in the Test Book, select a starting point based on an estimate of the examinee's present level of math skill. When prompted, give the examinee a pencil with an eraser and the SRB. These materials may be given prior to the prompt if the examinee requests them or appears to need them. Test by complete pages until the examinee correctly answers the six lowest-numbered items administered, or until you have administered the page with Item 1. Continue testing by complete pages until the examinee misses the six highest-numbered items administered or until you have administered the page with the last item. Upon request by the examinee, any item may be repeated. Rapid Reference 2.10 lists the key administration points for Applied Problems.

=== Rapid Reference 2.10

Key Administration Points for Test 10: Applied Problems

- *Materials needed:* Standard Battery Test Book, Test Record, SRB, and two pencils.
- Use Suggested Starting Points.
- Follow basal/ceiling rules: six consecutive correct/six consecutive incorrect.
- Test by complete pages.
- Provide the SRB and pencil when prompted, or earlier if needed.
- Repeat items if they are requested by the examinee.

Item Scoring

Score each correct response 1 and each incorrect response 0.

Common Examiner Errors

Common examiner errors include forgetting to test by complete pages or not repeating items upon request.

Test 11: Writing Samples

Administration

This test may be administered to a small group of two or three individuals at one time if, in your judgment, this procedure will not affect any individual's performance. Select a starting point based on an estimate of the examinee's present level of writing ability.

Administer the appropriate block of items as indicated on the table in the Test Book on the page after the Writing Samples tab. When prompted, give the examinee a pencil with an eraser and the SRB. If an examinee's response to an item is illegible or difficult to read, ask him or her to write as neatly as possible. You may read any words during this test or may repeat the instructions if requested by the examinee. When an examinee asks if spelling is important or how to spell a word, encourage the examinee to just do the best he or she can. Rapid Reference 2.11 lists the key administration points for Writing Samples.

Item Scoring

Score Writing Samples after testing is completed. Items may be scored 0, .5, 1, 1.5, or 2 points using a modified holistic procedure that requires judgment. Because scoring of this test is more involved and subjective than scoring other WJ

≡ *Rapid Reference 2.11*

Key Administration Points for Test 11: Writing Samples

- *Materials needed:* Standard Battery Test Book, Test Record, SRB, and two pencils.
- Use the examinee's estimated writing ability to select a block of items to administer.
- Score the items after the testing is complete.
- Administer additional items if the examinee's score falls in a shaded area.
- Read words to the examinee as he or she requests.
- Do not spell any words for the examinee.
- Do not ask the examinee to read his or her response for scoring purposes.
- Be sure the raw score is based on only one of the established blocks of items.
- Encourage examinee to attempt a response to each item in the block.

III ACH tests, special rating and scoring procedures are provided in Appendix B of the *WJ III Tests of Achievement Examiner's Manual* that accompanies the test. This section presents a summary of item-scoring procedures, and Chapter 3 presents additional details regarding scoring.

2 Points. A 2-point response is a superior response. Excluding beginning items, it is a complete sentence that satisfies task demands and includes additional descriptive words and embellishments.

1.5 Points. A response of 1.5 points is a borderline response that does not fit the exact pattern of the Scoring Guide. If it is not clear whether a response is superior (2 points) or standard (1 point), credit the response with a score of 1.5 points.

1 Point. A 1-point response is a standard response. Excluding beginning items, it is a complete sentence with adequate content.

0.5 Points. A response of 0.5 points is a borderline response that does not fit the exact pattern of the Scoring Guide. If it is not clear whether a response is standard (1 point) or inadequate (0 points), credit the response with a score of 0.5 points.

0 Points. A no-credit response is an inadequate response. It may be an incomplete sentence, a sentence with minimal content, an illegible response, or a sentence that does not follow task demands.

If the individual's raw score falls within one of the seven shaded areas in the scoring table, consider administering the additional items that are noted in the "Adjusted Item Blocks" chart in the Test Record. This will provide a more accurate representation of the examinee's writing ability.

Common Examiner Errors

Common examiner errors include (a) failing to administer the appropriate block of items, (b) scoring the items incorrectly, (c) being too lenient or harsh when evaluating responses, (d) failing to administer additional items when necessary, (e) calculating the raw score incorrectly, and (f) asking the examinee to read his or her response for scoring purposes.

Test 12: Story Recall-Delayed

Administration

Only administer this test if you have already administered Test 3: Story Recall. Be sure to administer the same stories that were presented on Test 3: Story Recall. Record the date and time of administration so that the correct delay interval is calculated. Rapid Reference 2.12 lists the key administration points for Test 12: Story Recall-Delayed.

Item Scoring

Score this test the same as Test 3: Story Recall. On the Test Record, check off the parts of the story that the examinee recalls accurately. Do not score the points that are used as the prompts for the recall of the story.

Common Examiner Errors

A common examiner error is adding in points for the prompts that are read by the examiner.

≡ Rapid Reference 2.12

Key Administration Points for Test 12: Story Recall-Delayed

- *Materials needed:* Standard Battery Test Book and Test Record.
- Administer this test only if Test 3: Story Recall has already been given.
- Administer only the stories that were previously given on Test 3.
- Record the date and time you administered Test 12.
- Do not include the prompts you read in the raw score.

ADMINISTRATION OF THE EXTENDED BATTERY, FORM A AND FORM B

Test 13: Word Attack

Administration

Review the correct pronunciation of all items before administering this test. Pronunciation for more difficult items follows in parentheses. Refer to the pronunciation guide in the test's manual or the Test Book. If the examinee has any special speech characteristics resulting from articulation errors or dialect, an examiner who is familiar with the examinee's speech pattern should administer this test.

Using the table in the Test Book, select a starting point based on an estimate of the individual's present level of reading skill. Test by complete pages until the examinee has missed six consecutive items, or until you have administered the last item.

If a response to a specific item is unclear, do not ask the examinee to repeat the specific item. Instead, complete the entire page and then ask the examinee to repeat all of the items on that page. Score only the item in question; do not re-score the other items.

If the examinee pronounces the word phoneme by phoneme or syllable by syllable instead of reading it in a natural and fluent way, score the item 0 and suggest that the examinee "first read the word silently and then say the word smoothly." Give this reminder only once during the administration of this test. However, if the examinee first sounds out the stimulus word and then pronounces it correctly, score the item 1. Score the last response given. Record incorrect responses for error analysis. Rapid Reference 2.13 lists the key administration points for Word Attack.

Item Scoring

Score each correct response 1 and each incorrect response 0. Do not penalize the examinee for mispronunciations resulting from articulation errors, dialects, or regional speech patterns.

Common Examiner Errors

Examiner errors include (a) failing to know the correct pronunciation of the items, (b) accepting responses that are sounded out and not blended to-

≡Rapid Reference 2.13

Key Administration Points for Test 13: Word Attack

- *Materials needed:* Extended Battery Test Book and Test Record.
- Know pronunciation of all items prior to administering this test.
- Use Suggested Starting Points.
- Follow basal/ceiling rules: six consecutive correct/six consecutive incorrect.
- Test by complete pages.
- Do not tell the examinee any letters or words.
- Only accept correct responses that are pronounced as a complete word.
- Do not ask the examinee to repeat a specific word. Instead, have the examinee repeat entire page and re-score only the item in question.
- Record errors for analysis after testing is completed.
- Score the last response given on each item.

gether, and (c) failing to have examinee repeat an entire page when one response was not heard.

Test 14: Picture Vocabulary

Administration

Be sure to know the correct pronunciation of the items. Pronunciation for more difficult items follows in parentheses. Refer to the pronunciation guide in the manual and the Test Books, or refer to any standard dictionary. Select a starting point based on an estimate of the individual's present level of oral language skill. Point to the appropriate picture or the specific part of the picture as directed in the instructions for each item in the Test Book. Complete any query listed in the Test Book. Test by complete pages until the examinee correctly answers the six lowest-numbered items administered or until you have administered the page with Item 1. Continue testing by complete pages until the examinee misses the six highest-numbered items administered or until you have administered the page with the last item. Rapid Reference 2.14 lists the key administration points for Picture Vocabulary.

Item Scoring

Score each correct response 1 and each incorrect response 0. Do not penalize an examinee for mispronunciations resulting from articulation errors, dialects, or regional speech patterns.

Common Examiner Errors

Examiner errors include (a) failing to point to the picture or specific picture part as directed, (b) failing to complete queries, and (c) failing to test by complete pages.

=Rapid Reference 2.14

Key Administration Points for Test 14: Picture Vocabulary

- *Materials needed:* Extended Battery Test Book and Test Record.
- Know the pronunciation of all test items.
- Use Suggested Starting Points.
- Follow basal/ceiling rules: six consecutive correct/six consecutive incorrect.
- Test by complete pages.
- Complete all queries as indicated in the Test Book.
- Be sure to point to the picture or picture part as directed.
- Record errors for further analysis.

Test 15: Oral Comprehension

Administration

Administer Sample Items A and B to all examinees and then select a starting point based on an estimate of the examinee's present oral language skill. Present Sample Items A and B orally. Present Sample Items C and D and all test items using the audio recording. In rare cases, you may present the items orally. Attempt to say the sentence in exactly the same manner that it is presented on the audio recording.

Test by complete pages until the examinee correctly answers the six lowest-numbered items administered or until you have administered the page with Item 1. Continue testing by complete pages until the examinee misses the six highest-numbered items administered or until you have administered the page with the last item. Rapid Reference 2.15 lists the key administration points for Oral Comprehension.

Item Scoring

Score each correct response 1 and each incorrect response 0. Unless noted, only one-word responses are acceptable. If a person gives a two-word or

---

≡ *Rapid Reference 2.15*

Key Administration Points for Test 15: Oral Comprehension

- *Materials needed:* Extended Battery Test Book, Test Record, audio recording, and audio equipment.
- Use Suggested Starting Points.
- Orally administer Samples A and B to all examinees.
- Use audio recording for Samples C and D and all test items.
- Follow basal/ceiling rules: six consecutive correct / six consecutive incorrect.
- Test by complete pages.
- Accept only one-word responses unless otherwise noted.
- Request one-word responses if examinee gives longer responses.
- Do not penalize for articulation errors or regional/dialectical speech differences.
- Do not penalize for responses that differ in tense or number.
- Do not accept responses that are a different part of speech.

longer response, ask for a one-word answer. Responses are correct when they differ from the correct response only in verb tense or number (singular/plural). A response is incorrect if the examinee substitutes a different part of speech, such as a noun for a verb. Do not penalize for mispronunciations resulting from articulation errors, dialects, or regional speech patterns.

Common Examiner Errors

Examiner errors include (a) failing to use the test audio recording, (b) failing to ask for one-word responses when a longer response is given, and (c) failing to imitate the tape when administering the test orally.

Test 16: Editing

Administration

Administer Sample Items A through D to all individuals and then select a starting point based on an estimate of the examinee's present level of writing ability. Test by complete pages until the examinee correctly answers six lowest-numbered items administered or until you have administered the page with Item 1. If the examinee has a score of 0 correct on the four sample items or on Items 1 through 4, discontinue testing and record a score of 0. Test by complete pages until the examinee misses the six highest-numbered items administered or until you have administered the page with the last item.

If the examinee requests it, read individual words; however, do not read an entire item. If an examinee reads the sentence aloud and inadvertently corrects the error in context, you may say, "Tell me how to correct the error." If the examinee indicates the error without explaining how to correct it, you may say, "How would you correct that mistake?" Unless the examinee can both identify and correct the error in the passage, score the item as incorrect. Rapid Reference 2.16 lists the key administration points for Editing.

Item Scoring

Score each correct response 1 and each incorrect response 0. For a response to be correct, the examinee must indicate both where the error is located and how it should be corrected.

≡Rapid Reference 2.16

Key Administration Points for Test 16: Editing

- *Materials needed:* Extended Battery Test Book and Test Record.
- Administer Samples A through D to all individuals.
- Select a starting point based on the individual's estimated writing ability.
- Follow basal/ceiling rules: six consecutive correct/six consecutive incorrect.
- Test by complete pages.
- Discontinue testing if an individual has a 0 on Samples A through D, or Items 1 through 4.
- Upon request, you may tell the examinee individual words. Do not read an entire item.
- Be sure to query when necessary.
- Do not give credit unless the examinee identifies and corrects the error.

Common Examiner Errors

Common examiner errors include (a) failing to read individual words when requested by the examinee, (b) failing to have the examinee both *identify and correct* the error, and (c) failing to query when necessary.

Test 17: Reading Vocabulary

Administration

Review the correct pronunciation of all items while learning to administer the test. Examiners may wish to make note of oral reading errors for error analysis. After administering the sample items, do not read any other items or tell the examinee any other words. All three subtests (Synonyms, Antonyms, and Analogies) must be administered to obtain a raw score for this test. For each subtest, administer the sample items to all examinees and then select a starting point based on an estimate of current reading ability. For each subtest, test by complete pages until the examinee correctly answers the four lowest-numbered items administered or until you have administered the page with Item 1. For each subtest, test by complete pages until the examinee misses the four highest-numbered items administered or until you have administered the

≡ Rapid Reference 2.17

Key Administration Points for Test 17: Reading Vocabulary

- *Materials needed:* Extended Battery Test Book and Test Record.
- Know the pronunciation of each item.
- Administer all three subtests.
- Administer sample items for each subtest to all examinees.
- Select an appropriate starting point for each subtest based on the examinee's current reading ability.
- Follow the basal/ceiling rules for each subtest: four consecutive correct/four consecutive incorrect.
- Test by complete pages.
- Do not tell the examinee any words in the test items.
- Unless noted, only one-word responses are acceptable.
- Record errors for further analysis.

page with the last item. Rapid Reference 2.17 lists the key administration points for Reading Vocabulary.

Item Scoring

Score each correct response 1 and each incorrect response 0. Unless noted, only one-word responses are acceptable. If a person gives a two-word or longer response, ask for a one-word answer. Responses are correct when they differ from the correct response only in verb tense or number (singular/plural). A response is incorrect if the examinee substitutes a different part of speech, such as a noun for a verb. If an examinee responds to an antonym item by giving the stimulus word preceded by "non" or "un," ask for another answer unless otherwise indicated by the scoring key. Do not penalize for mispronunciations resulting from articulation errors, dialects, or regional speech patterns.

Common Examiner Errors

Examiner errors include (a) reading items to examinees, (b) failing to administer all three subtests, (c) failing to apply the basal/ceiling rules to each subtest, and (d) miscalculating the total score.

Test 18: Quantitative Concepts

Administration

Both subtests (18A: Concepts and 18B: Number Series) must be administered to obtain a raw score for this test. For each subtest, select a starting point based on an estimate of the examinee's present level of math skill. For subtest 18B: Number Series, administer the sample item to all individuals. When prompted, give the examinee a sharpened pencil with an eraser and the SRB. If the examinee requests, any item may be repeated.

For 18A: Concepts, test by complete pages until the examinee correctly answers the four lowest-numbered items administered or until you have administered the page with Item 1. Continue testing by complete pages until the examinee misses the four highest-numbered items administered or until you have administered the page with the last item.

For 18B: Number Series, test by complete pages until the examinee correctly answers the three lowest-numbered items administered or until you have administered the page with Item 1. Continue testing by complete pages until the examinee misses the three highest-numbered items administered or until you have administered the page with the last item. Give the examinee 1 minute to respond to each item. Rapid Reference 2.18 lists the key administration points for Quantitative Concepts.

Item Scoring

Score each correct response 1 and each incorrect response 0. Several items require more than one response to receive credit. For example, the examinee may be asked to point to the smallest triangle, then to the largest triangle.

Common Examiner Errors

Examiner errors include (a) failing to administer both parts to obtain a raw score, (b) failing to apply the correct basal/ceiling rule to each part, and (c) forgetting to give a 1 minute time limit to each item in 18B: Number Series.

Test 19: Academic Knowledge

Administration

Review the exact pronunciation for all the words while learning to administer to this test. The pronunciation for more difficult items follows in parentheses.

≡Rapid Reference 2.18

Key Administration Points for Test 18: Quantitative Concepts

- *Materials needed:* Extended Battery Test Book, Test Record, SRB, and two pencils.
- Administer both subtests (18A and 18B) to obtain a raw score.
- Select a starting point for each subtest based on the individual's current level of math skill.
- Follow the basal/ceiling rules for each subtest: (18A) four consecutive correct / four consecutive incorrect; (18B) three consecutive correct/three consecutive incorrect.
- Test by complete pages.
- Repeat any item upon request by the examinee.
- Allow 1 minute for each item in 18B: Number Series.
- On items with multiple-part answers, be sure all parts of the answer are given to score item 1.

For other items, consult the pronunciation guide in the Test Book and *Manual* or consult a standard dictionary. Administer all three subtests (Science, Social Studies, and Humanities) to obtain a raw score for this test. Select a starting point for each subtest based on an estimate of the individual's present achievement level. For each subtest, test by complete pages until the examinee correctly answers the three lowest-numbered items administered or until you have administered the page with Item 1. For each subtest, test by complete pages until the examinee misses the three highest-numbered items administered or until you have administered the page with the last item. Any item may be repeated if the examinee requests. Rapid Reference 2.19 lists key administration points for Academic Knowledge.

Item Scoring
Score each correct response 1 and each incorrect response 0. Do not penalize for mispronunciations resulting from articulation errors, dialects, or regional speech patterns.

Common Examiner Errors
Examiner errors include (a) mispronouncing items, (b) failing to administer all three parts, and (c) failing to apply basal/ceiling rules to each part of the test.

≡*Rapid Reference 2.19*

Key Administration Points for Test 19: Academic Knowledge

- *Materials needed:* Extended Battery Test Book and Test Record.
- Know the pronunciation of all items.
- Administer all three subtests to obtain a raw score.
- Select starting point for each subtest based on examinee's present achievement level.
- Follow basal/ceiling rules for each subtest: three consecutive correct/three consecutive incorrect.
- Test by complete pages.
- Repeat any item upon request of examinee.
- Do not penalize for articulation errors or regional or dialectical speech differences.

Test 20: Spelling of Sounds

Administration

Present Sample Items A through D and Items 1 through 5 orally. When a letter is printed within slashes, such as /m/, say the most common sound (phoneme) of the letter, not the letter name. Present the remaining items using the audio recording. Before beginning the test, locate Item 6 on the audio recording and adjust the volume to a comfortably loud level. When prompted, give the examinee a sharpened pencil with an eraser and the SRB.

Select a starting point based on an estimate of the examinee's present achievement level. Test until the examinee correctly answers the four lowest-numbered items administered or until you have administered Item 1. Test until the examinee scores a 0 on the four highest-numbered items administered or until you have administered the last test item. If the examinee has a score of 0 on Items 1 through 4, discontinue testing and record a score of 0 in the Spelling of Sounds Number Correct box in the Test Record.

Although the audio recording provides adequate time for most individuals to write responses, pause or stop the audio recording if the examinee needs more time. If the examinee requests it, replay an item on the tape. Rapid Reference 2.20 lists key administration points for Spelling of Sounds.

≡Rapid Reference 2.20

Key Administration Points for Test 20: Spelling of Sounds

- *Materials needed:* Extended Battery Test Book, Test Record, SRB, audio recording, audio equipment, and two pencils.
- Know pronunciation of samples and Items 1 through 5 before administering the test.
- Select starting point based on examinee's current achievement level.
- Administer Samples A through D and Items 1 through 5 orally.
- Use the audio recording beginning with Item 6.
- Give the examinee the SRB and pencil when prompted.
- Follow the basal/ceiling rules: four consecutive correct/four consecutive incorrect.
- Score Items 6 through 12 as multiple-point responses. Score all other items 1 or 0.
- Use only the answers listed in the Test Book as correct responses.
- Repeat items if the examinee requests.

Item Scoring

The responses listed in the Test Book are the *only* correct answers. Although a response may seem like a reasonable sound spelling, the intent of this test is to measure both phonological coding skills and sensitivity to the most commonly occurring orthographic patterns (visual sequences of letters) in the English language. For example, the sound /kr/ is most typically spelled in English with the letters "cr" rather than "kr."

The first five items require single letter responses and, if correct, are scored with 1 point each. On Items 6 through 12, the examinee receives points for each correctly written and sequenced letter or word part. Points are deducted for sounds that are not present, as well as for sounds that have been altered by the inclusion of additional letters. The specific scoring of these items is indicated both in the Test Book and on the Test Record. After Item 12, all remaining items are scored 1 point each. Chapter 3 presents further details regarding item scoring.

Analysis of errors can help to determine if the examinee is able to sequence sounds correctly but has difficulty assimilating or recalling common orthographic patterns.

Do not penalize for reversed letters as long as the letter does not become a new letter. For example, a reversed lowercase "c" would not be penalized, whereas a reversed lowercase letter "b" would be penalized because it becomes a new letter "d."

Common Examiner Errors

Examiner errors include (a) incorrectly scoring items, (b) failing to use the answers provided in the Test Book as the only correct responses, and (c) failing to replay items if examinee requests.

Test 21: Sound Awareness

Administration

Administer all four subtests (Rhyming, Deletion, Substitution, and Reversal) to obtain a raw score for this test. Administer the sample items for each subtest to all individuals and then continue with the test items. For subtests 21A: Rhyming and 21B: Deletion, test until the examinee misses the four highest-numbered items administered or until you have administered the last item. For subtests 21C: Substitution and 21D: Reversal, test until the examinee misses the three highest-numbered items administered or until you have administered the last item.

Administer subtest 21A: Rhyming orally. For subtest 21B: Deletion, administer Sample Item A orally and all other items from the audio recording. For subtest 21C: Substitution, administer Sample Items A and B and Items 1 through 3 orally. Administer Sample Items C and D and Items 4 through 9 from the audio recording. For subtest 21D: Reversal, administer Sample Item A and Items 1 through 9 orally. Administer Sample Item B from the audio recording.

Letters printed within slashes, such as /s/, indicate that the examiner should say the most common sound of the letter (the phoneme), not the letter name. Consider recording errors for later error analysis. Rapid Reference 2.21 lists the key administration points for Sound Awareness.

Item Scoring

Score each correct response 1 and each incorrect response 0. Responses must be real words to receive credit. Do not penalize for mispronunciations resulting from articulation errors, dialects, or regional speech patterns.

≡Rapid Reference 2.21

Key Administration Points for Test 21: Sound Awareness

- Materials needed: Extended Battery Test Book, Test Record, audio recording, and audio equipment.
- Administer all four subtests to obtain a raw score.
- Know the pronunciation of samples and items that are presented orally.
- Administer the sample items to all individuals for each subtest.
- Begin with Item 1 on each subtest.
- Follow the ceiling rules for each subtest: (21A and 21B) four consecutive incorrect; (21C and 21D) three consecutive incorrect.
- Responses must be real words to receive credit.
- Record errors for further analysis.
- Use the audio recording as directed.

Common Examiner Errors

A common error is mispronouncing the samples and items that are presented orally.

Test 22: Punctuation and Capitalization

Administration

CAUTION

On 21D: Sound Awareness Reversal, only Sample B is on the audiotape. All test items are presented orally by the examiner. Items 4–9 are pronounced as complete words, therefore, a taped administration is not necessary.

While learning to administer the test, review the pronunciation of all test items. Use the pronunciation guides provided in the test materials or consult a standard dictionary. When prompted, give the examinee a sharpened pencil with an eraser and the SRB. Select a starting point based on an estimate of the examinee's present level of achievement. Test until the examinee correctly answers the six lowest-numbered items administered or until you have administered Item 1. Continue testing until the examinee misses the six highest-numbered items administered or until you have administered the last test. Although the examinee is asked to print responses, cursive responses are also acceptable. The letter "P" in parentheses after the item number indicates that the item is a punctuation item. The letter "C" in parentheses after the item

≡ *Rapid Reference 2.22*

Key Administration Points for Test 22: Punctuation and Capitalization

- *Materials needed:* Extended Battery Test Book, Test Record, SRB, and two pencils.
- Know pronunciation of items.
- Use starting point based on examinee's current achievement level.
- Follow basal/ceiling rules: six consecutive correct/six consecutive incorrect.
- Ask examinee to print responses, although cursive is acceptable.
- Do not penalize for spelling errors.
- Note that items marked "P" measure punctuation and items marked "C" measure capitalization.

number indicates that the item is a capitalization item. Rapid Reference 2.22 lists the key administration points for Punctuation and Capitalization.

Item Scoring

Score each correct response 1 and each incorrect response 0. Incorrectly spelled responses are acceptable for this test as long as they are legible. Do not penalize for poorly formed or reversed letters as long as the letter does not become a new letter. For example, a reversed lowercase "c" would not be penalized, whereas a reversed lowercase letter "b" would be penalized because it becomes a new letter "d."

Common Examiner Errors

Examiner errors include (a) mispronouncing items and (b) scoring items incorrectly (e.g., penalizing for spelling errors).

Handwriting Evaluation

The WJ III ACH offers two tools for evaluating handwriting and writing skill in more depth. Examiners may use the Handwriting Legibility Scale in Appendix C of the *WJ III Tests of Achievement Examiner's Manual* and the Handwriting Elements Checklist in the Test Record. To use either approach, select a page of the examinee's handwriting from Test 11: Writing Samples in the SRB or select samples of handwriting from other sources.

For the standardized evaluation using the Handwriting Legibility Scale, match the appearance of the examinee's handwriting to the samples on the scale in Appendix C. Consider both the legibility and the general appearance of the handwriting. Do not let an examinee's individual style, such as a back-hand slant, influence judgment about the legibility or appearance of the sample. The focus is on identifying the sample that is most like the examinee's typical handwriting. The samples are arranged along a 100-point scale ranging from illegible to artistic in 10-point increments.

The Handwriting Elements Checklist, located in the Test Record, can be used to analyze six elements that affect handwriting quality: slant, spacing, size, horizontal alignment, letter formation, and line quality. Evaluation of the six elements of handwriting aids in planning or recommending instructional

◆ Rapid Reference 2.23

Steps for Using the Writing Evaluation Scale

1. Select one or more samples of the individual's writing (e.g., story, essay, or report).
2. Record the writer's name, the date, and the type of writing to be evaluated on the WES.
3. Read the entire sample to form an overall impression of organization and content.
4. Reread the sample and mark all errors directly on the sample. Note mistakes in usage, spelling, punctuation, and capitalization.
5. Judge the sample by selecting the most appropriate ratings for the writing skill components on the WES. Do not rate elements that are not present.
6. Review and attempt to categorize the types of errors.
7. If desired, repeat the evaluation process using a different writing sample.
8. Referring to the strengths and weaknesses identified by the WES, develop appropriate instructional goals for the individual.
9. Attach the writing sample to the completed WES and file them in the individual's writing folder or portfolio. Refer to these materials to monitor progress.

procedures. While judging each of the six elements of writing quality, identify specific areas of need and record comments relevant to instructional planning.

Writing Evaluation Scale

The Writing Evaluation Scale (WES), a resource for evaluating longer, more complex examples of an individual's writing, is located in Appendix D of the WJ III ACH Examiner's Manual. Permission is granted to reproduce the WES for use with examinees. This scale provides a procedure for monitoring and assessing written language over time. Using the WJ III ACH writing tests in combination with the WES helps identify the individual's writing skills that need improvement, establish personal writing goals, and monitor growth in writing skill. The WES can be used as a tool to involve the writer actively in the evaluation process.

The WES uses an analytic scoring method that rates several different components of writing skill and assigns scores (Huot, 1990). In contrast to holistic scores, analytic scores provide more specific information regarding a writer's strengths and weaknesses in writing skill (Diederich, 1974). Rapid Reference 2.23 illustrates the steps to follow in rating a written product using the WES.

🖜 TEST YOURSELF 🖜

1. **All tests in the Standard Battery must be administered before using the Extended Battery.** True or False?

2. **List the four tests that have multiple parts that must be administered to get the score.**

3. **List the tests that require the audio recording.**

4. **List the timed tests.**

5. **All reading tests have the same basal/ceiling rules.** True or False?

6. **List the tests that require the use of the SRB.**

7. **The WJ III Tests of Achievement may not be used if the individual has physical or sensory impairments.** True or False?

8. **What materials that are not included with the test kit may be needed to administer some of the tests?**

9. **On Letter-Word Identification, an examiner began the test with Item 33. The examinee got Items 33 to 37 correct, but missed Item 38. What should the examiner do?**

   (a) Continue testing until the examinee misses six in a row.

   (b) Discontinue testing and give the examinee a 0.

   (c) Go back to Item 1 and administer Items 1 to 6.

   (d) Complete the page (Items 39–40) and then turn back one page and administer all items on that page beginning with the first item (Items 25–32).

10. **How should the following items be scored (using a 1 or a 0 for each item)?**

    (a) On Calculation—correct answer is 14, examinee wrote "41."

    (b) On Calculation—correct answer is 3, examinee wrote a backward "3."

    (c) On Oral Comprehension—correct answer is "cars," examinee said "car."

    (d) On Passage Comprehension—correct answer is "lie," examinee said "liar."

    (e) On Letter-Word Identification—correct answer is "island," examinee said "i . . . i . . . land" and did not pronounce the whole word.

    (f) On Spelling of Sounds—correct answer is "gat," examinee wrote "gate" (score using 0, 1, 2, or 3).

    (g) On Spelling—correct answer is "table," examinee wrote "tadle."

11. **When a letter is shown between slashes as /m/, the examiner should say the most common sound for that letter, not the letter name.** True or False?

12. **Which tests require that the score be based on a block of items?**

13. **If an examiner intends to give Story Recall-Delayed, which of the following things must he or she do?**

    (a) Administer Test 3: Story Recall at least 30 minutes in advance.

    (b) When giving Test 3, tell the examinee that you will be administering the delayed recall test later.

    (c) Exclude points used to prompt recall.

    (d) Only administer the items that were missed during the administration of Test 3.

14. **The Test Session Observations Checklist is a reproducible page located in an appendix of the *Examiner's Manual*.** True or False?

(continued)

15. The WES is a reproducible page located in an appendix of the *Examiner's Manual*. True or False?

Answers: 1. False; 2. Test 17: Reading Vocabulary, Test 18: Quantitative Concepts, Test 19: Academic Knowledge, Test 21: Sound Awareness; 3. Test 3: Story Recall, Test 4: Understanding Directions, Test 15: Oral Comprehension, Test 20: Spelling of Sounds, Test 21: Sound Awareness; 4. Test 2: Reading Fluency, Test 6: Math Fluency, Test 8: Writing Fluency, 18B: Quantitative Concepts-Number Series; 5. False; 6. Test 2: Reading Fluency, Test 5: Calculation, Test 6: Math Fluency, Test 7: Spelling, Test 8: Writing Fluency, Test 10: Applied Problems, Test 11: Writing Samples, Test 18: Quantitative Concepts, Test 20: Spelling of Sounds, Test 22: Punctuation and Capitalization; 7. False; 8. stopwatch, audio player, pencils; 9. D; 10. a. 0, b. 1, c. 1, d. 0, e. 0, f. 2, g. 0; 11. True; 12. Test 3: Story Recall and Test 11: Writing Samples; 13. a and c; 14. False; 15. True

Three

HOW TO SCORE THE WJ III ACH

The WJ III Tests of Achievement provide a wide array of scores: raw scores, age equivalents, grade equivalents, standard scores, percentile ranks, relative proficiency indexes (RPIs), and instructional zones. A unique aspect of the WJ III ACH is that it provides both age and grade norms. The age norms are presented in 1-month intervals from ages 2-0 through 18-11 and then by 1-year intervals from ages 19-0 through 95+ years. The grade norms are available by tenths of a year from K.0 through 18.0.

Due to the precision and variety of scores available on the WJ III, a computer-scoring program is included with each test kit. The only scores that the examiner needs to calculate manually are the raw scores. If desired, the examiner may manually obtain estimates of the age and grade equivalents for each test by using the scoring tables in the Test Record. All other scores are generated using the *WJ III Compuscore and Profiles Program* (Schrank & Woodcock, 2001).

ITEM SCORING

Because the individual's pattern of correct and incorrect responses is needed to determine basal and ceiling levels or appropriate blocks of items, item scoring is done during test administration. The number correct, or raw score, is usually calculated after testing is completed.

On most of the tests, each item administered is scored by writing 1 or 0 in the appropriate space in the Test Record (1 = correct, 0 = incorrect). The examiner should leave spaces blank that correspond to items not administered. After completing a test, the only spaces that will be blank are items below the basal, above the ceiling, or not in the assigned block of items. Rapid Reference 3.1 lists notations that examiners may find helpful when recording items.

≡Rapid Reference 3.1

Notations for Recording Responses

1:   correct response
0:   incorrect, or no response
Q: indicates a query
DK: indicates the response of "Don't Know"
NR: indicates "No Response"
SC: indicates a self-correction

Correct and Incorrect Keys

The Test Books include "correct" and "incorrect" keys that serve as guides for scoring certain responses. The keys show the most frequently given correct or incorrect answers. On occasion an examinee's response will not be listed in the key. In these cases, the examiner will need to use judgment in determining whether the response is correct or incorrect.

Responses Requiring More Information

Sometimes more information is needed before a response can be scored as correct or incorrect. For some responses, a "query" is designed to elicit another answer from the examinee. If the prompted response still does not fall clearly into the correct or incorrect category, the examiner should record the response and score it after testing has been completed. The examiner should use professional judgment in querying responses that are not listed in the query key.

Responses Requiring Examiner Judgment

Occasionally a response does not require a query but, at the moment, it is hard to decide how to score the item. In this case, the clinician should record the actual response in the Test Record and score it later. The clinician should not use that item to determine a basal or ceiling and should continue testing until the basal or ceiling criterion is met. After testing has been completed, the clinician should return to the item or items in question and score the responses. If, after further consideration, it is still not clear how to score two responses, the clinician should balance the scores by scoring one item a 1 and the other a 0.

Scoring Multiple Responses

When an examinee provides more than one response to an item, the general principle to follow is to *score the last answer given*. The new response, whether correct or incorrect, is used as the final basis for scoring that item. The examiner should follow this procedure even if the examinee changes a response given much earlier in the testing session. In cases where the

examinee provides two answers simultaneously, the examiner should query the response by asking something like "Which one?" or "Give me just one answer."

TESTS REQUIRING SPECIAL SCORING PROCEDURES

Of the 22 tests in the WJ III ACH, 6 tests have special scoring procedures: Reading Fluency, Story Recall, Understanding Directions, Writing Samples, Story Recall-Delayed, and Spelling of Sounds. On several of these tests, the raw score is based only on a "block" of items, stories, or pictures. Two tests require multiple-point scoring. One test requires counting both number correct and number incorrect. The following section summarizes details for these six tests. It is recommended that the reader have a copy of the ACH Test Record in hand while studying the following section. For further information, the reader should consult the *WJ III ACH Examiner's Manual*.

Test 2: Reading Fluency

The score for Reading Fluency is based on both the number of correct responses and the number of incorrect responses. Skipped items and items that fall outside the range of attempted items are not included in the score. For example, if the examinee only completed Items 1 to 77, Items 78 to 98 would not be factored into the score.

When using the software program, the clinician should enter both the number correct and the number incorrect. When obtaining estimated age or grade equivalents, the clinician should subtract the number of errors from the number correct. If the result is a negative number, the clinician should use zero.

Test 3: Story Recall

The score for Story Recall is based on the number of correctly recalled elements from sets of stories administered. The clinician should first place a check above each correctly recalled element on the Test Record and should then count the number of check marks (1 point each) and record the total in the box on the Test Record following each story. For each set of two stories, there is an additional box to record the combined score.

There is a scoring summary to complete after Story 10 on the Test Record. The clinician should enter the score (Number of Points) for each set of stories administered and place an "X" in the blank for each set of stories not administered. This information is entered into the scoring program to generate derived scores. To obtain estimated age and grade equivalents, the clinician should use the total number of points for the stories administered. The clinician locates that number in the appropriate column of the Scoring Table in the Test Record. If the examiner administered more than four stories (two sets), he or she uses only the points from the last four stories administered to obtain the estimated age and grade equivalents.

CAUTION

Do not enter "X" in the software data entry screen if you have not administered these tests: Story Recall, Understanding Directions, or Story-Recall-Delayed. Leave the fields blank.

Test 4: Understanding Directions

This test's score is based on the number of correct responses the examinee has on the set of pictures administered. Each correct response is scored 1 and each incorrect response is scored 0. On the Test

Record, the examiner writes the number of points for each picture in the space provided. When indicated on the Test Record, the examiner records the cumulative total for the two pictures specified. In the Software Score Entry section on the Test Record, the examiner enters the number of points for each picture or set of pictures administered but should enter an "X" if the set is not administered. To obtain estimated age and grade equivalents, the examiner should locate the number of points in the appropriate column corresponding to the group of pictures administered. If the examiner administered more than one group of pictures, he or she should use the last group administered following the continuation instructions to estimate age and grade equivalents.

Test 11: Writing Samples

The examiner scores Writing Samples after administering a block of items. He or she uses the Scoring Guide in Appendix B of the *WJ III ACH Examiner Manual* to score responses. The guide includes several examples of 0 to 2 point responses that occurred frequently in the standardization. Clinicians should consult Chapter 2 of this book for a summary of item scoring guidelines.

Two Raters
When possible, the most desirable procedure for scoring Writing Samples is to have two individuals score the test. After independent scoring, the two individuals should attempt to resolve any score differences of more than one point. The examiner should average the two raw scores to obtain the final raw score.

Administering Additional Items
On occasion, an examiner may obtain a better estimate of an examinee's writing skill by administering additional items that are easier or more difficult. If it is apparent that the examinee is experiencing undue ease or difficulty with the assigned block of items, it would be appropriate to administer the additional items immediately. Because Writing Samples is usually scored after testing is completed, it may be necessary to administer the additional items at a convenient time within the next few days. The Writing Samples scoring table in the Test Record allows an examiner to determine if the most appropriate block of items has been administered. If the individual's raw score falls within one of the seven shaded areas in the scoring table, the examiner should consider ad-

CAUTION

Scoring Writing Samples

Examiners frequently score items too liberally on this test. Adhere to the samples and criteria in Appendix B of the Examiner's Manual.* In addition, if the score for the selected block falls in a shaded area of the scoring table, administer the additional items as directed. Base the score on the adjusted block indicated in the test record.

* When you cannot decide how to score an item (e.g., you can't decide if it is a 1 score or a .5) assign the lower score. On the next item in question, assign the higher score. If you always assign the higher score, the resulting score will be inflated.

ministering the additional items that are noted in the "Adjusted Item Blocks" chart in the Test Record. This chart also indicates the block of items to use for calculating the raw score. Figure 3.1 illustrates the scoring table and Adjusted Item Blocks chart for Writing Samples.

Calculating the Number of Points

Record the number of points for each item in the administered block in the Number of Points box on the Test Record. The raw score (number of points) is based only on the items in the assigned block. Do not give credit for items below or above this block. Raw scores that result in fractions of one-half are rounded to the nearest *even* number. For example, a score of 17.5 rounds to 18 and a score of 18.5 also rounds to 18. On the Test Record in the Software Score Entry section, enter the number of points for the most appropriate block of items administered. The score is based on a single block, even if more than one block is administered.

Test 12: Story Recall-Delayed

The score for Story Recall-Delayed is based on the number of correctly recalled elements from the set of stories previously administered in Test 3: Story Recall. Use only items that were actually administered to calculate the raw score. On the Test Record, count the number of check marks for correctly recalled elements for each story. Do not include points for the prompts used to facilitate recall of the story. Record the number of check marks (points) for each story in the appropriate box in the Test Record. For each set of two stories there is an additional box to record the combined score. After Story 10 on the Test Record, there is a scoring summary to complete. Enter the score

Adjusted Item Block

Note	Administer Additional Items	Base Number of Points on Items
①	7 to 12	1 to 12
②	13 to 18	7 to 18
③	1 to 6	1 to 12
④	19 to 24	13 to 24
⑤	7 to 12	7 to 18
⑥	25 to 30	19 to 30
⑦	13 to 18	13 to 24

When a score falls in a shaded area on the scoring table, use the Adjusted Item Block table above to determine what additional items to administer.

Test 11 Writing Samples
Scoring Table
Encircle row for the Number of Points.

		Number of Points				
Items 1–6	Items 1–12	Items 7–18	Items 13–24	Items 19–30	AE (Est)*	GE (Est)*
0	—				<5-3	<K.0
1	1				5-5	<K.0
2	2				5-8	K.2
3	3				5-11	K.6
—	4				6-1	K.8
4	—				6-2	K.9
—	5				6-3	1.0
5	—				6-5	1.1
—	6	③			6-5	1.2
6	7				6-7	1.3
—	—	2			6-8	1.4
—	8		⑤		6-9	1.4
7	9	3			6-11	1.5
—	10		2		7-1	1.6
8	—	4			7-2	1.7
—	11	—			7-3	1.7
—	12	5	3	⑦	7-4	1.8
—	—	—			7-5	1.9
—	—	6		2	7-6	1.9
9	13	—			7-7	2.0
—	—	7	4		7-8	2.1
—	14	—			7-9	2.1
—	—	—			7-10	2.2
—	—	—		3	7-11	2.2
—	—	8	5		8-0	2.3
15	—	—			8-2	2.4
—	—	9	—		8-3	2.5
10	—	—	6	4	8-4	2.6
16	—	—	—		8-6	2.7
①	—	10	—	—	8-6	2.8
—	—	—	7	—	8-8	3.0
—	—	—	—	5	8-10	3.2
—	—	11	—	—	8-11	3.2
17	—	—	—	—	8-11	3.3
—	—	—	8	—	9-1	3.5
—	—	12	—	—	9-4	3.7
—	—	—	—	6	9-4	3.8
18	—	—	—	—	9-6	4.0
—	—	13	—	—	9-7	4.1
—	—	—	9	—	9-10	4.3
—	—	—	—	7	10-0	4.6
—	—	—	10	—	10-3	4.8
19	14	—	—	—	10-6	5.1
—	—	—	—	8	10-10	5.4
—	—	—	11	—	11-0	5.6
—	15	—	—	—	11-4	5.9
—	—	—	—	9	11-9	6.4
—	—	—	12	—	11-11	6.5
20	16	—	—	—	12-0	6.6
—	—	—	—	—	12-5	7.0
—	—	—	—	10	12-10	7.4
17	—	—	—	—	13-0	7.6
—	—	—	13	—	13-8	8.3
—	—	—	—	11	14-0	8.7
—	—	—	—	—	14-3	8.9
21	—	—	14	—	14-4	9.0
—	18	—	—	—	15-3	9.9
—	—	—	—	12	15-4	10.0
—	—	—	15	—	15-7	10.3
—	—	—	—	13	16-11	11.5
—	19	—	—	—	17-4	11.9
22	—	—	16	—	17-5	11.9
—	—	—	—	14	18-7	12.8
—	—	—	—	—	19	12.9
②	—	—	17	—	20	13.0
—	20	—	—	—	>23	13.5
—	—	—	—	15	>23	14.5
—	18	—	—	—	>23	17.7
—	21-22	19-22	16-24	—	>23	>18.0
	④		⑥			

*AE and GE are estimates of the precise values provided by the software scoring program.

Figure 3.1 Writing Samples Scoring Table and Chart

Source: From the WJ III Tests of Achievement, by R. W. Woodcock, K. S. McGrew, and N. Mather, 2001, Itasca, IL: Riverside Publishing. Copyright © 2001 by The Riverside Publishing Company. Adapted with permission.

(Number of Points) for each set of stories administered and place an "X" in the blank for each set of stories not administered. This information will be entered into the scoring program.

The only score that is generated for Story Recall-Delayed is a z score. The objective of this test is to determine whether the individual's delayed recall score is within normal limits given age or grade, initial score (on Test 3: Story Recall), and delay interval (30 minutes to 8 days). The z score reports the discrepancy between the individual's predicted and actual delayed recall score.

To show z scores in the Score Report, select the "Options" tab and then the "Report Options" tab. Select z score as the additional score to be reported in the last column of the Score Report. Appendix C of this book presents a chart for converting z scores to percentile ranks and standard scores ($M = 100$, $SD = 15$). Estimated age and grade equivalents are not available for this test.

Test 20: Spelling of Sounds

This test has several unique scoring aspects: (a) The responses listed in the Test Book are the only correct answers allowed, (b) Items 6 to 12 have multiple points possible, and (c) points are subtracted if sounds are altered, added, or omitted on Items 6 to 12. All other items in this test are scored 1 or 0.

The answers shown in the Test Book represent the most commonly occurring orthographic patterns (visual sequences of letters) in the English language. Although some responses may appear to be correct sound spellings, if they do not represent the most common and frequent orthographic patterns they are incorrect. Use only the answers shown in the Test Book to award points. For example, the nonsense word "scritch" needs to be spelled as "scritch" rather than "skrich." Although "skrich" is a correct sound spelling, the /skr/ sound is nearly always spelled using the letters "scr" in the English language and the letters "tch" are the most common spelling pattern in a one syllable word with a short vowel sound.

The first five items require a single letter response and are scored 1 or 0. On Items 6 through 12 (the first seven pseudowords) the examinee receives points for each correctly written and sequenced letter or word part. For example, a correct spelling of the pseudoword "jong" is worth three points: one point for the letter "j," one point for the letter "o," and one point for the grapheme "ng."

The specific scoring of these responses is indicated both in the Test Book and on the Test Record. This scoring procedure adds more precision when evaluating young individuals or people with less advanced development and provides increased sensitivity to growth and development in reevaluations.

In most instances, the seven multi-point items (6 through 12) are easy to score. At times, an examinee may add, omit, or reverse one or more of the letters, thus requiring judgment in scoring the response. To receive a point, the grapheme or word part must be in the correct sequence and should not be "spoiled" by the addition of letters. Table 3.1 presents examples to illustrate the application of this scoring principle.

Again, the general principle is that points are deducted for sounds that are not present, as well as for spellings that have been altered by the inclusion of additional letters.

Do not penalize for reversed letters as long as the letter does not become a new letter. For example, a reversed lowercase "c" would not be penalized, whereas a reversed lowercase letter "b" would be penalized because it becomes a new letter "d."

Analysis of errors can help determine if the examinee is able to sequence sounds correctly but has difficulty assimilating or recalling common orthographic patterns.

STEP-BY-STEP: HOW TO SCORE THE WJ III ACH

1: Compute Raw Scores

With the exception of six tests, (Reading Fluency, Story Recall, Writing Samples, Understanding Directions, Story Recall-Delayed, and Spelling of Sounds) the procedure for computing raw scores is the same. The raw score is the number of correct responses plus a score of 1 for every item in the test below the basal. Be careful not to include scores for sample items in the calculation of raw scores. Although responses to the sample items are recorded in the Test Record, they appear in tinted panels and thus are clearly distinct from the actual test items.

After adding up the raw score, record this score in the Number Correct tinted box in each test section in the Test Record. The scoring for each test may

Table 3.1 Examples of How to Score Multi-Point Items in Test 20: Spelling of Sounds

Item (total points possible)	Examinee Response	Points Earned	Explanation of Scoring
gat (3 points)	gate	2 points	1 for "g." 1 for "t." 0 for "a" because the "e" spoils the vowel sound.
ift (3 points)	ifft	2 points	1 for "i." 1 for "t." 0 for "f" because the extra "f" spoils the most common orthographic spelling.
	efd	1 point	0 for "i" because "e" is the wrong sound. 1 for "f." 0 for "t" because "d" is the wrong sound.
pag (3 points)	paig	2 points	1 for "p." 1 for "g." 0 for "a" because the "i" spoils the vowel sound.
	peguh	1 point	1 for "p." 0 for "a" because the "e" spoils the short "a" sound. 0 for "g" because the additional letters spoil the sound.
foy (2 points)	voi	0 points	0 for "f" because "v" is the wrong sound. 0 for "oy" because the "oi" is not the most common orthographic spelling for that sound at the end of a word.
jong (3 points)	gonk	1 point	0 for "j" because "g" is the wrong sound. 1 for "o." 0 for "nk" because it is the wrong sound.
	gug	0 points	None of the sounds are correct.
glay (3 points)	cla	1 point	0 for "g" because "c" is the wrong sound. 1 for "l." 0 for "ay" because "a" is not how this long vowel sound is usually spelled at the end of a word.
	culay	1 point	0 for "g." 0 for "l" because the "u" spoils the blend. 1 for "ay."
pash (3 points)	pach	2 points	1 for "p." 1 for "a." 0 for "sh" because the "ch" is a different sound.

CAUTION

Common Errors in Calculating Raw Scores

• Forgetting to include credit for all items not administered below the basal
• Including the sample items in the raw score
• Making simple addition errors
• Transposing numbers
• Transferring the number correct incorrectly to the computer program or scoring table
• Neglecting to enter the raw scores for each subtest within a test, (i.e., Reading Vocabulary, Quantitative Concepts, Academic Knowledge, and Sound Awareness)
• Miscalculating scores for tests that have multiple point options (i.e., Writing Samples and Spelling of Sounds)
• Including points on more than the specified block or set of items (i.e., Writing Samples, Story Recall, and Story Recall-Delayed)

be completed before moving to the next test or as the examinee is working on a test like Calculation.

The six tests that are exceptions to the basic procedure are discussed in detail in the previous section (Tests Requiring Special Scoring Procedures). For Reading Fluency, the score is based on both the number correct and the number incorrect. For Story Recall, Understanding Directions, and Writing Samples, the raw score is based on the most appropriate block of stories, pictures, or items administered. For Story Recall-Delayed the raw score is based only on the items actually administered. Spelling of Sounds has multiple points possible for Items 6 to 12.

2: Obtain Estimated Age and Grade Equivalent Scores

This optional procedure is available for examiners who wish to obtain immediate developmental or instructional information. In the Test Record, there are scoring tables for each test except Test 12: Story Recall-Delayed. These scoring tables provide the estimated age (AE) and grade equivalents (GE). The estimated scores for certain tests may differ slightly (less than one standard error of measurement) from the actual AE and GE scores reported by the computer scoring program.

Once the raw score is calculated, locate that number in the first column of the test's scoring table in the Test Record and circle the entire row. The circled row includes the number correct, the estimated AE, and the estimated GE. Figure 3.2 illustrates the completion of this step for an 8th grade girl who obtained a raw score of 46 on Test 1: Letter-Word Identification.

Computing the number correct and checking the estimated age or grade equivalent scores provides immediate feedback regarding the individual's level of performance during the testing session. These results may refine the selection of starting points in later tests or suggest the need for further testing.

3: Use the WJ III Compuscore and Profiles Program

Complete the remainder of the scoring procedure using the WJ III Compuscore and Profiles Program, a computer software scoring program that is supplied as part of the test kit. This program includes the following features:

- Scores for all tests and clusters administered
- Age or Grade Profile (depending on whether age or grade norms are selected)
- Standard Score/Percentile Rank (SS/PR) Profile
- Summary narratives in English or Spanish
- Options to select age or grade norms, levels of discrepancies, and types of scores
- A brief text introduction for the Summary and Table of Scores
- Test Session Observations information from Test Record (optional)
- Easy integration into word processing systems for editing and customization
- Options to add research codes

In addition to saving time, computer scoring virtually eliminates the possibility of clerical errors. To obtain derived scores, enter the examinee identification information, the number correct for each test administered, and the Test Session Observations information if completed. Any single test or combination of WJ III tests may be scored.

A variety of report options are available. You can save options selected to

Test 1 Letter-Word Identification

Basal: 6 lowest correct
Ceiling: 6 highest incorrect

Score 1, 0

1 _____	P
2 _____	E
3 _____	B
4 _____	C
5 _____	k
6 _____	r
7 _____	A
8 _____	D
9 _____	G
10 _____	cat
11 _____	m
12 _____	h
13 _____	t
14 _____	b
15 _____	car
16 _____	on
17 _____	to
18 _____	dog
19 _____	in
20 _____	can
21 _____	as
22 _____	get
23 _____	was
24 _____	have
25 _____	they
26 _____	when
27 _____	there
28 _____	must
29 _____	about
30 _____	only
31 _____	part
32 _____	could
33 __/__	because
34 __/__	knew
35 __/__	own
36 __/__	whole
37 __/__	against
38 __/__	sentence
39 __0__	island
40 __/__	decide
41 __/__	since
42 __/__	distance
43 __/__	usually
44 __/__	scientist
45 __0__	bounties
46 __/__	fierce
47 __0__	experience
48 __0__	moustache
49 __0__	achieved
50 __0__	tremendous
51 __0__	systematic
52 __0__	urged
53 __0__	ancient
54 __/__	obviously
55 __0__	sufficient
56 __/__	particularly

57 __0__	domesticated
58 __0__	interpretation
59 __0__	therapeutic
60 __0__	bouquet
61 __0__	significance
62 __0__	provincial
63 __0__	aeronautic
64 __0__	conspicuous
65 _____	diacritical
66 _____	deficiencies
67 _____	pituitary
68 _____	trivialities
69 _____	debutante
70 _____	magnanimous
71 _____	homogenization
72 _____	indissolubly
73 _____	picaresque
74 _____	ubiquitous
75 _____	argot
76 _____	satiate

46 Number Correct (0–76)

Test 1 Letter-Word Identification
Scoring Table
Encircle row for the Number Correct.

Number Correct	AE (Est)*	GE (Est)*
0	<2-0	<K.0
1	2-0	<K.0
2	3-0	<K.0
3	3-8	<K.0
4	4-2	<K.0
5	4-5	<K.0
6	4-8	<K.0
7	4-11	<K.0
8	5-1	K.1
9	5-3	K.2
10	5-4	K.2
11	5-6	K.3
12	5-8	K.4
13	5-9	K.5
14	5-11	K.6
15	6-0	K.7
16	6-2	K.8
17	6-3	K.9
18	6-4	1.0
19	6-5	1.1
20	6-6	1.2
21	6-7	1.2
22	6-8	1.3
23	6-9	1.4
24	6-10	1.5
25	6-11	1.5
26	7-0	1.6
27	7-0	1.7
28	7-1	1.8
29	7-2	1.8
30	7-3	1.9
31	7-4	2.0
32	7-5	2.1
33	7-6	2.2
34	7-7	2.2
35	7-8	2.3
36	7-9	2.4
37	7-10	2.5
38	7-11	2.6
39	8-0	2.7
40	8-1	2.8
41	8-2	2.9
42	8-4	3.0
43	8-5	3.1
44	8-6	3.3
45	8-8	3.4
46	8-10	3.5
47	9-0	3.7
48	9-2	3.8
49	9-4	4.0
50	9-7	4.2
51	9-10	4.4
52	10-1	4.6
53	10-4	4.8
54	10-8	5.1
55	11-0	5.3
56	11-4	5.6
57	11-8	5.9
58	12-0	6.3
59	12-4	6.7
60	12-9	7.1
61	13-1	7.5
62	13-6	8.0
63	14-0	8.5
64	14-6	9.1
65	15-1	9.8
66	15-9	10.6
67	16-6	11.6
68	17-5	12.7
69	18-4	14.1
70	19	15.4
71	20	17.3
72	21	>18.0
>72	>22	>18.0

*AE and GE are estimates of the precise values provided by the software scoring program.

Figure 3.2 Obtaining the Estimated Age Equivalent and Grade Equivalent for a Number Correct of 46 on Test 1: Letter-Word Identification

Source: From the *WJ III Tests of Achievement,* by R. W. Woodcock, K. S. McGrew, and N. Mather, 2001, Itasca, IL: Riverside Publishing. Copyright © 2001 by The Riverside Publishing Company. Adapted with permission.

CAUTION

Overreliance on Computer-Generated Report

The summary report generated by the WJ III software program is not intended to serve as a final, comprehensive report. It provides a summary description of results but does not interpret results or provide recommendations.

ensure that future reports will use those same options. You can save the examinee data, narrative report, and table of scores. You can print the profiles (age/grade, SS/PR), but not save or export them. Only the narrative report and table of scores can be exported to a word processing program. Chapter 7 contains an example of a complete report and table of scores produced by this program.

SCORING REMINDERS FOR EACH TEST

Test 1: Letter-Word Identification
Range: 0–76
Scoring Reminders:
- Score correct responses 1, incorrect responses 0.
- Score 1 if response differs from correct answer in verb tense or number.
- Score 0 if response is a different part of speech from the correct answer.
- Enter the number of items answered correctly plus one point for each item below the basal in the Number Correct box.

Test 2: Reading Fluency
Range: 0–98
Scoring Reminders:
- Score correct responses 1, incorrect responses 0.
- Enter total number of items answered correctly within the time limit in the Number Correct box on the Test Record.
- Enter total number of items missed within the time limit in the Number Incorrect box on the Test Record. Do not include items as incorrect that fall beyond the last item the examinee attempted during the time limit.

- If obtaining estimated AE/GE, subtract the number incorrect from the number correct to calculate total points. If a negative number results, use 0.
- When using the software program, enter both the number correct and the number incorrect.

Test 3: Story Recall
Range: depends on which set of stories is administered
Scoring Reminders:
- Score correct responses 1, incorrect responses 0.
- Score 1 if the response is a synonym or a paraphrase for an element that is not in bold.
- Do not penalize for mispronunciations due to articulation errors or regional/dialectical speech differences.
- Score 0 if the response differs from a bold element in any way with two exceptions: Accept derivations of words and accept synonyms that are very close in meaning to the words in bold type.
- Count number of points earned in each story administered and record in the appropriate box.
- Enter cumulative scores for each set of stories administered in the appropriate box.
- Record an "X" for each set of stories not administered.
- If obtaining estimated AE/GE, combine the points for the last four stories administered and use the column corresponding to that set of stories.

Test 4: Understanding Directions
Range: depends on which group of pictures is administered
Scoring Reminders:
- Score correct responses 1, incorrect responses 0.
- All steps must be completed to score an item 1.
- Except where noted, examinee may point in any order to receive 1.
- Enter number of points for each picture administered in the appropriate box.
- Enter cumulative number of points for groups of pictures (as directed in the Test Record).

- In the Software Score Entry section, enter the number of points for each group of pictures administered or an "X" if not administered.
- If obtaining estimated AE/GE, combine the points for the last group of pictures administered and find the corresponding column.

Test 5: Calculation

Range: 0–45

Scoring Reminders:

- Score correct responses 1, incorrect responses 0.
- Score skipped items 0.
- Score correct responses that have poorly formed or reversed numerals 1.
- Score transposed numerals 0.
- Enter number of items answered correctly plus one point for each item below the basal in the Number Correct box.

Test 6: Math Fluency

Range: 0–160

Scoring Reminders:

- Score correct responses 1, incorrect responses 0.
- Score skipped items 0.
- Score correct responses that have poorly formed or reversed numerals 1.
- Enter number of items answered correctly within the time limit in the Number Correct box.

Test 7: Spelling

Range: 0–59

Scoring Reminders:

- Score correct responses 1, incorrect responses 0.
- Score correctly spelled responses that contain a reversed letter 1, unless the reversed letter makes a real letter (e.g., a reversed "b" is a "d").
- Enter the number of items answered correctly plus one point for all items below the basal in the Number Correct box.

Test 8: Writing Fluency
Range: 0–40
Scoring Reminders:
- Score correct responses 1, incorrect responses 0.
- Score skipped items 0.
- Score correct responses that have errors in spelling, punctuation, capitalization, or poor handwriting 1 as long as they are legible and meet criteria.
- Score 0 if one of the three stimulus words is not included in the sentence.
- Score 0 if one of the three stimulus words is changed in any way.
- Score 0 if a word critical to the meaning of the sentence is omitted.
- Score 1 if the sentence is awkward but the meaning is clear and meets all other criteria.
- Score 1 if the subject is an understood "you" and response meets all other criteria.
- Score 1 if the response is correct but accidentally omits minor words.
- Enter number of items answered correctly within the time limit in the Number Correct box.

Test 9: Passage Comprehension
Range: 0–47
Scoring Reminders:
- Score correct responses 1, incorrect responses 0.
- Score 1 if the response differs from the correct answer in verb tense or number.
- Score 0 if the response is a different part of speech from the correct answer.
- Unless noted otherwise, score two-word or longer responses 0.
- Enter the total number of items answered correctly plus one point for each item below the basal in the Number Correct box.

Test 10: Applied Problems
Range: 0–63
Scoring Reminders:
- Score correct responses 1, incorrect responses 0.
- Enter the number of items answered correctly plus one point for each item below the basal in the Number Correct box.

Test 11: Writing Samples

Range: 0–12 or 0–24 depending on block administered

Scoring Reminders:

- Score responses using the multiple-point rating guide (2, 1.5, 1, .5, or 0).
- Score 2 if the response is superior and meets all criteria.
- Score 1.5 if the response falls between average and superior.
- Score 1 if the response is average and meets criteria.
- Score .5 if the response falls between unacceptable and average.
- Score 0 if the response does not meet criteria or is illegible.
- Add points for items within the selected block to obtain number of points.
- If number of points falls in a shaded area on the scoring table, administer additional items as directed.
- Base final score on the most appropriate block of items regardless of how many blocks were administered. The most appropriate block is the one with number of points closest to the midrange of possible scores.
- Enter number of points and letter corresponding to that block of items when using the software program.
- If obtaining estimated AE/GE, circle the row for the number of points in the column corresponding to the block of items administered.

Test 12: Story Recall-Delayed

Range: depends on which sets of stories are administered

Scoring Reminders:

- Score correct responses 1, incorrect responses 0.
- Do *not* include points used to prompt recall.
- Record number of points for each story in the appropriate box.
- Combine points for stories in a set and record the total in the appropriate box.
- Record an "X" for sets not administered.
- Remember that estimated scores are not available.
- Choose z score as the additional score option in the software program.

Test 13: Word Attack
Range: 0–32
Scoring Reminders:
- Score correct responses 1, incorrect responses 0.
- Enter the number of items answered correctly plus one point for each item below the basal in the Number Correct box.

Test 14: Picture Vocabulary
Range: 0–44
Scoring Reminders:
- Score correct responses 1, incorrect responses 0.
- Enter the number of items answered correctly plus one point for each item below the basal in the Number Correct box.

Test 15: Oral Comprehension
Range: 0–34
Scoring Reminders:
- Score correct responses 1, incorrect responses 0.
- Score 1 if the response differs from the correct answer in verb tense or number.
- Score 0 if the response is a different part of speech from the correct answer.
- Unless noted otherwise, score two-word or longer responses 0.
- Enter the number of items answered correctly plus one point for each item below the basal in the Number Correct box.

Test 16: Editing
Range: 0–34
Scoring Reminders:
- Score correct responses 1, incorrect responses 0.
- Score 0 if the response does not identify *and* correct the error.
- Enter the number of items answered correctly plus one point for each item below the basal in the Number Correct box.

Test 17: Reading Vocabulary
Range: 0–73
Scoring Reminders:
- Score correct responses 1, incorrect responses 0.
- Score 1 if the response differs from correct answer in verb tense or number.

- Score 0 if the response is a different part of speech from the correct answer.
- Unless noted otherwise, score two-word or longer responses 0.
- For each subtest A to C, record the number of items answered correctly plus one point for each item below the basal in the Number Correct box.
- Enter the number correct for each subtest when using the software program.
- If obtaining estimated AE/GE, add together the scores for all subtests (A + B + C).

Test 18: Quantitative Concepts

Range: 0–57
Scoring Reminders:

- Score correct responses 1, incorrect responses 0.
- When noted, the response must contain all parts of an answer to score 1.
- For each subtest A and B, record the number of items answered correctly plus one point for each item below the basal in the Number Correct box.
- Enter the number correct for each subtest when using the software program.
- If obtaining estimated AE/GE, add together the scores for both subtests (A + B).

Test 19: Academic Knowledge

Range: 0–78 (Form B, 0–77)
Scoring Reminders:

- Score correct responses 1, incorrect responses 0.
- For each subtest A to C, record the number of items answered correctly plus one point for each item below the basal in the Number Correct box.
- Enter the number correct for each subtest when using the software program.
- If obtaining estimated AE/GE, add together the scores for all subtests (A + B + C).

Test 20: Spelling of Sounds

Range: 0–41 (Form B, 0–45)

Scoring Reminders:

- Score correct responses 1 and incorrect responses 0 for Items 1 to 5 and 13 to 28.
- Use multiple-point scoring for Items 6–12: 0, 1, 2, or 3 following the scoring guide. (Form B has two items—8 and 10—that have four and five possible points, respectively.)
- The only correct responses possible are shown in the Test Book.
- Score correctly spelled responses that contain a reversed letter 1, unless the reversed letter makes a real letter (e.g., a reversed "b" is a "d").
- Enter the total number of all items answered correctly plus one point for each item below the basal in the Number of Points box on the Test Record.

Test 21: Sound Awareness

Range: 0–45

Scoring Reminders:

- Score correct responses 1, incorrect responses 0.
- For each subtest A to D, record the number of items answered correctly in the Number Correct box.
- Enter the number correct for each subtest when using the software program.
- If obtaining estimated AE/GE, add together the scores for all subtests (A + B + C + D).

Test 22: Punctuation and Capitalization

Range: 0–36

Scoring Reminders:

- Score correct responses 1, incorrect responses 0.
- Score responses that contain a reversed letter 1, unless the reversed letter makes a real letter (e.g., a reversed "b" is a "d").
- Score correct responses that are misspelled 1.
- Enter the number of items answered correctly plus one point for each item below the basal in the Number Correct box on the Test Record.

DON'T FORGET

Computer Generated Scores

Use the software program that comes with the test to generate all derived scores. Only estimated AEs and GEs for the individual tests can be obtained manually. Cluster scores, based on the tests administered, are only available using the computer program.

Evaluating Test Behavior

It is important to determine whether the test results accurately reflect the individual's abilities. During the testing process, be alert for signs in the examinee's behavior that indicate the test results may be of questionable validity. The question on the front page of each Test Record assists examiners in documenting the issue, "Do these test results provide a fair representation of the subject's present functioning?" If there is some reason for questioning the test results, mark the "No" box and provide an explanation in the space provided. Possible reasons for questioning validity include (a) an examinee's problems with hearing or vision, (b) behavioral or attentional difficulties that interfere with the examinee's ability to concentrate, and (c) certain background factors (e.g., limited English proficiency). Note any unusual test behaviors or answers encountered during the session because this type of qualitative information can take on unexpected significance when analyzing the test results. As described in Chapter 2, a test observation form is provided in the Test Record to assist in recording observations systematically throughout the testing session.

TEST YOURSELF

1. **All derived scores may be calculated manually or by using the computer program that accompanies the test.** True or False?

2. **Indicate incorrect responses with an "X."** True or False?

3. **For which test are items not administered below the basal included in the raw score?**
   (a) Story Recall
   (b) Understanding Directions
   (c) Quantitative Concepts
   (d) Reading Fluency

4. **Sample items should not be included in the raw score.** True or False?

5. **Which tests have subtests that must be added together to obtain estimated age and grade equivalents?**

    (a) Sound Awareness

    (b) Spelling of Sounds

    (c) Applied Problems

    (d) Reading Vocabulary

    (e) Story Recall

6. **On Writing Samples, how would a score of 20.5 be recorded?**

7. **Which tests have multiple points possible on individual items?**

8. **On Test 20: Spelling of Sounds, how would the following responses be scored (scoring from 0 to 3 points)?**

    (a) Correct response is "hig." Response is "hep."

    (b) Correct response is "tash." Response is "tach."

    (c) Correct response is "jang." Response is "jayng."

    (d) Correct response is "wib." Response is "mid."

9. **All cluster scores can only be obtained using the computer program.** True or False?

10. **Which test requires entry of both the number correct and the number incorrect to obtain the derived scores?**

Answers: 1. False; 2. False; 3. c; 4. True; 5. a and d; 6. 20 (round to nearest even value); 7. Writing Samples and Spelling of Sounds; 8. a. 1, b. 2, c. 2, d. 1; 9. True; 10. Reading Fluency

Four

The WJ III ACH provides a rich variety of interpretive options and scores. Examiners must know what scores are available, when to use the various scores, and how to interpret those scores. The purpose of the assessment dictates the scores that are most appropriate to use. In addition, examiners need to know what each test and cluster measure, what skills and abilities are required to perform the tasks, and what implications may be derived. Interpreting the WJ III ACH requires a higher level of skill than administering the test.

AGE- AND GRADE-BASED NORMS

The WJ III ACH provides the option to use either grade- or age-based norms. When making school-based decisions, grade norms are generally preferable. Age norms may be more applicable in clinical settings or with adults, and they must be used in cases where results will be compared to scores from another test that only provides age norms (e.g., comparing WISC-III to WJ III ACH). Selection of age or grade norms does not affect the obtained AEs and GEs, but differences will be noted on the standard scores, percentile ranks, and relative proficiency index scores. The WJ III Compuscore and Profiles Program (Schrank & Woodcock, 2001) provides the option to make age comparisons or grade comparisons. Selection of age or grade norms determines which profile (age or grade) is generated. Examiners should clearly indicate in reports which norm group was used.

TYPES OF SCORES

When reporting results to parents, teachers, and examinees, clinicians should select the scores that are most meaningful and easily explained. Some metrics are easier to interpret than others. Age and grade equivalents are most useful for discussions with parents and teachers who may more easily understand these types of scores than standard scores. These scores are also useful when examiners are attempting to determine an appropriate level of instructional materials.

The next section presents a detailed description of the scores available in the WJ III ACH. This overview includes AEs, GEs, relative proficiency indexes, instructional zones, Cognitive Academic Language Proficiency (CALP) levels, percentile ranks, and standard scores. It also presents additional optional standard score scales (i.e., normal curve equivalents (NCE), stanines, T scores, and z scores). All of the derived scores, as well as all profiles, are generated by the software scoring program.

> **DON'T FORGET**
>
> ### Assessment Creates Opportunity
>
> Examiners have an opportunity to observe how an individual approaches tasks during an assessment. The purpose of the testing should not be limited to determining eligibility for services or diagnosing a disability. Through qualitative observation, you can observe many facets of academic performance as well as the strategies an individual employs.

> **CAUTION**
>
> ### Use the Same Type of Norm Group
>
> When comparing results from two different tests, be sure to use the same type of norm reference group (i.e., age to age or grade to grade).

Raw Score / Number Correct

For most tests, the raw score is the number of correct responses, each receiving one point. Two tests (Test 11: Writing Samples, Test 20: Spelling of Sounds) use multiple-point scoring. The number correct is listed in the first column on the left in the scoring table that appears for each test in the Test Record (see Figure 4.1). Chapter 3 presents procedures for calculating the number correct.

Zero Scores

In cases where an individual receives a 0 on any test, the examiner must decide as to whether that score represents a true assessment of ability or reflects an in-

Test 1   Letter-Word Identification
Scoring Table
Encircle row for the Number Correct.

Number Correct	AE (Est)*	GE (Est)*
0	<2-0	<K.0
1	2-0	<K.0
2	3-0	<K.0
3	3-8	<K.0
4	4-2	<K.0
5	4-5	<K.0
6	4-8	<K.0
7	4-11	<K.0
8	5-1	K.1
9	5-3	K.2
10	5-4	K.2
11	5-6	K.3
12	5-8	K.4
13	5-9	K.5
14	5-11	K.6
15	6-0	K.7
16	6-2	K.8
17	6-3	K.9
18	6-4	1.0
19	6-5	1.1
20	6-6	1.2
21	6-7	1.2
22	6-8	1.3

Figure 4.1 Scoring Table for Test 1: Letter-Word Identification from the Test Record

ability to perform the task. If the individual has not been exposed to the type of task in question, it may be more appropriate to report that the examinee has no score for the test rather than interpreting a zero raw score. For example, if a 5th-grade student had a score of 0 on the Word Attack test, that score may represent the student's ability accurately and, therefore, should be interpreted. However, if a kindergarten student obtained a 0 on the Word Attack test, the score may indicate that the child has not yet been exposed to phoneme/grapheme relationships and, therefore, a score of 0 should not be interpreted. Even when a "zero score" is considered an accurate reflection of ability and is entered into the software program, it produces only age and grade equivalents. Because of the problems associated with interpretation, no other derived scores are available for zero scores at the individual test level. All derived scores, however, are reported for clusters that include a test with zero raw score. If all tests within a cluster have a zero raw score, then no derived scores are reported.

W Score

In the WJ III, the *W* score is not visible to examiners. The software converts raw scores into *W* scores (Woodcock, 1978; Woodcock & Dahl, 1971). If desired, the software program can produce *W* scores when needed for use in statistical procedures. The *W* score is a special transformation of the Rasch ability scale (Rasch, 1960; Wright & Stone, 1979). The *W* scale for each test is centered on a value of 500, which is set to approximate the average performance at age 10-0. Cluster scores are the average (arithmetic mean) *W* score of the tests included in that cluster. For example, the cluster score for Broad Written Language is the average *W* score of Test 7: Spelling, Test 8: Writing Fluency, and Test 11: Writing Samples.

Age and Grade Equivalents

An AE, or age score, reflects performance in terms of the age level in the norm sample at which the average score is the same as the examinee's score. Age equivalents may be more useful in some applications than grade equivalents, especially as they relate to the abilities of young children or adults not attending school.

A GE, or grade score, reflects the examinee's performance in terms of the grade level in the norm sample at which the average score is the same as the examinee's score. In other words, if the average *W* score on a test for students in the sixth month of the second grade is 488, then an individual who scores 488 would receive 2.6 as a grade score. The grade equivalents on tests like the WJ III ACH represent the midpoint of the individual's instructional zone and can be used for instructional planning. Because the test includes items distributed over a wide range of difficulty (rather than a limited range typically found on group-administered tests) the grade and age scores reflect the actual level of task difficulty an individual can perform.

At the lower ends of the age and grade scales, less than (<) signs are used for levels of performance that fall below the average score of the lowest age or grade group reported. Greater than (>) signs are used for levels above the average for the age or grade of peak performance. For example, if the age of peak performance is 34 years, an examinee who scored above the average for that age group receives an age score of > 34.

Examiners can use hand-scoring to approximate age and grade equivalents. The age and grade equivalents in the scoring table for each test in the Test Record (as shown in Figure 4.1) are only estimates (Est.). Precise age or grade equivalents for tests are reported in the computer-generated score report. Both age equivalents and grade equivalents can be displayed in the same score report by selecting the additional score option. For example, if the examiner is using grade norms, the score report automatically displays grade equivalents. To add age equivalents, the examiner should select the additional score option (AE/GE) and the age equivalents will appear in the last column. Age and grade equivalent scores for clusters are available only when using the software program.

W Difference Score

The *W* difference scores are based on the difference between an examinee's test or cluster *W* score and the average test or cluster *W* score for the reference group in the norming sample (same age or same grade) with which comparison is being made. Some scores such as the relative proficiency index and the standard score, are based on test or cluster *W* difference scores.

Relative Proficiency Index

The relative proficiency index (RPI) was called the relative mastery index (RMI) in the WJ-R (Woodcock & Johnson, 1989). The RPI allows statements to be generated about an examinee's predicted quality of performance on tasks similar to the ones tested. The RPI is expressed as a fraction. The denominator is a constant of 90. The numerator ranges from 0 to 100 and reflects the examinee's performance.

RPIs are based on the distance along the *W* scale that an individual's score falls above or below the average score for the reference group. Examiners should interpret an RPI of 45/90 to mean that the examinee is half as proficient on the task as average age- or grade-mates. When others at the examinee's age or grade show 90% success, the examinee is predicted to show only 45% success on similar tasks. On the other hand, if the examinee's RPI was 99/90, examiners should predict that the examinee would perform with 99% success those tasks that average age- or grade-mates perform with 90% success. Rapid Reference 4.1 provides verbal labels for describing performance when using the RPI.

Instructional Zone

A special application of the RPI, the instructional zone, identifies an individual's present level of functioning from easy (the independent level) to difficult (the frustration level). The instructional zone extends from an RPI of 96/90 to an RPI of 75/90. An individual will perceive tasks that fall at an RPI of 96/90 as "easy" (EASY), whereas he or she will perceive tasks that fall at an

≡Rapid Reference 4.1

Relationship between RPI and CALP Levels

CALP Level		RPI	English-Language Demands of Instruction will be:
5	Advanced	98/90 to 100/90	Very Easy
(4.5)	Fluent to Advanced	96/90 to 97/90	Easy
4	Fluent	82/90 to 95/90	Manageable
(3.5)	Limited to Fluent	68/90 to 81/90	Difficult
3	Limited	34/90 to 67/90	Very Difficult
(2.5)	Very Limited to Limited	19/90 to 33/90	Very Difficult to Extremely Difficult
2	Very Limited	5/90 to 18/90	Extremely Difficult
(1.5)	Negligible to Very Limited	3/90 to 4/90	Extremely Difficult to Impossible
1	Negligible	0/90 to 2/90	Impossible

RPI of 75/90 be as "difficult" (DIFF). When examiners use the software program the instructional zone is printed on the Age or Grade Profile.

CALP Levels

Cognitive Academic Language Proficiency (CALP) levels, another application of the RPI, are helpful in determining an individual's language proficiency. CALP is defined as language proficiency in academic situations and includes those aspects of language that emerge with formal schooling. Aspects of language that are acquired naturally, without formal schooling, are referred to as Basic Interpersonal Communication Skills (BICS). Cummins (1984) formalized this distinction between these two types of language proficiency (BICS and CALP). When evaluating English Language Learners or native English speakers with delayed or limited language, consideration of an individual's CALP levels will be helpful in planning an appropriate educational program.

CALP levels are available for eight clusters: Oral Language-Standard, Oral Language-Extended, Listening Comprehension, Broad Reading, Reading Comprehension, Broad Written Language, Written Expression, and Academic Knowledge. To display CALP levels for any of these clusters, examiners should select the additional score option (CALP) when using the software program. Rapid Reference 4.1 illustrates the CALP levels available, the relationship to the RPI, and the instructional implication of each.

DON'T FORGET

Determine Individual's Level of English Language Proficiency

Use the CALP levels to consider the individual's language proficiency before interpreting test results or making instructional recommendations. In addition, you can use CALP levels to help determine eligibility for ESL or bilingual programs. Use the broadest clusters (i.e., Oral Language-Extended, Broad Reading, Broad Written Language) when making entrance or exit decisions.

Percentile Rank

A percentile rank uses a scale from 1 to 99 to describe performance relative to a specific age- or grade-level segment in the norm sample. The examinee's percentile rank indicates the percentage of people in the selected segment of the norm sample who had scores the same as or lower than the examinee's score. Percentile ranks are particularly useful for describing a person's relative standing in the population.

Extended percentile ranks (Woodcock, 1987) provide scores that extend down to a percentile rank of one tenth (0.1) and up to a percentile rank of ninety-nine and nine tenths (99.9). If an individual's percentile rank is 0.2, this indicates that only 2 persons out of 1,000 (0.2%) would have a score as low or lower. If an individual's percentile rank is 99.8, this indicates that the person's performance was as good as or better than that of 998 persons out of 1,000 (99.8%) in the reference group, or that 2 persons out of 1,000 would have a score as high or higher. Extending the percentile rank scale adds discriminating measurement to the range of a traditional percentile rank scale—about three fourths of a standard deviation at the top and three fourths of a standard deviation at the bottom.

Standard Score

The standard score scale used in the WJ III is based on a mean of 100 and a standard deviation of 15. This scale is the same as most deviation-IQ scales and may be used to relate standard scores from the WJ III to other test scores based on the same mean and standard deviation. The WJ III standard score range (0 to 200+) provides more discrimination at the ends of the scale. Because standard scores are more difficult for parents and other nonprofessionals to understand, examiners may use the more meaningful and equivalent percentile rank to interpret the standard score.

In writing reports or communicating test results to parents and others, an examiner may prefer to use verbal labels rather than numbers to describe test performance. Rapid Reference 4.2 provides suggested verbal labels examiners may use when describing test results. Examiners should exercise care when using descriptors of a disability. Use the descriptor as a prepositional phrase (an individual "with severe mental retardation") rather than as an adjective ("a severely mentally retarded" individual). Use caution and professional judgment in the selection and application of verbal labels to describe a range of scores. Although labels may assist in communicating test results, the terminology is at times ambiguous or the meaning of the labels is misunderstood.

Four other types of standard scores: z scores, T scores, stanines, and normal curve equivalents (NCEs) are available when using the software program. To display any of these scores, examiners should select the additional score option

Rapid Reference 4.2

Verbal Labels for Standard Score and Percentile Rank Ranges

Standard Score	Percentile Rank	Verbal Label
151 and above	Above 99.9	Exceptionally Superior
131 to 150	98 to 99.9	Very Superior, Very High
121 to 130	92 to 97	Superior, High
111 to 120	76 to 91	High-average, Above Average
90 to 110	25 to 75	Average
80 to 89	9 to 24	Low-average, Below Average
70 to 79	3 to 8	Low, Well Below Average
50 to 69	0.1 to 2	Very Low
49 and below	Below 0.1	Exceptionally Low

Rapid Reference 4.3

Means and Standard Deviations for Standard Scores in WJ III ACH

Score	Mean	Standard Deviation
z	0	1
T	50	10
Stanine	5	2
NCE	50	21.06
SS	100	15

and choose the desired score. Only one additional score type can be displayed at a time. The additional standard score selected appears for all tests and clusters. The z score must be selected to obtain a score for Test 12: Story Recall-Delayed. A z score indicates how much above or below the mean an individual's score falls and it can be translated into a percentile rank. Rapid Reference 4.3 shows the means and standard deviations for each standard score available in the WJ III ACH.

Standard Error of Measurement

The standard error of measurement (SEM) is used to determine the range of scores and provides an indication of the degree of confidence professionals can have in an obtained score. Rather than using an average SEM, every different raw score in the WJ III has a unique SEM reported. These SEMs are primarily used to provide confidence bands for standard scores and percentile ranks.

LEVELS OF INTERPRETIVE INFORMATION

The WJ III provides four hierarchical levels of information in an interpretive framework. Information from one level cannot be used interchangeably with information from another. Each level provides unique information about a person's test performance and builds on information from the previous level. An examiner should consider information from all four levels when describing a person's performance. Rapid Reference 4.4 provides a brief summary of the four levels of information.

Level 1 information is useful in interpreting results and planning the appropriate instructional program. Informal and qualitative in nature, this information is obtained through behavioral observations during testing and through error analysis of responses to individual items. A framework for recording behavioral observations, the Test Session Observations Checklist, is located on

⪜ Rapid Reference 4.4

Four Hierarchical Levels of Information

Level	Score or Source of Information	Application
1	Qualitative, error analysis	Aids instructional planning
	Test Session Observations Checklist	Aids behavioral observations
2	Age Equivalents	Helps to determine level of development
	Grade Equivalents	Helps to determine level of instruction
3	RPI, CALP	Helps to determine level of proficiency
	Instructional Zone	Provides a range (easy to difficult)
4	Standard Scores	Shows relative standing with peers
	Percentile Ranks	

DON'T FORGET

Include Qualitative Information in the Report

Describe the following categories for each examinee:

Level of attention/concentration

Behaviors

Attitude

Motivation

Level of engagement

Persistence/effort

Response style

Record and analyze errors:

Look for patterns

Identify strengths and weaknesses

the first page of each WJ III Test Record.

Level 2 information indicates an individual's stage of development and is expressed as age or grade equivalents. Examiners can use these scores to help determine an appropriate developmental or instructional level.

Level 3 information indicates the quality of a person's performance on criterion tasks of a given difficulty level. The RPI compares the examinee's proficiency on a task to the proficiency of average age- or grade-mates. The RPI can be used to help determine an appropriate instructional level. The instructional zone, based on the RPI, defines the range of tasks that a person would perceive as quite easy (96% successful) to a level that a person would perceive as quite difficult (75% successful). This is similar to the independent and frustration levels typically found on informal reading inventories (IRI). CALP levels, also determined by the RPI, can be helpful in describing an individual's language proficiency.

Level 4 information provides a basis for making peer comparisons. In educational and clinical settings, percentile ranks and standard scores are the metrics most commonly used to describe an individual's relative standing in comparison to grade- or age-peers.

INTERPRETING TESTS

The interpretation of test results is a complex process. Simply reporting the derived scores is not interpretation. An analysis of the individual's performance on a test must consider the stimulus material, task demands, task complexity, language requirements needed to complete the task, developmental nature of the task, and any factors that may have impacted performance.

≡Rapid Reference 4.5

Definition of CHC Factors

Reading/Writing Ability *(Grw)*—Depth of lexical knowledge, including spelling, language comprehension, and English language usage.

Quantitative Knowledge *(Gq)*—Store of acquired quantitative declarative and procedural knowledge.

Comprehension-Knowledge *(Gc)*—Breadth and depth of a person's acquired knowledge of a culture and the effective application of this knowledge (i.e., crystallized intelligence).

Fluid Reasoning *(Gf)*—Mental operations an individual uses when faced with a novel task that cannot be performed automatically. Inductive and deductive reasoning are indicators of *Gf*.

Long-Term Retrieval *(Glr)*—Storage of information in long-term memory and fluent retrieval of it later through association. This is not the store of *knowledge (Gc or Gq)* but rather the *process* of storing and retrieving that information.

Short-Term Memory *(Gsm)*—Apprehension and retention of information in immediate awareness and then use of it within a few seconds (i.e., "use it or lose it" memory).

Processing Speed *(Gs)*—Fluent performance of cognitive tasks automatically, especially when under pressure to maintain focused attention and concentration.

Auditory Processing *(Ga)*—Perception, analysis, and synthesis of auditory stimuli (includes phonological awareness abilities).

Visual-Spatial Thinking *(Gv)*—Perception, analysis, synthesis, and manipulation of visual stimuli (includes thinking with visual patterns).

Understanding the Cattell-Horn-Carroll Theory of Cognitive Abilities (CHC theory) (Cattell, 1963; Horn, 1988, 1991; Horn & Cattell, 1966; Woodcock, 1990) can provide guidance in interpreting test results. Rapid Reference 4.5 provides definitions of the various factors in the CHC theory.

INTERPRETING THE READING TESTS

Many children find learning to read a formidable task. For about 20% to 30% of children, learning to read is the most difficult challenge they face (Lyon, 1998). Because reading is a major foundational skill for all school-based learn-

≡ Rapid Reference 4.6

Characteristics of Individuals with Low Reading Achievement

An individual with low basic reading skills

has poor phonological awareness.

has trouble learning sight words.

has difficulty sounding out words.

has trouble applying strategies for word analysis.

overrelies on content clues.

reads slowly.

avoids reading.

loses place when asked to read aloud.

misreads words.

An individual with low reading comprehension skills

has difficulty recalling what is read.

has trouble using syntactic and semantic cues.

has trouble understanding what is read.

becomes easily frustrated with tasks requiring reading.

may read well orally but does not comprehend.

has difficulty with all academic tasks involving reading.

ing, it is critical that examiners evaluate reading performance and plan appropriate instructional programs. Rapid Reference 4.6 provides a list of some of the common characteristics of individuals with low reading performance.

Interpretation of the reading tests requires the examiner to be aware of the skills involved in each task, to know what abilities underlie each test, and to recognize additional factors that facilitate or inhibit performance. Examiners should consider the impact of oral language when evaluating reading performance as well as the relationships between reading and written language performance.

The skills measured in the five reading tests range from lower-level (less complex) abilities, such as recognizing letters in isolation, to higher-level (more complex) abilities, such as comprehending connected discourse. Figure 4.2 displays an interpretive model of the various skills measured by the WJ III

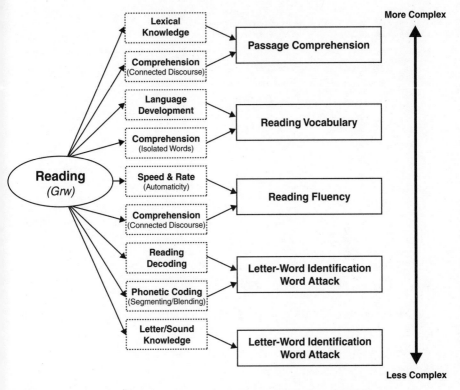

Figure 4.2 Various Skills Measured by the WJ III ACH Reading Tests

reading tests. Using the framework of the CHC theory to interpret the reading tests shows that the tests are primarily measures of reading ability, an aspect of reading/writing *(Grw)*.

Other aspects of processing, particularly auditory processing *(Ga)* and comprehension-knowledge *(Gc)*, are measured by several of the reading tests. Mc-Grew and Flanagan (1998) report that *Ga, Gc,* and *Gsm* have a consistent, significant relationship with reading achievement. Phonetic coding, an aspect of auditory processing *(Ga)*, is especially important at grades K through 3. The significance of comprehension-knowledge *(Gc)* to reading achievement increases with age. Short-term memory *(Gsm)* appears to contribute to reading achievement. This seems to be particularly true as it relates to memory span (the ability to attend to and immediately recall temporally ordered items). In addition, naming facility, an aspect of long term retrieval *(Glr)* appears to be an

DON'T FORGET

Difference between Phonological and Orthographic Awareness

Phonological awareness involves the ability to manipulate language sounds (phonemes). Orthographic awareness involves the ability to re-call letters and letter strings (graphemes).

important predictor of early reading failure. Fluid reasoning *(Gf)* is important to comprehension but not to decoding. Processing speed *(Gs)* adds significantly to the explanation of reading performance. Visual spatial thinking abilities *(Gv)* have little significance in explaining or predicting reading achievement. However, some visual abilities, such as orthographic coding, the ability to recall letters and letter strings (Berninger, 1990), are important to reading success.

Test 1: Letter-Word Identification

This test requires the individual to read isolated letters and words orally. It is a measure of reading decoding (sight recognition), including reading readiness skills. The items are presented in a list rather than in context. It is not necessary to know the meaning of the words.

Individuals with good sight-word recognition skills recognize the letters and words rapidly and with little effort. Automatic and fluent sight-word identification facilitates reading comprehension (Stanovich, 1982).

Individuals with inefficient or nonexistent strategies for word identification typically have low performance on this test. These individuals may identify several words accurately but require increased time and greater attention to phonic analysis to determine the correct response. Word identification skills are not automatic. Individuals with poor sight vocabulary tend to read slowly and make numerous errors (Mather, 1991). They may be unwilling to try, are easily frustrated, or are afraid to risk making an error. Examiners should evaluate the types of errors the individual made during testing. Table 4.1 indicates the task demands and categories of the phonic elements for a sampling of items in Forms A and B.

Compare results of this test and Reading Vocabulary to develop insights into the individual's acquisition of reading skills with and without the context of meaning. Both tests require word identification, but Reading Vocabulary also requires knowledge of word meanings. Compare results of Letter-Word

Table 4.1 Sample of Tasks and Phonic Elements for Items in Test 1: Letter-Word Identification (Forms A and B)

Task/Phonic Element	Item	Form A	Form B	Response Mode
Letter Recognition	1	P	L	Pointing
	2	E	A	
	3	B	W	
	4	C	S	
	5	k	i	
	6	r	y	
Letter Identification	7	A	R	Oral
	8	D	N	
	9	G	k	
	11	m	Q	
	12	h	p	
	13	t	b	
	14	b	u	
Word Recognition	10	cat	red	Pointing
	15	car	see	
Word Identification	16	on	the	Oral
	17	to	is	
	18	dog	and	
	19	in	go	
	23	was		
Short Vowel	20	can	will	Oral
	21	as	not	
	22	get	but	
	24	have	had	
Long Vowel	30	only		Oral
	32		use	
	36	whole		
Consonant Blend	23		from	Oral
	28	must		
	37	against	built	
	44	scientist	diagram	
	58	interpretation		

(continued)

Table 4.1 (Continued)

Task/Phonic Element	Item	Form A	Form B	Response Mode
Consonant Digraph	26	when		Oral
	27	there	with	
	30		which	
	60	bouquet		
	66		paraphernalia	
Vowel Diagraph	25	they	keep	Oral
	33	because		
	34	knew	young	
	46		fierce	
	48	moustache	authority	
Diphthong	29	about		Oral
	35		point	
	38		however	
	45	bounties		

Identification and Word Attack to determine differences between word identification and phonic skills.

Test 2: Reading Fluency

This test requires the individual to read simple sentences quickly and indicate if the statement is true or false by circling "yes" or "no." It is a measure of reading speed, automaticity, and rate of test taking.

Low performance on Reading Fluency may be a result of limited basic reading skills, slow perceptual speed, comprehension difficulties, or an inability to sustain concentration.

An individual's processing speed *(Gs)* (see Processing Speed Cluster from WJ III COG) may facilitate or inhibit performance on this test. The speed and fluency with which an individual performs basic skills influence performance on higher-level skills.

Test 9: Passage Comprehension

This test requires the individual to read a passage silently, comprehend the information, and provide a missing word. It is a measure of reading comprehension and lexical knowledge. This modified cloze task requires the ability to use syntactic and semantic clues in comprehending contextual information.

Low performance on Passage Comprehension may be a function of limited basic reading skills, comprehension difficulties, or both. Analysis of the types of errors made will help to determine the most appropriate instructional plan. Mather (1991) suggested three types of errors to consider: syntactically correct but semantically incorrect, semantically correct but syntactically incorrect, and both incorrect.

Examiners can compare results from Passage Comprehension directly to Oral Comprehension to determine whether poor performance is a result of limited language comprehension. Test 15: Oral Comprehension is a similar task but does not require reading. If the individual does well on the oral test, then language comprehension is not likely to be the reason for poor performance on the reading test. If the individual does poorly on Oral Comprehension, then limited language comprehension must also be considered as a contributing factor to poor reading performance.

Some individuals with learning disabilities appear to be inflexible and inefficient in applying problem-solving strategies that are required for tasks such as reading comprehension (Meltzer, 1994). Considering the impact of fluid reasoning *(Gf)* measured in the WJ III COG or in Test 17C: Reading Vocabulary-Analogies may help in interpreting reasons for low reading comprehension.

Test 13: Word Attack

This test requires the individual to read phonically regular nonsense words orally. Word Attack measures aspects of orthographic and phonological coding. Knowledge of phoneme/grapheme relationships is necessary to perform well on this test.

Low performance on Word Attack may result from poor decoding skills and strategies, lack of fluency, poor auditory processing, or limited phoneme/grapheme knowledge. Impaired decoding is frequently thought to be the basis of reading problems. Examiners should evaluate the types of errors the individual makes on this test in order to make the most appropriate instructional recommendations. Table 4.2 shows the tasks and phonic elements for a sampling of items on Word Attack, Forms A and B.

To evaluate the individual's phonological awareness, examiners should administer Test 21: Sound Awareness and the Phonemic Awareness cluster from

Table 4.2 Sample of Tasks and Phonic Elements for Items in Test 13: Word Attack (Forms A and B)

Task/Phonic Element	Item	Form A	Form B	Response Mode
Letter Recognition	1	p	r	Pointing
Sound Identification	2	k	s	Oral
	3	n	m	
Short Vowel	4	tiff	hap	Oral
	5		mell	
	6	nan	fim	
	7	rox	ven	
	9	ep		
Long Vowel	23		gnobe	Oral
Consonant Blend	9		floxy	Oral
	12	gusp	distrum	
	14	snirk		
	15		gradly	
	17	thrept		
Consonant Digraph	8	lish		Oral
	13		chur	
	20	wheeg		
	27		phintober	
	28	phigh		
	32		querpostonious	
Vowel Digraph	5	zoop		Oral
	11	feap	pawk	
	16	tayed	loast	
	18	grawl		
	20		koodoo	
	21		baunted	
	26	saist		
Diphthong	13	foy		Oral
	24	knoink		
	26		wroutch	
	30	doitibility		

the WJ III COG. An individual who has strong auditory processing *(Ga)* but does poorly on Word Attack has an excellent prognosis for improvement. The underlying abilities to analyze and synthesize sounds are intact.

An individual who has poor auditory processing *(Ga)* in addition to poor performance on Word Attack would benefit from an instructional program that focuses on developing phonological awareness. Research suggests that individuals need a prerequisite amount of phonological awareness to develop decoding skills (Juel, Griffith, & Gough, 1986). Specific training in sound blending and phonemic segmentation, in particular, improves decoding skills (Bradley & Bryant, 1985). Focused instruction can help an individual develop the relationship between sounds (phonemes) and symbols (graphemes).

Test 17: Reading Vocabulary

This test has three parts: 17A:Synonyms, 17B:Antonyms, and 17C:Analogies. The individual is required to read words and to supply (orally) synonyms in 17A and antonyms in 17B. In 17C, each item requires the individual to read three words and to provide a fourth word to complete the analogy.

Low performance on this test may result from poor basic reading skills, limited vocabulary, or both. If the individual reads the stimulus words correctly but provides an incorrect response, he or she may be better at decoding than comprehending. If the individual misreads the stimulus words but provides the correct response, he or she may be better at comprehending than decoding. Poor performance may also result when individuals are limited in both decoding and comprehending.

Results from Reading Vocabulary can be directly compared to the individual's performance on Verbal Comprehension in the WJ III COG, a similar task that does not require reading. If the individual's performance is good on the oral task but poor on the reading task, then the focus of instruction should be on developing basic reading skills. If the individual's performance is poor on both the oral task and the reading task, then the focus of instruction should be on developing oral vocabulary.

Reading Clusters

Three reading clusters are available in the WJ III ACH: Broad Reading, Basic Reading Skills, and Reading Comprehension. Each of these clusters can be

Rapid Reference 4.7

Instructional Implications for Individuals with Low Reading Achievement

- Match materials to individual's reading level.
- Provide support so individual can succeed while skills are being developed.
- Match instruction to specific needs of the individual.
- Provide instruction in phonological awareness and phoneme/grapheme relationships.
- Provide direct instruction to develop basic reading skills (both sight words and phonic skills).
- Develop oral language abilities.
- Teach comprehension strategies.
- Teach appropriate strategies and self-monitoring techniques.

used when calculating intra-achievement or ability/achievement discrepancies. Rapid Reference 4.7 illustrates some of the instructional implications for individuals with reading difficulties.

Broad Reading Cluster

Comprised of three tests, Letter-Word Identification, Reading Fluency, and Passage Comprehension, this cluster provides a broad overview of the individual's overall reading level. Because it is a mix of three different aspects of reading (basic skills, fluency, and comprehension) interpretation of this cluster is most meaningful when performance is similar on all three tests.

Basic Reading Skills Cluster

Comprised of Letter-Word Identification and Word Attack, this cluster provides a broad view of the individual's basic reading skills—a fundamental component of reading skill (Chall, 1983; Perfetti, 1985; Siegel, 1989; Stanovich, 1986, 1991a, 1991b). Measuring both sight-word recognition and phonic skills, this cluster can be used for diagnostic and instructional purposes. Comparing the results of the two tests will help determine if sight-word recognition skills, phonic skills, or both are limited and require remediation. Analysis of errors made in both tests helps target specific elements for instruction.

If an individual expends most of his or her energy decoding words, few resources will be left for comprehension. Slow, labored reading with many miscues may have a negative impact on comprehension. Poor decoding may put stress on short-term memory, overloading the system. Therefore, analyzing an individual's performance on the basic reading skill tests is important to the interpretation of the reading comprehension tests. The examiner should rule out decoding problems before identifying a problem in reading comprehension.

Reading Comprehension Cluster

Comprised of Passage Comprehension and Reading Vocabulary, this cluster provides a broad view of the individual's reading comprehension skill. Comparing the results of these two tests will help determine if the context of language helps or interferes with the individual's comprehension. Passage Comprehension measures comprehension in the context of connected discourse. Reading Vocabulary measures comprehension in a decontextualized format, that is, words in isolation.

The examiner should compare results of the Reading Comprehension cluster to the Basic Reading Skills, Listening Comprehension, and Academic Knowledge clusters. Low performance on reading comprehension tasks may result from low basic reading skills or limited oral language or background knowledge. Considering the impact of these various factors will help determine the most appropriate instructional program for the individual.

INTERPRETING THE ORAL LANGUAGE TESTS

Interpretation of the oral language tests requires the examiner to be aware of the skills involved in each task, know what abilities underlie each test, and recognize additional factors that affect performance. The examiner should consider the impact of oral language when interpreting all test results. Oral language is positively related to success in reading, math, and written language (Gregg, 2001; Litowitz, 1981; Perfetti, 1985; Stanovich, 1986; Wiig & Semel, 1984). Rapid Reference 4.8 shows characteristics of individuals with limited oral language.

The skills measured in the five oral language tests range from lower-level abilities, such as identification of isolated pictures, to higher-level abilities, such as comprehension and recall of connected discourse. Figure 4.3 is an interpretive model of the various skills measured in the WJ III oral language tests.

≡ Rapid Reference 4.8

Characteristics of Individuals with Low Oral Language Ability

An individual with low receptive language

asks to have oral information repeated.

has limited experience, stimulation, and exposure.

has difficulty understanding what is heard (e.g., lectures, directions, and conversations).

has difficulty following conversations.

has poor reasoning, especially with abstract, conceptual information.

has difficulty with social interactions.

An individual with low expressive language

has trouble thinking of specific words.

uses simple or immature sentences, vague pronoun referents, and immature vocabulary.

has difficulty formulating sentences.

seems disorganized when speaking (e.g., events out of sequence).

has trouble expressing him- or herself verbally or participating in discussions.

Using the CHC theory as the interpretive framework, the oral language tests are primarily measures of comprehension-knowledge *(Gc)*. The narrow abilities measured include language development, listening ability, and lexical knowledge. Knowledge and exposure to the prevalent culture facilitates or inhibits performance on oral language and comprehension-knowledge tasks. In addition, aspects of short-term memory *(Gsm)*, fluid reasoning *(Gf)*, auditory processing *(Ga)*, and long-term retrieval *(Glr)* are measured by some of the oral language tests.

Test 3: Story Recall

This test requires the individual to listen to a story and then recall the elements of that story. Both receptive and expressive language skills are required to perform this story-retelling task. Story Recall measures linguistic competency, listening comprehension, meaningful memory, and language development.

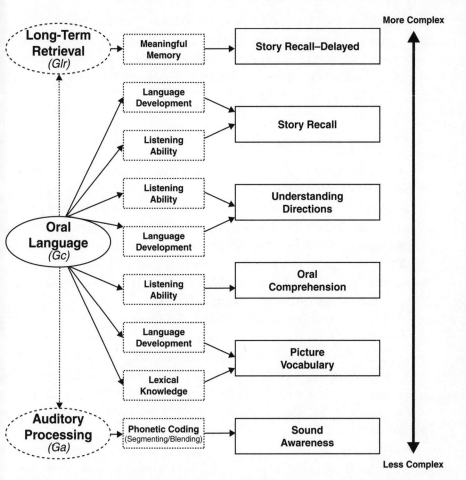

Figure 4.3 Various Skills Measured by the WJ III ACH Oral Language Tests

Limited vocabulary, limited comprehension, poor expressive language, or poor attention skills may negatively impact performance on this test. An individual with word retrieval problems may have difficulty recalling elements on demand.

Test 4: Understanding Directions

This test requires the individual to listen to a sequence of audio-recorded instructions and then follow the directions by pointing to various objects in a colored picture. This test measures listening ability and language development, both aspects of comprehension-knowledge *(Gc)*. Test 4: Understanding Directions also measures memory span, an aspect of short-term memory *(Gsm)*.

Limited vocabulary, comprehension, attention, or memory span can have a negative impact on performance.

Test 12: Story Recall-Delayed

This test requires that the individual recall elements of stories presented earlier. A measure of meaningful memory (an aspect of long-term retrieval *(Glr)*, Story Recall-Delayed may be administered from 30 minutes to 8 days after the administration of Test 3: Story Recall. Interpretation of the delayed recall score is based upon the difference between the individual's obtained score on Test 12 and a predicted score. The predicted score is based on the individual's age or grade, initial score on Test 3: Story Recall, and the delay interval (30 minutes to 8 days). The z score produced for this test indicates whether the delayed score was lower (negative z) than predicted or higher (positive z) than predicted. The purpose of the delayed recall score is to determine if the individual's performance is within normal limits. Scores between -1.00 (percentile rank [PR] $= 16$) and $+1.00$ (PR $= 84$) may be considered "within normal limits." The examiner may use other criteria such as, -1.30 (PR $= 10$) and $+1.30$ (PR $= 90$), or -1.50 (PR $= 7$) and $+1.50$ (PR $= 93$), or -2.0 (PR $= 2$) and $+2.00$ (PR $= 98$). These options are available in the software program and can be selected by the examiner.

Low performance on this test may result from limited language, poor attention, limited associative memory, or difficulty retrieving previously learned information.

Test 14: Picture Vocabulary

This test requires the individual to name pictured objects, ranging from the familiar to less familiar. Early items only require a pointing response. All other items require an oral response. This test measures vocabulary, verbal ability, and knowledge of culture, all aspects of comprehension-knowledge *(Gc)*. Picture Vocabulary is primarily an expressive vocabulary or semantic task. It does not measure syntax or morphology.

Low performance may result from limited vocabulary, limited exposure to the prevalent culture, or word retrieval problems. Analysis of the errors will help determine if poor performance is a result of limited vocabulary or retrieval problems. Errors that are related to the correct response (e.g., describe an attribute or function), may indicate a retrieval problem. For example, a person may describe "hinges" as the things that let the door swing back and forth. Errors that are not directly associated with the correct response may indicate a weakness in vocabulary development.

Test 15: Oral Comprehension

This test requires the individual to listen to a short passage and then provide the final word to complete the passage. This task measures listening ability and language development, both aspects of comprehension-knowledge *(Gc)*. The individual must use previously acquired knowledge, syntax, and context clues to identify the missing word. Oral Comprehension is primarily a receptive language task.

Low performance may result from limited semantic or syntactic knowledge or poor attention. This oral task is similar to Test 9: Passage Comprehension. Comparing the results of these two tests will help determine whether limited oral language or decoding skill are impacting reading comprehension performance.

Test 21: Sound Awareness

This test requires the individual to analyze and manipulate phonemes by performing rhyming, deleting, substituting, and reversal tasks. No reading is required. Sound Awareness measures the analysis and synthesis processes involved in decoding and spelling. Because this test measures aspects of phonological awareness, it will be particularly useful in evaluating both beginning readers and individuals who are experiencing difficulty in reading.

Examiners should compare the results of this test and Test 13: Word Attack to determine if problems are with phonological awareness, phoneme/grapheme knowledge, or a result of difficulty in both areas.

Oral Language Clusters

Four oral language clusters are available in the WJ III ACH: Oral Language-Standard, Oral Language-Extended, Oral Expression, and Listening Comprehension. Examiners can use any of these clusters when calculating intra-achievement or ability/achievement discrepancies. WJ III ACH provides an option to use oral language as a predictor score in the ability/achievement discrepancy calculation. Only the Oral Language-Extended cluster score may be used in that capacity.

Professionals should consider performance on the oral language clusters in relation to performance on the reading, math, and written language tests. Rapid Reference 4.9 lists possible instructional implications for individuals with limited oral language ability.

Oral Language-Standard and Extended

Two broad oral language clusters exist, standard and extended. The standard cluster is composed of two tests in the Standard Battery, Story Recall and Un-

---

≡Rapid Reference 4.9

Instructional Implications for Individuals with Limited Oral Language

- Consider impact on reading, math, and written language performance.
- Refer the individual to the speech/language specialist for a comprehensive language evaluation.
- Develop oral vocabulary and oral language skills prior to or simultaneously with instruction in other academic areas.
- Use concrete examples.
- Demonstrate or model what is expected of the individual.
- Encourage use of gestures.
- Limit length of instructions.
- Provide visual, graphic reminders (e.g., outlines, pictures, graphs, story frames).
- Provide exposure to language (e.g., read aloud or converse with the individual).
- Provide additional time for the individual to respond or speak.
- Pre-teach important vocabulary words related to assignment.
- Pair the individual with a peer who will encourage and facilitate verbal communication.
- Build on individual's interests and strengths.
- Exempt him or her from foreign language requirements.

derstanding Directions. The extended cluster is composed of four tests—the two in the Standard Battery plus two from the Extended Battery, Picture Vocabulary and Oral Comprehension.

Oral Expression

This cluster is composed of two tests, Story Recall and Picture Vocabulary. It measures linguistic competency and vocabulary knowledge. A significant difference between the two tests comprising this cluster may indicate whether increased contextual information helps or interferes with performance.

Listening Comprehension

This cluster is composed of two tests, Understanding Directions and Oral Comprehension and measures both listening ability and verbal comprehension. A significant difference between the two tests in this cluster can help determine if performance varies depending on the receptive or expressive nature of the task.

DON'T FORGET
....

Importance of Oral Language Proficiency

Be sure to consider the individual's oral language proficiency when interpreting any of the achievement tests. Aspects of oral language, such as vocabulary, underlie performance in reading, written language, math reasoning, and content/knowledge areas.

INTERPRETING THE MATHEMATICS TESTS

Interpretation of the mathematics tests requires the examiner to be aware of the skills involved in each task, know what abilities underlie each test, and recognize additional factors that influence performance. Rapid Reference 4.10 indicates characteristics of individuals with low math achievement.

The four mathematics tests measure skills that range from lower-level abilities, such as writing numerals, to higher-level abilities, such as analyzing and solving problems. Figure 4.4 is an interpretive model of the various skills measured by the WJ III mathematics tests.

Using the CHC theory as the interpretive framework, the mathematics tests primarily measure quantitative knowledge *(Gq)*. Some of the tests also measure aspects of fluid reasoning *(Gf)*, comprehension-knowledge *(Gc)*,

=====Rapid Reference 4.10

Characteristics of Individuals with Low Math Achievement

An individual with low basic math skills

   appears anxious or resistant to solving math problems.

   lacks confidence when presented with math problems.

   uses finger counting long after it is developmentally appropriate.

   reverses and transposes numbers (e.g., 12 for 21).

   does not attend to signs.

   has difficulty aligning numbers when performing calculations.

   has difficulty remembering steps in computing or solving problems.

An individual with low math reasoning skills

   has limited math vocabulary.

   lacks age-appropriate quantitative concepts.

   has trouble with estimation.

   has limited strategies for solving math problems.

   does not recognize or self-correct errors.

   has difficulty recognizing relevant information in word problems.

   has difficulty eliminating extraneous information from word problems.

processing speed *(Gs)*, and visual-spatial thinking *(Gv)*. McGrew and Hessler (1995) found that *Gf*, *Gc*, and *Gs* abilities were correlated consistently and significantly with mathematics achievement although there were developmental differences. The *Gc* relationship increases with age while the *Gs* relationship decreases with age. *Gf* was related consistently and significantly across all ages. *Gv* appears to be related to math tasks that require higher-level skills and thinking but is not related to basic math skills (McGrew & Flanagan, 1998).

Test 5: Calculation

This test requires the individual to perform a variety of calculations ranging from simple addition to complex calculus. Tasks include (a) basic addition, subtraction, multiplication, and division; (b) advanced calculations of each op-

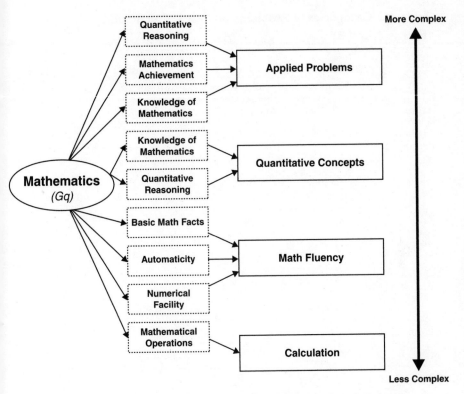

Figure 4.4 Various Skills Measured by the WJ III ACH Mathematics Tests

eration with regrouping; (c) advanced calculation of each operation with negative numbers (except division); (d) fractions; (e) percentages; (f) algebra; (g) trigonometry; (h) logarithms; and (i) calculus.

Calculation measures the ability to perform mathematical computations that are fundamental to more complex math reasoning and problem solving. Fluency with calculation is fundamental to more complex math (Cawley, 1985; Hasselbring, Goin, & Bransford, 1987; Kirby & Becker, 1988).

Low performance may result from limited basic math skill, limited short-term memory, limited fluency or automaticity, limited instruction, or lack of attention. Examiners should observe the examinee's behaviors, categorize errors that are made, note which concepts are known and unknown, and interview the examinee. Table 4.3 indicates the categories for each problem in Forms A and B.

Table 4.3 Categories of Problems on Test 5: Calculation (Forms A and B)

	Basic Addition	Basic Subtraction	Basic Multiplication	Basic Division
Form A	1–5, 10	6–9, 11, 12	13, 16	15, 21
Form B	1–4, 10	5–8, 11, 12	13, 17	15, 18

	Advanced (+) Regrouping & Negative #s	Advanced (–) Regrouping & Negative #s	Advanced (×) Regrouping & Negative #s	Advanced (÷) Regrouping
Form A	14, 28	18	17, 19, 26, 29	22, 24
Form B	9, 14	16, 20	19, 27, 28	22, 25

	Fractions	Percentages	Algebra	Trigonometry Logarithms, Calculus
Form A	20, 23, 25, 27, 30, 36	34	32, 33, 35, 38	31, 37, 39–45
Form B	21, 23, 29–31, 35	32	24, 26, 33, 34, 36, 37, 39	38, 40–45

Test 6: Math Fluency

This test requires the individual to solve simple addition, subtraction, and multiplication facts quickly. Low performance on this test may result from limited basic math skills, lack of automaticity, limited attention, or slow processing speed *(Gs)*.

Test 10: Applied Problems

This test requires the individual to analyze and solve practical math problems. It is a measure of quantitative reasoning, math achievement, and math knowledge. Because no reading is required, low performance will likely be related to limits in mathematical knowledge. Low performance may result from limited fluid reasoning *(Gf)*, limited math skills, or comprehension difficulties.

Examiners should compare results on this test to reading and writing clusters to determine if the individual does better when no reading is required. Oral

Table 4.4 Categories of Problems on Test 10: Applied Problems (Forms A and B)

	Number Concepts	Addition	Subtraction	Multiplication
Form A	1–8, 10–13	17, 18, 22, 25, 27, 29, 33, 36	9, 14–16, 20, 23, 28, 30, 32, 35, 36	31, 37, 40, 46
Form B	1–9, 11, 12	17, 19, 21, 22, 25, 29, 32, 33, 38	10, 13–16, 18, 24, 30, 44	28, 31, 38, 41, 43

	Money	Time	Percents/Fractions	Interest
Form A	24, 25, 27, 29, 32, 33, 35, 36	19, 21, 44	39, 42, 43, 45, 47, 49, 50, 52, 57	52, 57
Form B	21, 24, 25, 29, 31, 32, 33	20, 23, 27, 35, 39, 40	36, 45–47, 49, 50	51, 50, 59

	Measurement	Averaging	Probability	Algebra/ Geometry
Form A	26, 38, 43, 46, 48		60	41, 42, 51, 53–56, 58, 59, 61–63
Form B	31	42, 53	54	48, 52, 55–58, 60–63

	Division	Extraneous Information
Form A	34, 38, 45, 48	28, 30, 37, 40
Form B	26, 34, 37	30, 32, 33, 34, 41, 46, 59

language (limited vocabulary) and fluid reasoning *Gf* can impact performance on Applied Problems. Categorizing the individual's errors may help determine instructional planning. Table 4.4 indicates the categories for the problems in Forms A and B.

Test 18: Quantitative Concepts

This test has two parts, 18A: Concepts and 18B: Number Series, that measure mathematical knowledge and quantitative reasoning. The tasks in 18A: Concepts require the individual to count and identify numbers, shapes, and se-

Table 4.5 Categories of Problems in Test 18A: Quantitative Concepts-Concepts (Forms A and B)

	Counting	Geometric Shapes	Vocabulary
Form A	1, 2, 4, 14	5	6, 8, 10, 28, 34
Form B	1, 3, 4	5	7–13, 17, 20, 34

	Number Identity	Symbols	Money
Form A	3, 7, 9	11, 12, 17, 18, 26, 29, 32, 33	13
Form B	2, 6	14, 15, 16, 23, 28, 32	

	Sequences	Abbreviations	Fractions
Form A	8, 10	19, 20	21, 23
Form B	9–13, 17	19	22, 24, 26, 27

	Time/Measurement	Algebra/Geometry	Rounding
Form A	15, 16, 27	22, 24, 27, 28	25
Form B	12, 17	18, 25, 28	21

	Trigonometry/Calculus
Form A	29–34
Form B	29–34

quences. Some items require knowledge of mathematical terms and formulas. The tasks in Number Series require the individual to look at a series of numbers, figure out the pattern, and provide the missing number.

Low performance on this test may result from limited vocabulary, insufficient concept development, or limited fluid reasoning *(Gf)*. Categorizing the errors may help determine the most appropriate instructional program. Table 4.5 indicates the categories for each problem in 18A: Concepts, Forms A and B.

Math Clusters

Three math clusters are available for interpretation in the WJ III ACH, Broad Math, Math Calculation Skills, and Math Reasoning. Each of these clusters

≡ Rapid Reference 4.11

Instructional Implications for Individuals with Low Math Achievement

- Match materials to individual's instructional level.
- Provide a high-interest, success-oriented environment.
- Use manipulatives to help teach concepts.
- Reduce the number of problems.
- Provide additional time for completion of assignments.
- Teach the use of a calculator.
- Use graph paper to aid alignment and organization of calculation problems.
- Provide systematic and extended practice to reinforce learning.
- Be sure the individual understands the task by monitoring performance closely.
- Use fact charts.
- Teach meaningful applications of mathematics.
- Develop math vocabulary.
- Teach functional mathematics.

may be used in intra-achievement or ability/achievement discrepancy calculations. Rapid Reference 4.11 lists possible instructional implications for individuals with low math achievement.

Broad Math

This cluster is composed of three tests, Calculation, Math Fluency, and Applied Problems. It provides a broad, comprehensive view of the individual's math achievement level. The Broad Math cluster measures problem solving, number facility, automaticity, and reasoning. Because this cluster measures several different aspects of math ability, interpretation is most meaningful when performance is similar on all three tests.

Math Calculation Skills

This cluster is composed of two tests, Calculation and Math Fluency. It provides a measure of basic math skills including computational skills and automaticity with basic math facts. Rapid and automatic calculation is an important variable in predicting math performance (Meltzer, 1994). Examiners should compare the results of the two tests in this cluster to help determine if processing speed *(Gs)* or mastery of basic facts is impacting performance.

Math Reasoning

This cluster is composed of two tests, Applied Problems and Quantitative Concepts. It provides a measure of mathematical knowledge and reasoning, including problem solving, analysis, and vocabulary.

Examiners can compare results of this cluster to the Math Calculation Skills cluster to help determine whether basic math skills are impacting performance. In addition, results of this cluster can be compared to oral language and (if using the WJ III COG) comprehension-knowledge *(Gc)* and fluid reasoning *(Gf)* clusters. Individuals with low oral language may have difficulty with quantitative terminology or the vocabulary of math. Individuals with low comprehension-knowledge may lack prerequisite knowledge for acquiring and identifying mathematical concepts. Individuals with low fluid reasoning may have difficulty identifying and thinking through the steps of a mathematical problem.

INTERPRETING WRITTEN LANGUAGE TESTS

Interpretation of the written language tests requires the examiner to be aware of the skills involved in each task, to know what abilities underlie each test, and to recognize additional factors that are affecting performance. Rapid Reference 4.12 shows characteristics of individuals with low written language performance.

The skills measured in the six written language tests range from lower-level abilities, such as copying shapes, to higher-level abilities, such as expressing ideas in writing. The WJ III ACH measures six aspects of writing skill: punctuation and capitalization, spelling, usage, quality of handwriting, writing fluency, and quality of written expression. Figure 4.5 is an interpretive model of the various skills measured by the WJ III written language tests.

Using the CHC theory as the interpretive framework, the written language tests primarily measure writing ability, an aspect of reading/writing ability *(Grw)*. Some of the tests also measure aspects of comprehension-knowledge *(Gc)*, processing speed *(Gs)*, auditory processing *(Ga)*, and visual-spatial thinking *(Gv)*.

≡ *Rapid Reference 4.12*

Characteristics of Individuals with Low Written Language Achievement

An individual with low basic writing skills

has poor basic reading skills.

has poor handwriting.

reverses or transposes letters.

has poor spelling.

fails to self-monitor errors.

uses simple vocabulary to avoid misspellings.

does poorly under time constraints.

has limited proofreading skill.

An individual with low written expression

appears to resist writing tasks.

has a poor attitude toward writing tasks.

has limited background knowledge, limited experiences, and low vocabulary.

has low oral language abilities.

has poor organizational skills.

has low reasoning abilities.

Test 7: Spelling

This test requires the individual to produce, in writing, single letters or words in response to oral prompts. Several factors that may influence performance include handwriting, fine-motor skill, phonological coding, and orthographic coding. This test measures prewriting skills and spelling.

Test 8: Writing Fluency

This test requires the individual to produce, in writing, legible, simple sentences with acceptable English syntax. Low performance on this test may result from limited concentration, poor motor control, limited spelling or reading skills, limited processing speed *(Gs)*, or may result from a response style that interferes with performance (slow and accurate, fast and inaccurate, slow and inaccurate, etc.).

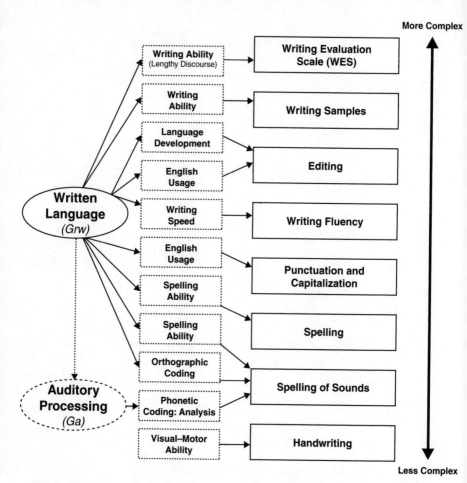

Figure 4.5 Various Skills Measured by the WJ III ACH Written Language Tests

Test 11: Writing Samples

This test requires the individual to produce meaningful written sentences in response to a variety of tasks. Low performance may result from limits in (a) oral language, (b) vocabulary, (c) organizational ability, (d) world knowledge, or (e) spelling skill. The individual's attitude toward writing may also influence performance.

Test 16: Editing

This test requires the ability to identify and correct errors in punctuation, capitalization, spelling, and usage in short written passages. Low performance may result from limited instruction, lack of knowledge, failure to self-monitor or self-correct errors, or poor reading skill.

Test 20: Spelling of Sounds

This test requires the individual to spell nonsense words that conform to conventional phonics and spelling rules. Both phonological coding *(Ga)* and orthographic coding are measured by this test. Low performance may result from lack of attention, poor phonological processing, poor orthographic awareness, or poor phoneme/grapheme knowledge. The examiner can compare results from this test to Sound Awareness and Word Attack to help determine if difficulties result from phonological problems or limited knowledge of phoneme/grapheme relationships.

Test 22: Punctuation and Capitalization

This test requires the ability to identify and correct mistakes in punctuation and capitalization and measures knowledge of English writing conventions. Low performance may result from limited knowledge of English language use, limited reading skill, or poor error monitoring.

Written Language Clusters

Three written language clusters are available in the WJ III ACH: Broad Written Language, Basic Writing Skills, and Written Expression. All of these clusters may be used when calculating intra-achievement and ability/achievement discrepancies. Rapid Reference 4.13 lists possible instructional implications for individuals with low written language performance.

Broad Written Language

This cluster is comprised of three tests: Spelling, Writing Fluency, and Writing Samples. It provides a broad, comprehensive view of the individual's written language achievement. Task demands include spelling single-word responses, writing simple sentences quickly, and expressing ideas well. The examiner should compare results from this cluster to results on the Broad Reading and Oral Language-Standard or Extended clusters to help determine the impact of oral language or reading skills on written language performance.

≡Rapid Reference 4.13

Instructional Implications for Individuals with Low Written Language Achievement

- Match instruction to developmental level.
- Teach the use of a computer, including spell-check feature.
- Provide alternatives to writing (e.g., oral responses).
- Provide preferential seating for copying tasks, or limit or omit copying tasks.
- Simplify or shorten spelling lists or other written assignments.
- Teach high-frequency words.
- Teach word-study strategies.
- Teach proofreading skills.
- Provide extended time for completing written tasks.
- Provide practice activities.
- Teach sentence structure.
- Use sentence-combining exercises.
- Help the individual develop vocabulary and other oral language abilities.
- Help the individual develop reading skills (vocabulary, comprehension, and strategies).
- Use story frames or other graphic organizers.

Basic Writing Skills

This cluster is comprised of two tests, Spelling and Editing. It provides a measure of basic writing skills in isolated and context-based formats. Task demands include writing letters, spelling single words, and identifying and correcting errors in spelling, usage, capitalization, and punctuation. Examiners should compare results of this cluster with the Written Expression cluster to determine if basic skills are impacting performance. Fluent and automatic basic skills are a fundamental part of complex meaningful written expression (Gerber & Hall, 1987). Error analysis of the two tests in this cluster will help identify the individual's developmental level in spelling.

Written Expression

This cluster is comprised of two tests, Writing Samples and Writing Fluency. It provides a measure of meaningful written expression and fluency. Examiners should compare results of this cluster to the results on the Oral Expression, Reading Comprehension, and Basic Writing Skills clusters. Low performance may result from limited oral language, limited basic writing skills, or limited reading skills.

INTERPRETING THE SPECIAL PURPOSE CLUSTERS

Academic Knowledge

Test 19: Academic Knowledge requires the individual to respond orally to prompts in the areas of science, social studies, and humanities. Early items require the examinee only to point to a response. This test measures acquired curricular knowledge, an aspect of comprehension-knowledge (Gc). A broad sample of the individual's range of scientific knowledge, general knowledge, cultural knowledge, and geographic knowledge is measured by this test. Due to the comprehensiveness of this test, it also serves as the Academic Knowledge cluster.

Low performance may result from limited vocabulary, limited exposure to curricular areas, or both. This test/cluster can provide valuable insights into the interests of the individual as well as his or her level of crystallized intelligence. No reading is required to perform this task. Therefore, the results can help determine whether the individual's knowledge base is impacting performance in the other academic areas. If the WJ III COG has been administered, results from this test can be compared to the comprehension-knowledge (Gc) cluster. In addition, this test can be combined with General Information from the WJ III COG to form a Knowledge cluster.

Total Achievement Cluster

This cluster is composed of nine tests in the Standard Battery: Letter-Word Identification, Reading Fluency, Passage Comprehension, Calculation, Math Fluency, Applied Problems, Spelling, Writing Fluency, and Writing Samples. These nine tests are used to create the Broad Reading, Broad Math, and Broad Written Language clusters.

The purpose of the Total Achievement cluster is to provide a general academic proficiency score. The cluster can be used to identify students with very

CAUTION

Interpretation of Global Scores

Exercise care when interpreting global scores that are composed of tests measuring many different skills or abilities, such as the Total Achievement score. Although this score provides an estimate of general academic performance, it reveals little about the underlying scores upon which it is based. An examiner should complete a profile analysis to obtain information about the examinee's unique achievement patterns.

limited or advanced performance levels across curricular areas. It is also helpful when examiners need a global view of the individual's overall performance across the various achievement domains. The tests required for obtaining the Total Achievement cluster also yield the three additional cross-academic clusters described below.

Academic Skills Cluster

This cross-academic cluster is composed of the three basic skill tests, Letter-Word Identification, Calculation, and Spelling. It provides a general, basic skills achievement level and can help determine if the individual's level of basic skills is similar or variable across academic areas. Examiners should consider whether basic skills facilitate or inhibit the individual's performance. Low performance may suggest particular curricular adaptations, such as use of a calculator during math activities.

Academic Fluency Cluster

This cross-academic cluster is composed of the three fluency tests, Reading Fluency, Math Fluency, and Writing Fluency. It provides a general academic fluency level. This cluster can help determine if the individual's level of automaticity with basic skills is facilitating or inhibiting academic performance. Examiners should note if the individual's speed of performance is similar or variable across academic areas. Low performance may suggest a need for extended time.

Academic Applications Cluster

This cross-academic cluster is composed of the three application tests, Passage Comprehension, Applied Problems, and Writing Samples. It provides a general measure of the individual's ability to apply academic knowledge. Examiners should note if the individual's performance on the tests in this cluster is similar or variable, and they should consider the impact of basic skills, fluency, and oral language proficiency when interpreting this cluster. Low performance may suggest a need for adjusting the difficulty level of materials.

Phoneme/Grapheme Knowledge

This cluster is a combination of two tests, Word Attack and Spelling of Sounds, and may be used to evaluate the individual's proficiency with phonic and orthographic elements. The tasks require the individual to decode (read) and encode (spell) pseudowords. Low performance may result from limited phonological skills, limited orthographic skills, or both. To help pinpoint an individual's low performance, comparisons should be made to Sound Awareness and, if using the WJ III COG, the auditory processing *(Ga)* and Phonemic Awareness clusters. The Phoneme/Grapheme cluster is especially helpful in documenting specific reading disabilities (dyslexia).

INTERPRETING PROFILES

A graphic representation of a person's performance can be helpful in explaining or interpreting results. The WJ III ACH offers two types of profiles for interpretation, Age/Grade and the Standard Score/Percentile Rank. The WJ III Compuscore and Profiles Program generates both types of profiles. The Age/Grade Profiles report an examinee's instructional zone. The Standard Score / Percentile Rank Profiles provide a comparison to the norm group and illustrate the confidence band around each obtained score.

Analyzing an individual's pattern of scores provides information about his or her academic strengths and weaknesses, which helps develop hypotheses about present levels of academic functioning. Some profiles may show extreme variability, whereas others may show minimal variability. Some examples of various types of profiles include

1. A flat profile with all scores much above average. This suggests that the student is advanced academically and may profit from an enrichment program.

2. A flat profile with scores all much below average. This suggests that the student has low academic performance and may need specific accommodations as well as specialized instruction.
3. An uneven profile. This suggests special strengths and weaknesses and may provide insights about the student's learning style, and learning abilities and disabilities. This type of profile may also help determine possible interventions.
4. A profile of scores within the average range. This suggests that intervention is unnecessary.

INTERPRETING THE AGE/GRADE PROFILE

The Age/Grade Profiles are graphic representations of the examinee's instructional zones. When planning instructional or service needs or presenting results to nonprofessionals, these profiles can provide a meaningful interpretation of test performance. When using the software program, the norm reference group selected determines which profile is generated: Age norms create age profiles, grade norms create grade profiles. A vertical line is plotted automatically, representing either the examinee's chronological age or grade placement.

The instructional zone for each test or cluster is represented by a shaded area extending from the point at which the examinee perceives the related task as "easy" to the point at which the examinee perceives the task as "difficult." The easy point is equivalent to an RPI of 96/90. The difficult point is equivalent to an RPI of 75/90. The midpoint corresponds to the obtained age equivalent or grade equivalent and represents the instructional level. For example, on Basic Reading Skills, a 6th-grade student obtained an easy level of performance (approximately the middle of Grade 2) and a difficult level of performance (approximately the beginning of Grade 4). This student would have little success on grade-level tasks requiring the use of basic reading skills. To ensure success and classroom participation, the level of instructional material will need to be adapted.

In addition, the bands on the Age/Grade Profile depict the rate of growth in a particular ability at a particular point in time. A narrow band means that growth is rapid during a stage of development, whereas a wide band means that growth is slow. For example, the band on the Word Attack test for a 9th-grade student is wide because the student's ability to pronounce pseudowords (phonically regular nonsense words) is not changing much during this time. In contrast, a test like Picture Vocabulary has a narrow band because knowledge of word meanings in-

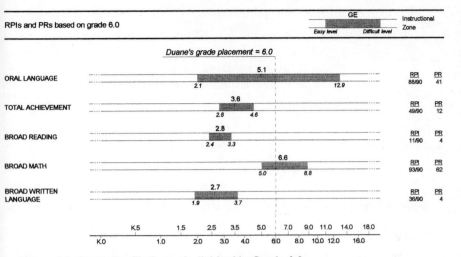

Figure 4.6 Grade Profile for an Individual in Grade 6.0

Note: Profiles generated by the Compuscore and Profile Programs, 2001, Riverside Publishing.

creases at a steady rate across the school years. Figure 4.6 illustrates a portion of the achievement cluster Grade Profile for an individual in Grade 6.0.

Interpretation of the bands is similar to the criteria used on many informal reading inventories. The easy level of the band represents the independent level of performance where the student needs no assistance. The midpoint represents the instructional level, the appropriate level for the student when some support is provided. The difficult level is comparable to the frustration level and the tasks will be too hard for the individual.

Vygotsky's (1978) zone of proximal development (zpd) is a concept similar to the instructional zone. The zpd represents the distance between an individual's actual developmental level and his or her level of potential development when assisted by a more knowledgeable other. The concept of developmental ranges is helpful in planning instruction to support growth.

INTERPRETING STANDARD SCORE/ PERCENTILE RANK PROFILES

Viewing a test score on a profile is generally preferred to interpreting single scores or points. The Standard Score/Percentile Rank Profile (SS/PR Profile)

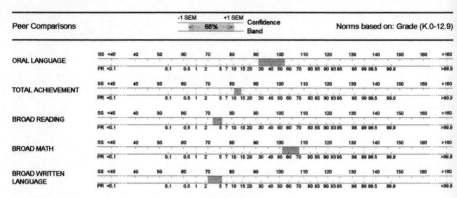

Figure 4.7 SS/PR Profile for an Individual in Grade 6.0

Note: Profiles generated by the Compuscore and Profiles Program, 2001, Riverside Publishing.

simultaneously portrays the ±1 SEM confidence band for the standard scores and the percentile ranks. This band, extending from a point 1 SEM below the individual's obtained score to a point 1 SEM above the individual's obtained score, is the zone in which the true score falls two out of three times, or the 68% confidence band. If a higher degree of confidence is desired, the software program provides an option to select a 90% or 95% level of confidence. A 95% confidence band (±2 SEM) represents the region in which an individual's true ability would fall 19 times out of 20. Figure 4.7 illustrates a portion of the achievement cluster SS/PR Profile for an individual in Grade 6.0.

Examiners can use the SS/PR Profile to evaluate differences in an individual's performance on administered tests. Examiners should use caution when interpreting these differences because some degree of variability in performance is to be expected. The significance of observed differences decreases as the number of comparisons increases. In addition, examiners must determine whether statistically significant differences have any practical or educational implication. A statistically significant discrepancy may exist between measures but have little educational relevance. For example, a child's standard score of 100 on Broad Mathematics may be significantly lower than his advanced performance in other areas of achievement. The child however, is not likely to need intervention because this ability falls within the average range. As a general rule, examiners should not use scores on individual tests to attempt precise descriptions of specific academic skills; rather, they should use them to generate hypotheses about academic performance. Examiners can derive more reliable estimates of achievement from cluster scores than from individual test scores.

One way to approach test or cluster profile analysis is to evaluate the scores in reference to the norm group. On the SS/PR Profile, the reference point is a mean of 100 (coupled with a standard deviation of 15). For analysis purposes, (a) standard scores above 115 always indicate a strength (one or more standard deviations above the mean), (b) standard scores of 85 to 115 always indicate average ability (within one standard deviation from the mean), and (c) standard scores below 85 always indicate a weakness (one or more standard deviations below the mean). Sometimes, clinicians may discuss "relative" strengths and weaknesses. For example, a person may obtain a standard score of 80 in Broad Reading and 60 in Broad Mathematics. Although both scores are below average, reading could be described as a "relative" strength.

Because all of the WJ III ACH clusters and tests have a mean of 100 and standard deviation of 15, profiles across the clusters and across the test scores can be evaluated statistically. To say that one score is meaningfully (i.e., statistically significantly) higher than another score, examiners first need to determine that the difference between the two scores does not represent chance variation. It is not possible to simply look at two scores and say that one is statistically higher or lower than the other score. A statistically significant difference indicates a high probability that the academic skills measured by the two scores differ. In other words, the difference is greater than that which is expected to occur simply by chance.

The questions to ask are:

- Do the individual's scores on the clusters differ significantly from each other?
- Do the individual's test scores differ significantly from one another?

The following section provides guidelines for determining the likelihood that a true difference in abilities is represented by the difference between the point scores on any two tests or any two clusters.

1. *If the 68% confidence bands for any two tests or clusters overlap at all, assume no difference exists between the person's two abilities.*
2. *If a separation exists between the ends of two test bands that is less than the width of the wider of the two bands, assume that a possible difference exists be-*

tween the individual's two abilities. A difference this size would occur on average about 8 times in 100 if a single comparison is made and if the two abilities are actually the same. A common practice with batteries such as the WJ III ACH is to compare more than one pair of tests at a time or to look only at the most extreme examples. Under these conditions, the probability increases that at least one difference will be observed even though the two abilities are the same. For example, if 10 comparisons are being made, a difference of this size would occur by chance about 57 times in 100.

3. *If the separation between the two bands is greater than the width of the wider band, assume that a real difference exists between the subject's two abilities.* A difference this size would occur on average about 2 times in 1,000 if a single comparison is being made and if the two abilities are actually the same. (The actual probability ranges from 0 to 5 times in 1,000 depending on the amount of separation.) If 10 comparisons were being made, a difference this size would occur by chance about 20 times in 1,000.

The goal of profile analysis is to generate hypotheses about a person's achievement. The hypotheses generated need to be compared with other information gathered about the examinee. When the hypotheses are reasonable, they can be used to (a) clarify the specific nature of an individual's academic performance, (b) clarify the severity of any problems in academic development, (c) develop treatment recommendations, (d) select appropriate educational programs, or (e) consider an appropriate academic or vocational placement.

To determine the factors that might account for a certain pattern of scores, examiners should consider both the extrinsic (or external) factors, as well as the intrinsic (or internal) factors. Extrinsic factors include the person's socioeconomic status, education, special training, social and physical environment,

CAUTION

Do Not Overinterpret Differences in Scores or Profiles

A certain amount of variability is expected in the general population. The significance of observed differences decreases as the number of comparisons increases. You must determine whether observed differences have any practical applications or educational implications.

family background, temperament, and so forth. In some cases, differences among scores may be factors associated with examiner characteristics or factors associated with the assessment situation. Internal factors include the health status of the examinee, as well as physical and mental status.

INTERPRETING DISCREPANCIES

Two basic types of discrepancy procedures are available in the WJ III: intra-ability (discrepancies among abilities) and ability/achievement (discrepancies between a predictor score and measured academic performance). The primary purpose of the intra-ability discrepancy procedures is diagnosis, whereas the primary function of the ability/achievement discrepancy procedures is prediction. The following section describes these options in more detail. Table 4.6 indicates the discrepancies that are available when using the WJ III ACH and/or the WJ III COG.

Because all norms for the WJ III ACH and the WJ III COG are based on data from the same sample, actual discrepancy norms are available. This eliminates the need to estimate the discrepancy by using a regression equation or a table based on the equation. The co-norming of the WJ III also provides an accurate means for evaluating the significance of a discrepancy. These advantages are available to the examiner when using any of the discrepancy procedures shown in Table 4.6.

Interpreting the Significance of a Discrepancy

Understanding the "significance" of a discrepancy is based upon interpretation of either of two scores: the *discrepancy percentile rank* (Discrepancy PR) or

Table 4.6 Discrepancy Calculations Available in the WJ III

Intra-Ability Discrepancy		Ability/Achievement Discrepancy	
Intra-achievement	(ACH only)	Oral Language/ Achievement	(ACH only)
Intra-cognitive	(COG only)	GIA/Achievement	(COG & ACH)
Intra-individual	(COG & ACH)	Predicted Achievement/ Achievement	(COG & ACH)

DON'T FORGET
....

Purpose of WJ III Discrepancy Procedures

Intra-ability discrepancies are designed for diagnosis.

Use to display strengths and weaknesses.

Use to help with early identification of problems.

Ability/achievement discrepancies are designed for prediction.

Use to estimate expected performance in the near term.

Use to illustrate performance relative to peers.

the *discrepancy standard deviation* (Discrepancy SD). These scores help interpret the presence and severity of the discrepancies. The Discrepancy PR reflects the percent of the population that possesses a discrepancy or difference score of that magnitude, such as 1% or 95%. The Discrepancy SD is a standardized z score that reports the same discrepancy into standard deviation units, related to a criterion such as -1.5 standard deviations. The Discrepancy PR score differs from other percentile ranks in that it compares the person to age- or grade-mates of the same ability, not to the entire age or grade norm group.

Examiners should remember that when describing certain discrepancies, they should refer to differences as being "relative" (compared to the person's other abilities) strengths or weaknesses. For example, on the Intra-Achievement discrepancy procedure, a student scored in the low 60s on Broad Reading, Broad Mathematics, and Broad Written Language. In contrast, the student's score on Oral Language was 80. The computer printout identifies oral language as a significant strength. In the report or description of performance, examiners should describe this as a relative strength because none of the scores fall in the average range.

INTRA-ABILITY DISCREPANCY

The intra-ability discrepancy procedures are based on the practice of examining test performance to determine patterns of strengths and weaknesses. As noted in Table 4.6, three types of intra-ability discrepancies are available in the WJ III. With these discrepancies, equal interest exists in either strengths or weaknesses in one area relative to the average of all other areas being considered. Only one of the intra-ability discrepancies is available when using the WJ

III ACH. The others require using the WJ III COG alone or in conjunction with the achievement tests. The intra-achievement discrepancy procedure compares each achievement cluster to the average of the other clusters.

Intra-Achievement

The intra-achievement discrepancy allows examiners to analyze an individual's academic cluster scores and to explore covarying strengths and weaknesses. For example, a person may have a strength in reading, but a weakness in mathematics. These discrepancies within achievement can help determine a person's present educational needs.

Examiners can calculate intra-achievement discrepancies on four broad curricular areas (reading, oral language, mathematics, and writing) or nine specific areas of academic performance (Basic Reading Skills, Reading Comprehension, Basic Writing Skills, Written Expression, Math Calculation Skills, Math Reasoning, Oral Expression, Listening Comprehension, and Academic Knowledge). See Table 4.7 to determine which tests and clusters are required to calculate intra-achievement discrepancies.

Individuals who have specific achievement strengths or weaknesses, such as superior math skills relative to the average of all other achievement areas, exhibit an intra-achievement discrepancy. Table 4.8 illustrates results from a set of intra-achievement discrepancy calculations.

The Actual Standard Score (SS) column in Table 4.8 shows the standard score the individual actually obtained on the cluster. The Predicted SS column shows the individual's predicted SS and is based on the average of the other three achievement clusters. In this example, the individual has an average of 98 on the Broad Math, Broad Written Language, and Oral Language-Standard clusters ($115 + 79 + 100 = 294/3 = 98$). Therefore, the Predicted SS for Broad Reading is 98. Because the actual SS for the individual in this example is 79, a negative 19-point difference exists between the actual and predicted scores ($79 - 98 = -19$). This means that the individual's performance on Broad Reading was lower than predicted by performance on the other three achievement clusters.

The PR column shows the discrepancy percentile rank (Discrepancy PR). This score indicates the percentage of this individual's peer group that achieved as low or lower, (or as high or higher) as the individual achieved. For

Table 4.7 Tests and Clusters Required to Calculate Intra-Achievement Discrepancies

4 Clusters	11 Tests
Intra-Achievement Option 1 (requires tests in Standard Battery only)	
Broad Reading	Letter-Word Identification, Reading Fluency, Passage Comprehension
Broad Math	Calculation, Math Fluency, Applied Problems
Broad Written Language	Spelling, Writing Fluency, Writing Samples
Oral Language-Standard	Story Recall, Understanding Directions

9 Clusters	17 Tests
Intra-Achievement Option 2 (requires tests in Standard and Extended Batteries)	
Basic Reading Skills	Letter-Word Identification, Word Attack
Reading Comprehension	Passage Comprehension, Reading Vocabulary
Math Calculation Skills	Calculation, Math Fluency
Math Reasoning	Applied Problems, Quantitative Concepts
Basic Writing Skills	Spelling, Editing
Written Expression	Writing Fluency, Writing Samples
Oral Expression	Story Recall, Picture Vocabulary
Listening Comprehension	Understanding Directions, Oral Comprehension
Academic Knowledge	Academic Knowledge

Table 4.8 Intra-Achievement Discrepancy Calculations Using Broad Achievement Clusters

Achievement Area	Standard Scores			Discrepancy		Significant at ±1.5 SD
	Actual	Predicted	Difference	PR	SD	
Broad Reading	79	98	−19	5	−1.67	Yes
Broad Math	115	90	+25	99	+2.24	Yes
Broad Written Lang.	79	98	−19	4	−1.76	Yes
Oral Language-Std.	100	94	+6	69	+0.49	No

example, a Discrepancy PR of 98 indicates that only 2% of the individual's peer group (same age or grade *and* same predicted score) had an actual SS as high or higher in the target area. Another way to describe a Discrepancy PR of 98 is that the individual did as well or better than 98 out of 100 age- or grade-mates.

The SD column shows the difference, in units of the standard error of estimate, between the individual's actual and predicted scores. A negative value in the SD column indicates the individual's actual achievement was lower than expected. A positive value indicates the individual's actual achievement was higher than expected. This statement of significance (SD) can be used instead of the percentile rank in programs with selection criteria based on a difference equal to or greater than, for example, one and one-half times the standard deviation. Any individual who had a SD of −1.5 or lower would meet this selection criteria.

The results in Table 4.8 indicate that this individual has a significant strength in Broad Math (PR = 99, SD = +2.24) relative to the other achievement areas. Also, the individual has significant weaknesses in Broad Reading (PR = 5, SD = −1.67) and Broad Written Language (PR = 4, SD = −1.76) relative to the other achievement areas. The following section presents a few examples of how to discuss these scores in a report.

In Broad Written Language, only 4% of grade-peers with the same predicted achievement score would obtain a standard score of 79 or lower. (Discrepancy PR = 4).

When the Broad Math score of 115 is compared to the average of the other academic clusters, only 1 in 100 grade-peers (Discrepancy PR = 99) with the same predicted score would obtain a score the same or higher.

When the Broad Reading cluster score of 79 is compared to performance on the other broad academic clusters, only 5 out of 100 individuals (Discrepancy PR = 5) with the same predicted score would obtain a score the same or lower.

Although professionals must evaluate the examinee's entire performance, clinical history, and background information to arrive at the most reasonable hypothesis that accounts for significant differences among abilities, significant intra-achievement discrepancies may indicate one or more of the following:

- varied interests
- strengths or weaknesses in processing information

- strengths or weaknesses in academic performance
- strengths or weaknesses in oral language
- strengths or weaknesses in speed of processing (e.g., as demonstrated on the timed tests)
- sensory impairments
- learning disabilities
- language impairments
- limited educational opportunity

Other Intra-Ability Discrepancy Procedures

The two remaining procedures, intra-cognitive and intra-individual, require the WJ III COG. The WJ III COG intra-cognitive discrepancy procedure helps determine specific cognitive strengths and weaknesses and can be helpful in documenting specific cognitive strengths or impairments. The intra-individual discrepancy procedure requires both the WJ III COG and ACH batteries and allows examiners to analyze an individual's strengths and weaknesses across all academic and cognitive areas assessed. The intra-individual discrepancy may provide important information for diagnosing learning difficulties. For example, an examiner may determine that a 3rd-grade boy's reading problem is influenced by some underlying condition, such as poor phonetic coding skills. Furthermore, the examiner may determine that a weakness in the boy's long-term retrieval ability is negatively impacting his ability to associate, store, and retrieve new learning. The intra-individual discrepancy examines the relationship between achievement abilities in any particular domain in reference to cognitive abilities that may be related to and affect academic performance. One caution is needed. If the achievement areas are very low, the overall predicted score is lowered and significant cognitive discrepancies may not be apparent. In some cases, the examiner should use the intra-cognitive and intra-achievement discrepancy procedures instead.

ABILITY/ACHIEVEMENT DISCREPANCIES

Ability/achievement models use certain intellectual or linguistic abilities to predict academic performance. The three ability/achievement discrepancy procedures available in the WJ III provide a means for comparing an individual's current academic performance to the average academic performance for all others in the population with similar ability. Only one ability/achievement discrepancy option (oral language/achievement) is available when using the WJ III ACH. The other two procedures require the use of the WJ III COG and the WJ III ACH.

Oral Language Ability/Achievement Discrepancy

Oral language ability/achievement discrepancies can be calculated using only the WJ III ACH. The standard score from the Oral Language-Extended cluster, composed of 4 tests, is used to predict achievement on any of the broad, basic skills, or applied cluster scores. Individuals with a significant negative discrepancy (> –1.5) between oral language ability and achievement exhibit relative strengths in oral language with weaknesses in one or more achievement areas. Table 4.9 illustrates the oral language ability/achievement discrepancy calculations with three broad achievement clusters.

In the field of reading disabilities, one commonly proposed discrepancy model is to compare oral language abilities to specific domains of academic performance. Often individuals with "specific" reading and writing impairments are described as having a discrepancy between oral and written language abilities. The disability is called "specific" because it primarily affects the development of literacy. The person may struggle with reading, but have no trouble understanding mathematical concepts. The oral language ability/ achievement procedure has particular relevance for helping distinguish be-

Table 4.9 Oral Language/Achievement Discrepancy Calculations Using Broad Achievement Clusters

Achievement Area	Standard Scores			Discrepancy		Significant at ±1.5 SD
	Actual	Predicted	Difference	PR	SD	
Broad Reading	79	104	–25	3	–1.89	Yes
Broad Math	115	104	+11	80	+0.84	No
Broad Written Language	79	104	–25	3	–1.85	Yes

Note: These discrepancies based on Oral Language-Extended with ACH Broad Clusters

tween individuals who have adequate oral language capabilities but poor reading and writing abilities (i.e., specific reading disabilities), versus individuals whose oral language abilities are commensurate with their reading and writing performance. In the first case, intervention would focus on reading and writing development; in the second case, intervention would be directed toward all aspects of language development.

The results in Table 4.9 indicate that this individual has significant ability/achievement discrepancies in Broad Reading and Broad Written Language when Oral Language is used as the ability score. As noted previously, an individual with poor reading and writing abilities but adequate oral language may have a reading disability. Furthermore, the relative strength in Broad Math (SS = 115) indicates this individual does not have a flat profile that would be associated with generalized low academic performance.

Other Ability/Achievement Discrepancy Procedures

The remaining procedures require the use of the WJ III COG. Examiners may use either the General Intellectual Ability (GIA) Standard or Extended clusters or the Predicted Achievement clusters as the ability scores.

STEP BY STEP: HOW TO INTERPRET THE WJ III ACH

1. Interpret the Clusters

- Cluster scores are the most valid and reliable scores to interpret. They represent a more representative array of abilities as well as a larger number of items than are found in individual tests. Eighteen clusters are available.

  Reading: Broad Reading, Basic Reading Skills, Reading Comprehension

  Mathematics: Broad Mathematics, Basic Calculation Skills, Math Reasoning

  Written Language: Broad Written Language, Basic Writing Skills, Written Expression

  Oral Language: Oral Language, Oral Expression, Listening Comprehension

Special: Academic Knowledge, Phoneme/Grapheme Knowledge, Total Achievement

Cross-Academic: Academic Skills, Academic Fluency, Academic Applications

- Use the Total Achievement score as an estimate of academic abilities. This score gives a general indicator of overall classroom performance.
- Examine the Broad Achievement clusters.
- Compare results of clusters within an academic area. For example, when looking at a particular academic area such as reading, compare the scores from Basic Reading Skills to Reading Comprehension. Is performance low on all clusters (generalized) in the area? Is performance lower on Basic Skills than on Comprehension? Is performance lower on Comprehension cluster than on Basic Skills cluster?
- Compare results of clusters across academic areas. For example, compare reading clusters to written language, knowledge, or mathematics clusters. Using the cross-academic clusters can be helpful in determining if the individual has a generalized problem in basic skills, fluency, or application of the skills.
- Compare oral language performance to results in all other achievement areas.

2. Interpret the Discrepancies

- Determine whether there are significant intra-ability discrepancies by using the intra-achievement discrepancy procedure.
- Determine whether there are any significant ability/achievement discrepancies by using the oral language/achievement discrepancy procedure.
- Consider the implications of any significant discrepancies.

3. Interpret Profiles

- Examine the Age/Grade Profiles to determine instructional zones. For each cluster or test, an independent (easy), instructional, and frustration (difficult) level can be identified. The vertical line representing the individual's grade placement or chronological age provides a visual reference for interpreting and explaining test performance.

- Examine the SS/PR Profiles to determine relative standing in comparison to the peer group and scatter of the individual's performance. Interpretation of this profile helps identify statistically significant discrepancies in the individual's performance. Determine whether the discrepancy has instructional significance.
- Analyze the differences among cluster scores to develop hypotheses about strengths and weaknesses.
- Determine whether significant differences exist among cluster scores.
- Determine whether significant differences exist among the tests that comprise a specific cluster.
- Determine whether significant differences exist between individual test scores.

4. Interpret Individual Tests (22 possible tests)

- Consider the results of each test in each cluster obtained. Are the results similar or discrepant? It is often informative to analyze performance among the tests measuring a broad achievement area. For example, make comparisons among the three tests of the Broad Reading Cluster: Letter-Word Identification, Reading Fluency, and Passage Comprehension. Although these comparisons are open to the errors associated with multiple comparisons, they are valuable for generating hypotheses about the examinee's reading abilities. Evaluating results at the individual test level can help determine instructional objectives.
- Analyze the differences among all of the test scores to see the patterns that go across different domains. For example, it may be noted that a person responds slowly on all timed tests or has difficulty on all tasks involving basic skills.

5. Complete an Error Analysis

- Analyze the pattern of errors within each test. You may obtain important information from this analysis. Evaluating the quality of responses will help determine the individual's level of understanding.

Some responses are very close to being correct, whereas others reveal minimal understanding or limited knowledge. Within a test, the items are arranged in order of difficulty, which will help you to evaluate the pattern of successes and failures. An examinee may complete addition problems correctly but make errors on subtraction problems involving regrouping.

- Examine systematically correct and incorrect responses to individual items to help identify error patterns and determine instructional objectives. For example, it may be apparent on the reading and spelling tests that the individual has not learned all letter/sound correspondences.

6. Review and Summarize Behavioral Observations

- Review the information compiled when completing the Test Session Observations Checklist in the Test Record.
- Consider the individual's reaction to different tasks as well as response to increased difficulty of tasks. Is there a noticeable difference in attitude or behavior between academic areas? How does the individual handle increasingly difficult tasks? Does the individual respond carefully or impulsively; quickly or slowly; accurately or inaccurately?
- Consider the strategies used by the individual. Are they appropriate for the task? Is the individual flexible or rigid in applying strategies?
- Note if the individual used self-monitoring or self-correcting behaviors.
- Note any comments that were made by the examinee during the testing session.

🎣 TEST YOURSELF 🎣

1. What is the primary purpose of intra-ability discrepancy procedures?
2. What is the primary purpose of ability/achievement discrepancy procedures?
3. What cluster is used as the predictor score when calculating an ability/achievement discrepancy from just the WJ III Tests of Achievement?

(continued)

4. **What does an Age or Grade Profile illustrate?**

5. **Which two tests combine to form the Phoneme/Grapheme Knowledge cluster?**

6. **What does the SS/PR Profile illustrate?**

7. **What does it mean if two scores plotted on the SS/PR Profile have overlapping bands?**

8. **Write a statement describing an intra-achievement Discrepancy PR of .1 on Broad Reading for an individual in eighth grade.**

9. **On which written language test would a weakness in auditory processing have the greatest impact?**

    (a) Writing Fluency

    (b) Spelling of Sounds

    (c) Writing Samples

    (d) Editing

10. **Results from which oral language test should be compared directly to results from Passage Comprehension?**

Answers: 1. diagnosis, determination of strengths and weaknesses; 2. Prediction; 3. Oral Language-Extended; 4. display instructional or developmental levels; 5. Word Attack and Spelling of Sounds; 6. display a norm-referenced pattern of scores; 7. There is no statistically significant difference between the two scores. 8. Compared to grade-peers with the same predicted score, only 1 in 1,000 would have scored as low or lower on Broad Reading. 9. b; 10. Oral Comprehension

Five

STRENGTHS AND WEAKNESSES OF THE WJ III ACH

The WJ III ACH has many additions and improvements compared to the WJ-R. Because the WJ III ACH was only several months old when this book went to press, no published reviews or critiques existed. During the standardization, we reviewed the instrument carefully and from our initial use of this instrument, we have identified what appear to be its major strengths and limitations. We choose to present these findings and opinions in a format similar to Kaufman and Lichtenberger (1999) and have organized these strengths and weaknesses into the following areas: test development, standardization, reliability and validity, administration and scoring, and interpretation (see Rapid References 5.1, 5.2, 5.3, 5.4, 5.5).

We can note many significant strengths of the WJ III ACH, but do not note any weaknesses that seem of major significance. Although not a weakness per se, a concern could center around the complexity of the instrument, as considerable study is required for mastery. WJ-R ACH users, however, should have little difficulty in learning the new scoring and interpretive features.

The significant strengths include (a) excellent standardization sample, (b) co-norming with the WJ III COG, (c) high reliability of clusters and tests, (d) coverage of all major areas of school achievement, (e) four measures of oral language, (f) varied measures of skills, fluency, and application, (g) and enhanced interpretive options. The changes made in this latest version of the WJ have made it a more useful instrument for diagnosis, as well as for instructional planning. As with all test instruments and test scores, the WJ III ACH results need to be integrated with other data about the subject, including consideration of test behaviors, data from other assessments, results of informal procedures, information obtained from teachers, and classroom observations.

Rapid Reference 5.1

Strengths and Weaknesses of the WJ III ACH: Test Development

Strengths

- The easels are smaller and lighter.
- The overall appearance of the materials has been improved.
- The addition of oral language tests provides increased options.
- New fluency tests in reading and math have been added to measure varied aspects of automaticity.
- The addition of Spelling of Sounds enhances the assessment of an important aspect of spelling.
- The addition of Sound Awareness adds a broad-based measure of phonological awareness.
- The test provides broader coverage of each achievement area.
- Co-norming with WJ III COG provides a "best practice" approach for comparing performance on cognitive and achievement tests.
- Application of the Cattell-Horn-Carroll theory of cognitive abilities to the WJ III ACH creates a common framework for interpreting results.
- Parallel, alternate forms of the test facilitate pre- and posttesting.

Weaknesses

- Several WJ III ACH tests require the use of a tape recorder, increasing the amount of equipment needed for testing.
- Tests appropriate for use with the preschool population are not clearly identified.
- Two tests are identical in Form A and Form B, Sound Awareness and Punctuation and Capitalization.
- There is a limited number of items at specific age or grade levels due to wide range of coverage.
- Writing tasks only require single sentence responses. However, the test does provide the Writing Evaluation Scale to evaluate informally longer, more complex passages.

≡ Rapid Reference 5.2

Strengths and Weaknesses of the WJ III ACH: Standardization

Strengths

- The normative sample was stratified for 10 key individual and community variables.

- Bias toward any specific type of community was avoided by applying 13 socioeconomic status (SES) variables during the selection process. WJ III is one of the few tests to control for SES.

- Oversampling was done on minorities to ensure adequate representation.

- Normative data were collected on first-year graduate students, extending the grade range to 18.0.

- The WJ III ACH contains the largest nationally representative norm sample ($n = 8,818$) for an individually administered test.

- For school-age sample, the continuous-year procedure was used for gathering data.

- Age norms are reported by 1-month intervals from 2-0 to 18-11 and then by 1-year intervals from 19-0 to 95+ years of age.

- Grade norms are reported for each tenth of a year from grade K.0 through 18.0.

- The test provides a wide range of measurement, allowing examiners to use the same tests to assess the performance of individuals at various stages of development.

Weaknesses

- Data on the mean scores for various ethnic groups are not included in the manuals.

≡ Rapid Reference 5.3

Strengths and Weaknesses of the WJ III ACH: Reliability and Validity

Strengths

• The WJ III ACH is co-normed with the WJ III COG, providing information about a wide range of cognitive and achievement abilities. Co-norming also allows the examiners to more accurately predict a subject's achievement scores based on the General Intellectual Ability score (GIA) or the Predicted Achievement scores.

• Median split-half reliabilities for all clusters meet or exceed the .90 level except for three: Oral Language Standard (.87), Oral Expression (.85), and Listening Comprehension (.89).

• Median split-half reliabilities for all tests meet or exceed the .80 level except for two: Spelling of Sounds (.76) and Punctuation and Capitalization (.79).

• Numerous validity studies are reported in the *Technical Manual*. The *Manual* presents concurrent validity studies (e.g., WJ III ACH Reading Comprehension correlated .81 with KTEA Comprehension and .79 with WIAT Comprehension).

Weaknesses

• No counterbalanced studies of the WJ-R and WJ III are presented in the manuals. Users will not know how much change to expect when switching from the WJ-R ACH to WJ III.

• Split-half reliabilities are below .70 for the following tests at specific age groups: Story Recall (age 2), Story Recall-Delayed (ages 3, 4, 5, 70–79, and 80+), Understanding Directions (ages 16 and 17), Math Fluency (age 7).

• No reliability information is reported for grade levels.

≡ Rapid Reference 5.4

Strengths and Weaknesses of the WJ III ACH: Administration and Scoring

Strengths	Weaknesses
• The administration and scoring procedures are described clearly in the easel test books.	• Different scoring procedures are applied to different tests. Some have basal and ceiling rules and others have cutoffs and continuation procedures. New users may be confused by these different procedures.
• The scoring procedures are explained clearly in the *Manual*.	
• The WJ III ACH is computer-scored which enhances interpretive options and reduces the chance of error. Profiles may also be printed.	• The WJ III cannot be scored by hand, presenting a problem for those without access to a computer.
• Estimated age and grade equivalents are available on the Test Record, providing immediate feedback about instructional levels.	• A few tests require some judgment in scoring (Story Recall, Story Recall-Delayed, and Writing Samples).
• All tests in which the participant has to write responses are located in one Subject Response Booklet.	• The Story Recall-Delayed test provides only a z score. To obtain this score, the examiner must select the z score as an additional score option.
• An Examiner Training Workbook, included with each test kit, contains practice exercises and checklists to help build examiner competency.	
• The Test Record includes a Test Session Observations Checklist to assist in documenting the examinee's behavior and response style.	

Rapid Reference 5.5

Strengths and Weaknesses of the WJ III ACH: Interpretation

Strengths	Weaknesses
• The WJ III ACH is co-normed with the WJ III COG, providing more information about the interrelationships among an array of cognitive and academic abilities.	• Timed tasks may not be as important in settings when ample time is provided for completion of assignments.
• The addition of extra items on the reading tests lowers the floor making the tests more appropriate for young children and individuals who are low-functioning.	• Performance on timed tests may be influenced by cultural differences.
• The addition of Reading Fluency and Math Fluency allows for measurement of academic fluency (Reading, Math, and Writing Fluency) across three curricular domains.	• Some users may not understand the relevance of the oral language ability/achievement procedure for the diagnosis of reading and writing disabilities.
• The addition of four oral language tests provides an ability/achievement discrepancy procedure within the WJ III ACH.	• Several of the oral language tests are factorially complex. For example, the Understanding Directions and Story Recall tests measure both *Gc* and *Gsm.* Although this makes the tests clinically more useful, interpretation of performance may be more difficult.
• The Story Recall-Delayed test can be combined with Visual-Auditory Learning-Delayed on the WJ III COG to get a Delayed Recall cluster score, which may provide good neuropsychological data.	
• The Math Reasoning cluster has been expanded to include a Quantitative Concepts test (Concepts and Number Series subtest) in addition to the Applied Problems test.	
• The addition of several special purpose clusters (Total Achievement, Academic Skills, Academic Fluency, Academic Applications) enhances cross-academic analysis.	
• The *z* score for Story Recall-Delayed is interpreted as a personal discrepancy score. The individual's performance is compared to a predicted score (based on age or grade, initial test score, and delay interval). This is analogous to a focused norm frequently used in neuropsychology. It indicates whether the individual's delayed recall score is within normal limits.	

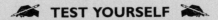 TEST YOURSELF

1. The addition of Sound Awareness enhances measurement of

(a) vocabulary.

(b) auditory discrimination.

(c) phonological awareness.

(d) spelling.

2. The Cattell-Horn-Carroll theory of cognitive abilities provides a framework for interpretation of the achievement tests. True or False?

3. The WJ III ACH grade norms were extended to

(a) 17.0.

(b) 16.9.

(c) 18.0.

(d) 18.9.

4. All tests have basal and ceiling rules. True or False?

5. The Story Recall and Understanding Directions tests are factorially complex. True or False?

6. The reliabilities of the WJ III ACH clusters are mostly

(a) .90 or above.

(b) .80 or above.

(c) .70 or above.

(d) .60 or above.

7. The oral language ability/achievement discrepancy procedure requires administration of the WJ III COG. True or False?

8. The oral language ability/achievement discrepancy procedure compares one area of achievement to the average of the person's other areas of achievement. True or False?

9. Both the SS/PR and Age/Grade Profiles may be plotted by hand on the Test Record. True or False?

10. A Delayed Recall score can be obtained by combining Story Recall-Delayed with Visual-Auditory Learning-Delayed in the WJ III COG. True or False?

Answers: 1. c; 2. True; 3. c; 4. False; 5. True; 6. a; 7. False; 8. False; 9. False; 10. True

Six

CLINICAL APPLICATIONS OF THE WJ III ACH

"Diagnosis must take second place to instruction, and must be made a tool of instruction, not an end in itself" (Cruickshank, 1977, p. 193).

The purposes of an educational evaluation are to identify an individual's strengths and weaknesses and then to design an educational program to meet this person's needs. This plan may include specific accommodations, such as oral testing and extended time on tests or it may include specific instructional materials. Although lists of instructional materials and recommendations are beyond the scope of this book, Chapter 4 does provide instructional implications for each academic area. Also, Mather and Jaffe (in press) provide lists of recommendations, summaries of instructional methods that can be appended to reports, and many illustrative case reports.

The focus of this chapter is on clinical applications of the WJ III ACH. The most common clinical use of the WJ III ACH is for the assessment of learning disabilities (LD), particularly for the diagnosis of reading, mathematics, and writing disabilities. The WJ III ACH is also used to help identify individuals with language impairments and individuals with exceptionally high or low academic performance. Additionally, an analysis of discrepancy information can help the evaluator determine strengths and weaknesses within academic performance, and whether oral language abilities are commensurate with other areas of school performance.

LEARNING DISABILITIES

The WJ III ACH can provide helpful information for documenting an LD. A learning disability is defined in the Individuals with Disabilities Education Act (IDEA) as "a disorder in one or more of the basic psychological processes." In order to be identified as having a learning disability, one of seven achievement areas must be significantly affected by the disorder and the individual must have a severe discrepancy between ability (measured by an intelligence test) and achievement. The seven areas of achievement include: oral expression, listening comprehension, written expression, basic reading skill, reading comprehension, mathematics calculation, and mathematics reasoning. The WJ III ACH provides cluster scores for each of the required LD areas as listed in Rapid Reference 6.1.

Even though Basic Writing Skills and Academic Knowledge are not included in the IDEA list, they are important areas that should be considered in an evaluation.

The primary criterion used for identifying a learning disability is a discrepancy between aptitude (described as potential for school success) and achievement (equated with present levels of academic performance). In other words, a specific learning disability is characterized as "unexpected" or "unexplained"

≡Rapid Reference 6.1

WJ III ACH Tests and Clusters Measuring the Seven IDEA Areas

Required LD Areas	Test	Cluster
Oral Expression	Story Recall Picture Vocabulary	Oral Expression
Listening Comprehension	Oral Comprehension Understanding Directions	Listening Comprehension
Written Expression	Writing Samples Writing Fluency	Written Expression
Basic Reading Skills	Letter-Word Identification Word Attack	Basic Reading Skills
Reading Comprehension	Passage Comprehension Reading Vocabulary	Reading Comprehension
Math Calculation	Calculation Math Fluency	Math Calculation Skills
Math Reasoning	Applied Problems Quantitative Concepts	Math Reasoning

DON'T FORGET

14 WJ III ACH Tests Needed for Seven Required IDEA Areas

Nine from Standard Battery: Tests 1, 3–6, 8–11

Letter-Word Identification, Story Recall, Understanding Directions, Calculation, Math Fluency, Writing Fluency, Passage Comprehension, Applied Problems, Writing Samples

Five from Extended Battery: Tests 13–15, 17, 18

Word Attack, Picture Vocabulary, Oral Comprehension, Reading Vocabulary, Quantitative Concepts

poor performance based upon observations of the person's other capabilities and not predicted by general intellectual competence.

Considerable controversy exists regarding the use and implementation of this criterion for LD identification. In fact, more than a decade of research has undermined the practice of using aptitude/achievement discrepancy as the sole criterion for learning disabilities (Mather & Healey, 1990; Stanovich, 1994). We agree with Stanovich when he states, "None of the critics of discrepancy definitions are denying the existence of severe reading disability per se or the importance of remedial help. Instead, they are questioning the rationale of differential treatment and resources being allocated on the basis of IQ-achievement discrepancy" (p. 355). We also agree with Fletcher and colleagues (1998) that evaluating both domain-specific achievement skills and the abilities related to these skills is a more appropriate approach to the identification of learning disabilities than an IQ-discrepancy model.

As with ADHD, there is no specific test or one specific score that will accurately diagnose LD. In addition to test scores, factors such as clinical skill, consideration of educational history, behavioral observations, informal work samples, and the results of other tests will help an evaluator make an accurate diagnosis.

Before diagnosing a student as having an LD many states require the identification of a processing disorder in addition to a discrepancy between ability and achievement. Determining the presence of a processing disorder generally involves using cognitive tests (e.g., tests of memory, language, auditory processing, or processing speed), which measure the abilities believed to underlie academic learning. The WJ III ACH includes several measures that can provide insights into information processing abilities, such as oral language and phonological awareness. When used with the co-normed WJ III COG, examiners can obtain comprehensive information about cognitive processing, academic performance, and discrepancy calculations using actual discrepancy norms. In addition to the WJ III COG, results from the WJ III ACH

DON'T FORGET

Application of WJ III ACH for LD Identification

The WJ III ACH can be used in conjunction with any intelligence test to determine if a discrepancy exists between overall ability and any of the seven areas for LD identification.

may also be compared to other intelligence tests. For these comparisons, examiners should score the WJ III ACH using age norms and should apply a correction for statistical regression.

READING

The WJ III ACH has five reading tests and one measure of phonological awareness, Letter-Word Identification, Reading Fluency, Passage Comprehension, Word Attack, Reading Vocabulary, and Sound Awareness. These tests provide important measures of various aspects of reading achievement. The Letter-Word Identification and Word Attack tests form a Basic Reading Skills cluster. Both measures of word identification (Letter-Word Identification) and nonword (pseudoword) pronunciation (Word Attack) are necessary in a comprehensive evaluation of reading (Siegel, 1989). The Passage Comprehension and Reading Vocabulary tests create the Reading Comprehension cluster. The Reading Fluency and Sound Awareness tests provide important information about speed of reading and phonological awareness. Rapid Reference 6.2 reviews the abilities measured by the WJ III ACH reading tests as well as which LD areas are assessed. Rapid Reference 6.3 lists possible reasons for low performance in basic reading skills and reading comprehension.

Early Identification of Children At-Risk for Reading Failure

Considerable research on the early identification of reading difficulties has focused on identifying measures to predict future reading achievement in

≡ *Rapid Reference 6.2*

Abilities Measured by WJ III ACH Reading Tests

Test	Ability	Required LD Area
Letter-Word Identification	Letter and word identification	Basic Reading Skills
Word Attack	Nonword reading	Basic Reading Skills
Passage Comprehension	Syntactic and semantic cues	Reading Comprehension
Reading Vocabulary	Lexical knowledge	Reading Comprehension
Reading Fluency	Automaticity	Basic Reading Skills
Sound Awareness	Phonological awareness	(oral language processing)

≡ *Rapid Reference 6.3*

Factors That Can Affect Reading Performance

Possible Reasons for Low Performance in Basic Reading Skills

- Poor phonological awareness
- Poor orthographic awareness
- Slow processing speed
- Limited alphabetic knowledge
- Trouble pronouncing multisyllabic words
- Limited instruction

Possible Reasons for Low Performance in Reading Comprehension

- Poor basic reading skills
- Lack of experiences and exposure
- Low motivation and interest
- Limited oral language
- Low vocabulary
- Low reasoning ability
- Limited self-monitoring
- Limited use of strategies
- Limited instruction

preschool or kindergarten children. Three abilities appear to be good predictors of risk for reading failure: letter/sound knowledge, phonological awareness (sensitivity to the sounds in spoken words), and rapid naming (the capacity to name arrays of letters, digits, colors, or pictured objects rapidly) (Wagner & Torgesen, 1987; Wolf, 1991). The WJ III ACH has several measures of letter/sound knowledge (Letter-Word Identification, Word Attack, and Spelling of Sounds) and several measures of phonological awareness and phonological coding (Sound Awareness, Word Attack, and Spelling of Sounds). An

> ## DON'T FORGET
>
> ### Best Predictors of Beginning Reading Achievement
>
> 1. Phonological Awareness/Phonological Coding—
>   WJ III ACH tests: Sound Awareness, Word Attack, Spelling of Sounds
>   WJ III COG tests: Sound Blending, Incomplete Words
> 2. Letter/sound Identification—
>   WJ III ACH tests: Letter-Word Identification, Spelling of Sounds
> 3. Rapid Naming—
>   WJ III COG test: Rapid Picture Naming

adapted measure of rapid naming is available in the WJ III COG. The Rapid Picture Naming test in the WJ III COG is designed to measure speed of lexical retrieval.

Dyslexia

The most common type of learning disability is dyslexia. Poor readers have trouble learning letter-sound correspondences, blending and segmenting phonemes, memorizing letter sequences, and recognizing words rapidly. One core deficit of dyslexia affects the use of phonological processes in reading (Rack, Snowling, & Olson, 1992; Stanovich, 1988). These phonological coding skills are the strongest predictor of reading disabilities; they are uniquely deficient in most readers with disabilities and the deficit is highly heritable (Wise & Olson, 1991). Rapid Reference 6.4 provides some of the most common symptoms of dyslexia.

Decoding (pronouncing words) and encoding (spelling words) involve similar processes, including knowledge of phoneme/grapheme relationships as well as the ability to recall letter strings and words. To pronounce a word, an

Rapid Reference 6.4

Symptoms of Dyslexia

- Poor phonological awareness
- Poor orthographic awareness (knowledge and recall of English spelling patterns)
- Trouble with word pronunciation
- Trouble sequencing sounds in spelling
- Trouble with rapid word recognition
- Slow reading and writing speed

individual needs to know how to break apart the sounds and then how to blend the sounds back together to make a word; to spell a word, an individual needs to be able to break pronunciations into the component sounds.

Another core deficit in dyslexia appears to affect automaticity or rapid symbol processing (Wolf, 1991). This type of problem seems to be more related to accuracy in pronouncing words and the rapid processing of words, rather than to phonological abilities. Students with slow symbol processing speeds do not recognize words easily and rapidly. Their lack of automaticity then affects their comprehension. This ability to recognize words rapidly by sight is the most important variable in predicting reading comprehension for individuals with LD (Meltzer, 1994).

When identifying individuals with dyslexia, examiners should consider the following to be the most relevant information from the WJ III ACH: (a) word identification (e.g., out-of-context word decoding of both real words and pseudowords), (b) measures of linguistic processes (e.g., phonological awareness), (c) measures of spelling (e.g., nonword spelling), and (d) measures of speed (e.g., reading fluency and academic fluency). Students with dyslexia who have not had systematic instruction will have low phoneme/grapheme knowledge and are likely to perform slowly on tasks involving rapid processing (e.g., the measures of academic fluency).

When analyzing the reading tests, an individual with dyslexia is likely to have higher scores on tests involving context and language comprehension and lower scores on measures of rate and phoneme/grapheme knowledge. For example, performance may be higher on Passage Comprehension and Reading Vocabulary than on Letter-Word Identification, Reading Fluency, or Word Attack.

Individuals with dyslexia suffer from a specific impairment that affects reading and spelling development. They require explicit instruction and practice in reading and spelling single words. They often require more repetition, more practice, and more review to acquire basic skills. Instruction needs to be more systematic and more carefully designed, aimed at improving the overall level of skill, as well as the efficiency of the learner. Effective strategies include the following components: (a) drills and probes, (b) provision of immediate feedback, (c) rapid pacing of instruction, and (d) carefully sequenced instruction (Swanson & Hoskyn, 1998). In addition, instruction needs to be adapted to the level of skill development.

Individuals with dyslexia often have strengths in other areas, including oral language, mathematics, or knowledge. Because the impairment does not affect all domains of functioning, individuals may have discrepancies within and among abilities (i.e., intra-ability discrepancies).

CAUTION

Consider Impact of Remediation

Some individuals with dyslexia who have had remediation may obtain average or above scores when reading a list of real words or pseudowords. Their performance declines, however, when asked to read text rapidly and fluently. In other words, their rate of reading is compromised.

CAUTION

Not Everyone with Reading Difficulties has Dyslexia

To identify dyslexia, look for a specific impairment in reading and spelling. In addition, the individual should show some areas of strength (e.g., oral language or math) as well as low phoneme/grapheme knowledge and low basic reading and writing skills.

WRITTEN LANGUAGE

The WJ III ACH contains six writing tests that measure different aspects of writing ability. Rapid Reference 6.5 reviews the abilities measured by the WJ III ACH writing tests. Under IDEA, all of these measures fall under the broad category of written expression. Only two tests Writing Samples and Writing Fluency, are required to obtain the Written Expression cluster. In addition, two

≡ Rapid Reference 6.5

Abilities Measured by WJ III ACH Written Language Tests

Test	Ability Measured	Required LD Area
Spelling	Spelling of real words	Written Expression
Writing Fluency	Automaticity with writing	"
Writing Samples	Expression of ideas in writing	"
Editing	Identification and correction of errors in written work	"
Spelling of Sounds	Spelling of pseudowords	"
Punctuation and Capitalization	Knowledge of punctuation and capitalization rules	"

procedures are included for evaluating handwriting and the Writing Evaluation Scale is included for evaluating longer, more complex writing samples.

Individuals who struggle with basic reading skills may also struggle with spelling. Individuals who have poor reading comprehension are likely to struggle with written expression. A few individuals have adequate or even advanced reading skills but they struggle with one or more aspects of written language development. Some individuals have adequate written expression, but struggle primarily with basic writing skills. Other individuals write with ease but have trouble coming up with ideas.

Dysgraphia, difficulty writing, is a disorder resulting from poor visual-motor integration. Individuals with dysgraphia have difficulty writing or copying letters, words, or numbers. These individuals can speak, read, and may even be able to spell orally, but have trouble with the motor response necessary for writing. The inability to copy text is a key to differentiating between dysgraphia and other types of writing problems. For example, some individuals with writing difficulties may be able to copy but have trouble reproducing words from memory. They recognize words when they see them and can copy and read, but they have trouble writing spontaneously or from dictation. Others have difficulties ordering words or expressing their ideas in writing. They can communicate orally, copy, and spell correctly, but they have trouble expressing their ideas and they make errors in writing that they do not make when speaking.

An evaluator should compare performance in Basic Writing Skills to Written Expression to determine which aspects of writing are difficult for an individual. Careful analysis of performance on the various written language tests can help pinpoint the examinee's specific writing difficulties. For example, the Spelling test affords an opportunity to look at copying and spelling, whereas the Writing Samples test looks at sentence construction and ideation. In addition, the normed Handwriting Scale provides a means for evaluating the visual-motor aspects of writing.

A more in-depth evaluation of written language performance can be obtained by analyzing several samples using the Writing Evaluation Scale in Appendix D in the *Examiner's Manual*. Rapid Reference 6.6 suggests pos-

≡ *Rapid Reference 6.6*

Factors That Can Affect Written Language Performance

Possible Reasons for Low Performance in Basic Writing Skills

- Poor phonological awareness
- Poor orthographic awareness
- Weak fine-motor skills
- Weak visual-spatial skills
- Limited alphabetic knowledge
- Limited instruction

Possible Reasons for Low Performance in Written Expression

- Weak fine-motor skills
- Limited basic writing skills
- Limited oral language
- Limited reading skills
- Lack of experiences and exposure
- Low motivation and interest
- Low reasoning ability
- Limited instruction

sible reasons for low performance in basic writing skills and written expression.

MATH

Although math problems have not been studied as thoroughly as reading problems, some attempts have also been made to identify specific disorders of mathematics. Most studies have focused on basic numeracy skills. Those studies indicate that 6 to 7% of the school-age population demonstrates persistent, grade-to-grade difficulties in basic arithmetic. Although other areas of mathematics need to be studied, we do know that acquisition of mathematical concepts, more than any other content area, is tied closely to the teacher's knowledge of mathematics and to the manner in which these concepts are taught (Lyon, 1996). Teachers who do not understand mathematical principles or know how to teach them may create learning difficulties for their students.

The complexity of mathematics increases the difficulty of documenting specific disorders. Some students seem to have trouble primarily with computational skills, such as adding, subtracting, and multiplying, whereas other students have trouble with the conceptual component, such as the abilities involved in learning mathematical concepts and solving story problems. Novick and Arnold (1988) found individuals who demonstrated deficits in fundamental arithmetic operations, even though they evidenced adequate reasoning, language, and visual-spatial skills. Other individuals demonstrated preserved computational skills but difficulties with the production and comprehension of numbers.

Dyscalculia, a neurologically based disability, is rare (Steeves, 1983) so the term tends to be misused. Novick and Arnold define dyscalculia as a "developmental arithmetic disorder, which refers to the failure to develop arithmetic competence" (p. 132). From an instructional point of view, it is not enough to label someone as having "dyscalculia." It is more appropriate to describe the specific areas of math affected for that individual.

On the WJ III ACH, an evaluator can compare performance in basic math skills and math application. This can help determine if the problem lies in knowledge of how to perform calculations, automaticity with basic math facts, or application of math concepts and knowledge to tasks involving problem

Rapid Reference 6.7

Abilities Measured by WJ III ACH Math Tests

Test	Ability Measured	Required Area
Calculation	Math computation	Math Calculation
Math Fluency	Automaticity with math facts	Math Calculation
Applied Problems	Problem solving	Math Reasoning
Quantitative Concepts	Vocabulary, concepts, and reasoning	Math Reasoning

solving. Rapid Reference 6.7 reviews the abilities measured by the WJ III ACH math tests as well as which LD areas are assessed.

Careful observation during the administration of the math tests may reveal characteristics typical of individuals with math disabilities. One of the most common characteristics is the use of immature problem-solving procedures, even when solving simple arithmetic problems. For example, an individual may count on his or her fingers well past the age of developmental appropriateness. Another common characteristic is difficulty memorizing and recalling math facts. Many individuals with learning disabilities have persistent trouble memorizing basic number facts in all four operations, despite great effort and adequate understanding (Fleischner, Garnett, & Shepherd, 1982).

As with reading comprehension and written expression, multiple factors can affect an individual's ability to solve math problems effectively. Oral language abilities play a key role, as does the ability to move back and forth between verbal and visual representations. Difficulty with the language aspects of math may result in confusion about terminology, difficulty following verbal explanations, and weak verbal skills for monitoring the steps of complex calculations. Disturbances in visual-spatial organization may result in weak understanding of concepts, poor number sense, difficulty with pictorial representations, confused arrangements of numerals and signs on the page, and poor handwriting. Individuals with memory problems may have difficulty learning math facts. Similar to success in reading comprehension and written language, success in mathematics depends largely upon background knowl-

≡Rapid Reference 6.8

Factors That Can Affect Math Performance

Possible Reasons for Low Basic Math Skills
- Poor memory
- Limited attention
- Weak fine-motor skills
- Poor visual-spatial abilities
- Limited language skills
- Limited knowledge of procedures
- Limited instruction

Possible Reasons for Low Math Reasoning
- Low basic skills
- Low oral language
- Limited background knowledge
- Poor visual-spatial thinking
- Poor reasoning abilities
- Limited instruction

edge, symbolic facility, and the use of strategic behaviors. Rapid Reference 6.8 lists factors that can affect math performance.

RESEARCH WITH WJ III ACH AND LEARNING DISABILITIES

Gregg and Hoy (McGrew & Woodcock, 2001) conducted a university study that included 200 students who were classified with and without learning disabilities. Mean score LD/non-LD comparisons were conducted on six WJ III ACH clusters and are reported in Table 6.1. The results indicate that the clusters do reveal significant differences between university students with and without LD. All but one of the six achievement clusters were significant at the .05 level, even after applying the Bonferroni adjustment procedure to control for overall error rate. This means there is a 95% probability the score differences are due to group status rather than chance. The LD students scored significantly lower than non-LD students on tasks requiring reading, writing,

Table 6.1 Means for LD and Non-LD University Sample

Cluster	LD	Non-LD	Significant
Broad Reading	86.5	102.4	Yes
Basic Reading Skills	84.3	98.2	Yes
Basic Writing Skills	86.5	104.3	Yes
Oral Expression	99.3	103.9	No
Phoneme/Grapheme	90.8	104.3	Yes
Academic Fluency	94.7	112.0	Yes

phoneme/grapheme knowledge, and academic fluency. Performance was not significantly different on the Oral Expression cluster. This finding provides support for the use of the WJ III in the classification of individuals as having learning disabilities.

ORAL LANGUAGE

Oral language abilities provide the foundation for success in tasks involving comprehension, problem solving, and self-monitoring. The WJ III ACH measures both receptive and expressive oral language abilities. Receptive oral language abilities refer to an individual's ability to understand what is being said to them. Listening is the major skill needed for success in the area of receptive oral language. Listening requires individuals to receive and interpret correctly the message that is being conveyed. Individuals with poor receptive language have difficulty understanding what has been said and difficulty following classroom directions. They become confused listening to lectures and have difficulty understanding what they read. Although they may decode and spell words accurately, they have limited knowledge of word meanings and limited experiential knowledge. When children are in school, teachers expect them to be able to follow verbal instructions, lectures, and guidelines. For students who have difficulties in listening, the ability to follow through on a given verbal task is a challenge. Poor receptive language can result in lower grades, gaps in a knowledge base, and the inability to work effectively with others. It can also affect social interactions due to difficulties listening to and understanding language. As children reach adulthood and become employed, poor receptive oral language abilities can hinder job performance. If the problem is severe enough, the individual may be classified as having a receptive language impairment.

Some students have adequate receptive language but poor expressive language. They understand what is said to them but have difficulty responding orally. Expressive oral language relates to our abilities to retrieve ideas and vocabulary and express these thoughts in an appropriate manner. Speaking is the major ability needed for success in the area of expressive oral language. Speaking requires developing an intention to speak and formulating thoughts into words and sentences. Deficiencies in the use of expressive language in preschool children have been found to predict subsequent academic difficulties. Individuals with weaknesses in expressive language have difficulty organizing their thoughts, choosing the right words, and expressing their ideas in a clear and fluent manner. They may understand what they hear but not be able to express what they know. These individuals may have trouble expressing their ideas in speaking, as well as in writing. If the problem is severe enough, the student may be classified as having an expressive language impairment.

Weaknesses in oral language affect performance in reading comprehension, written expression, and math problem solving. A student with weaknesses in oral language may perform adequately on basic skill tests, such as pronouncing and spelling words, but have difficulty on tasks involving the comprehension and use of language.

The WJ III ACH has four tests of oral language that are designed to measure different aspects of language functioning. Each of these tests varies in the receptive and expressive requirements. Two tests, Story Recall and Understanding Directions, measure both acquired knowledge and memory abilities. Rapid Reference 6.9 reviews the basic language requirements of the WJ III ACH oral language tests as well as which LD areas it assesses.

An individual who has low performance on oral language tests may require a more comprehensive evaluation from a speech/language therapist. This evaluation will help uncover the intrinsic and extrinsic factors affecting language development. Additionally, the therapist will develop a treatment plan. Rapid Reference 6.10 indicates some possible reasons for low performance on receptive or expressive language tasks.

≡Rapid Reference 6.9

Language Requirements of WJ III ACH Oral Language Tests

Test	Requirement	Required LD Area
Story Recall	Receptive/Expressive	Oral Expression
Understanding Directions	Receptive	Listening Comprehension
Picture Vocabulary	Expressive	Oral Expression
Oral Comprehension	Receptive/(Expressive)	Listening Comprehension

≡Rapid Reference 6.10

Factors That Can Affect Oral Language Performance

Possible Reasons for Low Performance in Receptive Language
- Auditory processing deficits
- Attention problems
- Lack of experience and opportunity
- Limited listening skills
- Difficulty with auditory comprehension

Possible Reasons for Low Performance in Expressive Language
- Poor receptive language
- Difficulty with articulation
- Cultural differences
- Poor word retrieval (inability to recall words that are known)
- Difficulty with formulation of ideas or organization of thoughts

GENERALIZED LOW OR HIGH PERFORMANCE

Some students do not show discrepancies among achievement areas or between abilities and may have generally low or high performance. This is important information to consider when evaluating an individual for a possible learning disability. Typically, if the individual has generalized low or high performance, the examiner should rule out an LD diagnosis. One or more do-main-specific difficulties are important indicators of a learning disability.

Generalized Low Performance

Students with low performance may be several years below grade level in all academic subjects, as well as oral language. These students require adaptations and adjustments in the curriculum. The difficulty level of the instructional materials has to be adapted to both their present performance levels and their level of oral language.

Examiners should consider extrinsic factors when a student has low academic performance and acquired knowledge. Some students come to school with very limited background knowledge. The reasons that they struggle in school are more related to a lack of educational opportunity than an intrinsic disability. These students have limited world knowledge, limited exposure, and, often, low vocabularies. Because vocabulary knowledge is needed for most academic tasks, the breadth and depth of an individual's vocabulary can affect school success. Although these students need help, they should not be described as having a disability. Rather than special instructional methods, these students often require a developmental curriculum that will provide language stimulation and enrichment within the general education setting. Rapid Reference 6.11 lists possible reasons for generally low academic performance.

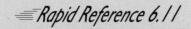

Rapid Reference 6.11

Possible Reasons for Generalized Low Academic Performance

- Limited educational opportunity
- Oral language impairments
- Cultural differences
- Poor reasoning abilities
- Mental retardation
- Linguistic differences
- Developmental delays
- Traumatic brain injury
- Lack of opportunity

Generalized High Performance

Other students are advanced in oral language and above grade-level in most academic subjects. Students with well established oral language and rich vocabularies tend to speak, read, and write more effectively than other students. Because they learn easily, these students often require an accelerated curriculum. They may take advanced courses, use higher-level textbooks, or complete special projects. In some cases, students with advanced academic performance participate in gifted and talented programs.

DISCREPANCY INTERPRETATION

Interpretation of WJ III ACH discrepancy information can aid in differentiating among learning

---

DON'T FORGET
....

Questions to Ask

- Does a comparison of achievement areas highlight certain patterns in academic performance, such as math reasoning is higher than basic math skills?
- Does a comparison of achievement areas highlight certain weaknesses in performance, such as performance is significantly lower on all timed tests or tests of basic skills?

---

disabilities (such as dyslexia), language impairments, and generalized low academic performance. Chapter 4 provides details regarding the discrepancy procedures available in the WJ III Tests of Achievement.

Intra-Achievement Discrepancies

The intra-achievement discrepancy analysis can help an evaluator determine and document both strengths and weaknesses in academic performance. The relationship between achievement abilities in any particular domain can be explored in reference to other academic abilities. Table 6.2 displays the intra-achievement discrepancies for Sarah, a 4th-grade student. With regard to academic performance, Sarah has significant weaknesses in basic reading skills and basic writing skills. She has significant strengths in math reasoning and academic knowledge. There is no discrepancy present in her oral language clusters (i.e., Oral Expression, Listening Comprehension). All of this is indicative of a specific learning disability in reading (significant weaknesses in domain-specific areas such as reading and writing skills, strengths in other domains such as math reasoning and academic knowledge, and average oral language).

After reviewing the intra-achievement discrepancies, the clinician can analyze cluster and test results to reveal possible underlying conditions influenc-

Table 6.2 Intra-Achievement Discrepancies for Sarah, 4th-Grade Student

| | Standard Scores | | | Discrepancy | | Significant |
Discrepancies	Actual	Predicted	Difference	PR	SD	at ± 1.50 SD
Basic Reading Skills	78	112	−34	< 0.1	−3.93	Yes
Reading Comp	100	108	−8	19	−0.88	No
Math Calc Skills	121	104	+17	91	+1.34	No
Math Reasoning	128	104	+24	99	+2.33	Yes
Basic Writing Skills	80	111	−31	0.2	−2.87	Yes
Written Expression	100	107	−7	26	−0.64	No
Oral Expression	117	105	+12	84	+1.01	No
Listening Comp	109	106	+3	58	+0.19	No
Academic Knowledge	134	103	+31	99.6	+2.70	Yes

ing performance. When using just the WJ III ACH, there are limited chances to explore underlying conditions. Many more opportunities are present when using the WJ III COG in conjunction with the ACH. However, within the WJ III ACH it is possible to consider the influence of oral language, phonological awareness, phoneme/grapheme knowledge, fluency, basic skills, thinking skills, and knowledge in general.

Table 6.3 illustrates a sampling of cluster and test results for Sarah. She is having particular difficulty with the acquisition of word identification and spelling skills, and as a result, obtains low scores on the Phoneme/Grapheme Knowledge cluster. Her scores on both Spelling of Sounds and Word Attack tests indicate a weakness in phonological and orthographic coding. Additionally, her performance on Academic Skills and Academic Fluency is lower than her performance on Academic Applications. This means that her difficulties have a greater impact on basic skills and fluency than on the higher-level thinking skills, or application areas. Both poor knowledge of sounds and symbols and a weakness in phonological awareness appear to be underlying conditions influencing Sarah's performance in basic reading and writing skills.

Table 6.3 Exploring Underlying Conditions Influencing Performance: Sample Cluster and Test Results

Cluster/Test	RAW	GE	EASY to DIFF	RPI	PR	SS (68% BAND)
Phoneme/Grapheme Knowledge	—	1.8	1.5 to 2.3	41/90	11	82 (79–85)
Spelling of Sounds	17	1.7	1.2 to 2.8	64/90	13	83 (79–88)
Word Attack	7	1.8	1.6 to 2.1	21/90	13	83 (79–86)
Academic Skills	—	2.7	2.3 to 3.2	44/90	11	82 (79–84)
Academic Fluency	—	3.9	3.0 to 5.0	89/90	48	99 (97–102)
Academic Apps	—	5.5	3.9 to 8.2	96/90	82	114 (110–118)
Sound Awareness	24	1.5	K.9 to 2.4	47/90	8	79 (75–82)

Oral Language Ability/Achievement Discrepancy

One important aspect of an LD evaluation is to distinguish children whose problems are specific to one or more cognitive domains from those whose problems result from a more pervasive impairment in language skills that may be more appropriately classified as an oral language disorder (Fletcher et al., 1998). Children who struggle in most aspects of language, as well as in many nonverbal domains may be more appropriately classified as having some degree of mental impairment (e.g., mild to moderate mental retardation).

The oral language ability/achievement procedure has particular relevance for helping evaluators distinguish between individuals with adequate oral language capabilities but poor reading and writing abilities (i.e., specific reading disabilities) versus individuals whose oral language abilities are commensurate with present levels of reading and writing performance. In the first case, when oral language performance is higher than reading ability, instructional recommendations would focus on reading and writing development. In the second case, instructional recommendations would be directed at all aspects of language development.

Table 6.4 illustrates the results of Sarah's oral language/achievement discrepancy calculations. When using oral language ability to predict academic performance, Sarah demonstrates a significant ability/achievement discrep-

Table 6.4 Oral Language/Achievement Discrepancies for Sarah, 4th-Grade Student

Discrepancies*	Standard Scores			Discrepancy		Significant at ±1.50 SD
	Actual	Predicted	Difference	PR	SD	
Broad Reading	86	106	−20	6	−1.58	Yes
Basic Reading Skills	78	107	−29	1	−2.40	Yes
Reading Comp	100	107	−7	29	−0.54	No
Broad Math	128	106	+22	95	+1.64	Yes
Math Calc Skills	121	105	+16	88	+1.17	No
Math Reasoning	128	108	+20	95	+1.66	Yes
Broad Written Language	87	107	−20	7	−1.48	No
Basic Writing Skills	80	106	−26	3	−1.89	Yes
Written Expression	100	105	−5	35	−0.38	No
Academic Knowledge	134	108	+26	99	+2.31	Yes

*These discrepancies based on Oral Language-Extended with ACH Broad, Basic, and Applied clusters

ancy in broad reading, basic reading, and basic writing. In addition, she demonstrates significant strengths in broad math, math reasoning, and academic knowledge. Sarah is an individual who has adequate oral language abilities but poor reading and writing skills. These results support the diagnosis that Sarah has a specific LD in reading.

As noted by Stanovich (1991a, 1991b), use of an oral language measure to predict reading and writing is often preferable to use of a general intelligence score because it is more in line with the concept of "potential" and "unexpected" failure. He further explains that using oral language ability as the aptitude measure moves us closer to a more principled definition of reading disability because it provides a more accurate estimate of what the person could achieve if the reading problem were entirely resolved. Essentially, what distinguishes the individual with a reading disability from other poor readers is that listening comprehension ability is higher than ability to decode words (Rack, Snowling, & Olson, 1992), and thus the difficulty is "unpredicted."

An individual with a learning disability may or may not exhibit an oral language ability/achievement discrepancy. For example, an older student with reading difficulties may have depressed performance in oral language because of his or her limited experiences with text. This lack of exposure to print contributes to reduced knowledge and vocabulary.

> # DON'T FORGET
> ....
> ### Value of the Oral Language/Achievement Discrepancy Procedure
>
> The WJ III ACH compares Oral Language-Extended to the achievement clusters. This comparison helps differentiate between individuals with generalized language impairments and individuals with domain specific learning disabilities.

Can the WJ III ACH Diagnose the Problem?

Achievement tests are designed primarily to determine academic levels, thereby limiting their diagnostic capability. When conducting a complete evaluation, examiners need to supplement any achievement test with other instruments designed to assess cognitive abilities, information processing, behavior, and so forth. However, information from the WJ III ACH can be helpful in diagnosing reasons for academic difficulties. Although the most common type of LD is a reading disability, some individuals have specific difficulties in writing or mathematics. Throughout this chapter, we have identified the tests, clusters, and abilities most sensitive to the main clinical applications presented. Table 6.5 shows a summary of some of the diagnostic information available from the WJ III ACH.

USE OF THE WJ III ACH ACROSS THE LIFE SPAN

The wide age span covered by the WJ III (ages 2-0 to 95+ years) makes it an ideal instrument for continuous measurement and longitudinal studies. The age span also provides evidence of developmental trends and differences in abilities measured by the test. For example, the *WJ III Technical Manual* reports

Table 6.5 Diagnostic Indicators of a Disability

Reading Disability	Writing Disability	Math Disability	Oral Language Impairment	Generalized Low Ability
Low reading, broad, basic, or comprehension.	Low written language, broad, basic skills, or expression.	Low math, broad, basic skills, or reasoning.	Low oral language (expressive or receptive).	Flat profile.
Slow on speeded tasks (look at fluency tests).	Limited language.	Limited oral language.	Limited experiences (look at Academic Knowledge).	No discrepancies.
Low Phonological Awareness (look at Sound Awareness).	Presence of an intra-achievement discrepancy in writing.	Presence of an intra-achievement discrepancy in math.	Basic academic skills higher than application tasks.	Generalized low performance in most areas.
Low Phoneme/Grapheme Knowledge.	Low reading skills and/or comprehension.	Strong concepts and weak basic skills.	Low reading comprehension, written expression, math reasoning.	
Low Basic Reading Skills.	Organizational difficulties.	Low basic reading skills.		
Presence of an intra-achievement discrepancy in reading.	Poor handwriting.	Difficulty memorizing and recalling basic math facts.		
Adequate oral language.	Difficulty with copying.	Low visual-spatial skills.		
Higher math than reading scores.	Difficulty formulating ideas in writing.			

Rapid Reference 6.12

Developmental Evidence in the WJ III ACH

- Reading decoding skills grow and are retained at a higher level throughout life than reading comprehension abilities.
- Basic writing skills grow at a faster rate than written expression abilities.
- Listening comprehension ability increases until about age 25 and then begins a slight decline across the age span.
- Oral expression abilities have a lower rate of growth than listening skills but continue to develop until about age 65.
- Math reasoning shows the most decline with age, possibly due to reduced need or opportunity to use and apply math knowledge during adult years (after age 25).

that abilities in reading, math, writing, and academic knowledge increase during the school years. Once an individual learns these abilities, he or she does not lose them in later years, but rather maintains them. Rapid Reference 6.12 provides information on the developmental trends noted in the WJ III ACH tests and clusters.

🖋 TEST YOURSELF 🖋

1. **What are the two types of discrepancy procedures on the WJ III ACH?**
2. **What is the difference between an expressive and a receptive language disorder?**
3. **List the seven LD areas measured by clusters on the WJ III ACH.**
4. **What is the primary criterion used for identifying LDs?**
5. **The WJ III ACH measures which two key predictors of risk for reading failure?**
6. **If WJ III ACH results are being compared to the WISC-III, the WJ III ACH should be scored by age norms.** True or False?
7. **How can the oral language/achievement discrepancy procedure help examiners differentiate between individuals with specific reading impairments and those with language impairments?**

(continued)

8. **The Phoneme/Grapheme Knowledge cluster score is often average or above for an examinee with dyslexia.** True or False?

9. **A domain-specific deficit must be present for an LD to be identified.** True or False?

10. **Which of these statements would not be consistent with a specific reading disability profile?**

    (a) low oral language

    (b) low basic reading skills

    (c) low phoneme/grapheme knowledge

    (d) low basic writing skills

Answers: 1. intra-ability and ability/achievement; 2. Expressive involves speaking and receptive involves listening. 3. Oral Expression, Listening Comprehension, Written Expression, Basic Reading Skills, Reading Comprehension, Math Calculation, Math Reasoning; 4. a discrepancy between intellectual ability and achievement; 5. Phonological Awareness and Letter Identification (letter/sound knowledge); 6. True; 7. Oral language is higher than reading performance while oral language is commensurate with reading performance. 8. False; 9. True; 10. a

Seven

ILLUSTRATIVE CASE REPORTS

The purpose of this chapter is to illustrate the use of the WJ III ACH in case study evaluations. Knowledge of the test content, administration, and scoring and interpretive options (presented in Chapters 1 through 6 of this book) is required to understand fully the information presented here. The first case report is an 11-year-old male, Raymond, who was referred due to concerns about his limited progress in reading and writing. Even though Raymond is currently in a special education placement for students with learning disabilities, more information was needed to establish his continued eligibility and to make recommendations for increasing his academic success. Although Raymond was administered the WJ III COG, the major focus of the report is the WJ III ACH. The second case is Stanley, a 7th-grade boy who was referred because of difficulties with organization and written language. This case discusses results from the WJ III COG in more depth. The third case is Alison, a high school senior who is seeking information about her difficulties in math courses. She was administered only the WJ III ACH battery.

Each report includes the reason for referral, background information, previous evaluations (if any), tests administered, behavioral observations, test results, and recommendations. However, the style of each report differs in order to illustrate various report-writing options. Most reports include key information, but the style is modified to fit the setting (e.g., public school or clinic), as well as to reflect individual preferences.

As examiners attempt to resolve referral questions and make appropriate recommendations, they must consider and integrate findings from behavioral observations, error analysis, and test scores. The report generated by the WJ III software can serve as a beginning point for the case report, but should not be used as a final report. It includes a description of test performance and

CAUTION

Do not use the WJ III computer-generated report as a final case report. The computer-generated report is strictly a beginning point.

observations (if entered) and can easily be exported into a word processing program. Examiners are responsible for interpreting results, integrating information from various sources, drawing conclusions, and making recommendations.

EDUCATIONAL EVALUATION FOR RAYMOND S.

Name: Raymond S.
Birthdate: 8/7/89
Chronological Age: 11-1
Grade: 5.0

Parents: Fred and Eva S.
School: Shaner Elementary
Examiner: B. J. Wendling
Test Dates: 9/12, 9/13, 9/14/00

Reason for Referral

Raymond was referred for testing to provide information to be considered in regard to his continued eligibility for special education services under the category of learning disabilities. In addition, the evaluation was conducted to provide further documentation of Raymond's strengths and weaknesses for the purpose of making instructional recommendations and accommodations. Although Raymond has continued to receive special services and accommodations in the general education setting, both his general education teachers and his parents are concerned about his limited progress in reading and writing.

DON'T FORGET

Key Information to Include in a Case Report

- Identifying Information
- Reason for Referral
- Background Information
- Tests Administered
- Behavioral Observations
- Test Results
- Examples of specific strengths and weaknesses
- Summary and Recommendations

Background Information

Prior to school entry, Raymond received speech/language services for articulation problems. During his preschool years, Raymond had many ear infections. Because of the recurrent ear infections, tubes were placed in his ears and were not removed until the end of second grade. In an interview his mother noted that even though Raymond appeared to have trouble pronouncing the sounds of language, his vocabulary and language concepts were always very advanced. By the age of 3, she noted that he could converse easily with adults.

At the age of 5, Raymond was diagnosed by a clinic at St. John's hospital as having moderate dysgraphia and problems with articulation. While attending kindergarten, he received both speech/language and occupational therapy services. On one occasion, his kindergarten teacher informed the parents that when it came to "talking" their son was a genius, but when it came to writing letters, he required tremendous assistance.

In first grade, the family moved to a new district. At that time, the multidisciplinary team recommended that Raymond receive LD, speech/language, and adaptive physical education services. In second grade, adaptive physical education and speech/language services were discontinued, but Raymond continued to receive LD services. In fourth grade, he received small group instruction in a resource setting for 30 minutes a day. At the end of fourth grade, his general education teacher wrote that his academic achievement was good in mathematics, but below expectation in both reading and written language. She raised the possibility that part of Raymond's difficulties were related to inattention. She noted that he seemed to have the most difficulty during oral discussions. Although he was cooperative in the classroom, she noted that he often seemed like he was "out in space."

In August of 2000, Raymond saw Dr. Michelle Roberts, a pediatrician specializing in behavior, regarding concerns about inattentiveness. From this evaluation, data collected from classroom observations, and a review of educational history, Dr. Roberts concluded that the diagnosis of Attention-deficit Hyperactivity Disorder was appropriate. She further suggested that based upon his school performance, Raymond might benefit from medical therapy as well as increased reading support. The parents agreed that additional reading support was needed and decided against a trial of medication until they could see how Raymond was adjusting to his 5th-grade classroom.

Previous Evaluations

On two past psychological assessments on the WISC-III, Raymond obtained scores in the high-average to superior ranges on both the Verbal and Performance Scales. His lowest score was on a test involving short-term memory (Digit Span scaled scores of 4 and 6) that involves the two tasks of repeating a series of digits forward and backward. Academic testing has consistently demonstrated average to above average mathematics performance and low performance in reading and writing. Throughout his school years, testing and observations have indicated an advanced vocabulary but poor performance on reading and writing tasks. In addition, concerns have been expressed in regard to articulation, attention, memory, and visual-motor development.

Tests Administered

Woodcock-Johnson III
Tests of Cognitive Abilities (WJ III COG)
Tests of Achievement (WJ III ACH) (Form A)
Informal reading inventory

Behavioral Observations

Raymond was cooperative throughout the testing, although at times he appeared restless. On several occasions, he asked if the testing was almost finished. Throughout testing, Raymond's advanced oral language abilities were apparent, as were his difficulties with reading and writing tasks. He commented that he loves tasks that involve using his hands but hates tasks that involve writing and spelling. At one point, when trying to write, he commented, "My hand just cannot keep up with my brain." He seemed to enjoy tests involving vocabulary and academic knowledge but expressed frustration during tasks involving listening to and then repeating information and tasks involving writing.

Test Results

The assessment was conducted in three sessions. Results from the WJ III were scored according to grade norms. A summary of scores is appended to this report (see Table 7.1 and Figure 7.1).

Cognitive Performance

Raymond's overall general intellectual ability is in the average range (GIA-Extended = 99). When compared to others at his grade level, he performs in

Table 7.1 TABLE OF SCORES: Woodcock-Johnson III Tests of Cognitive Abilities and Tests of Achievement Norms based on Grade 5.0

Cluster	RAW	GE	EASY to DIFF		RPI	PR	SS (68% BAND)
GIA-Ext	—	4.8	2.7	7.7	89/90	47	99 (97–101)
Verbal Ability-Ext	—	8.8	6.4	12.1	98/90	93	122 (117–127)
Thinking Ability-Ext	—	4.5	1.9	10.2	89/90	44	98 (95–100)
Cog Efficiency-Ext	—	3.0	2.2	4.1	59/90	12	82 (78–86)
Comp-Knowledge (*Gc*)	—	8.8	6.4	12.1	98/90	93	122 (117–127)
Long-term Retrieval (*Glr*)	—	2.0	K.3	8.1	80/90	7	77 (73–82)
Vis-Spatial Think (*Gv*)	—	14.9	5.5	>18.0	97/90	91	120 (114–125)
Auditory Process (*Ga*)	—	1.0	K.1	3.2	67/90	8	79 (74–84)
Fluid Reasoning (*Gf*)	—	6.3	3.9	9.9	94/90	63	105 (101–109)
Process Speed (*Gs*)	—	5.5	4.4	6.8	93/90	61	104 (100–108)
Short-Term Mem (*Gsm*)	—	K.8	K.1	1.5	13/90	2	68 (63–73)
Phonemic Aware	—	K.3	<K.0	1.8	54/90	3	71 (65–76)
Phonemic Aware III	—	K.9	K.1	2.1	49/90	2	69 (65–73)
Working Memory	—	1.8	1.0	2.7	35/90	6	76 (72–81)
Broad Attention	—	2.8	1.7	4.5	70/90	14	83 (80–87)

(continued)

Table 7.1 (Continued)

Cluster	RAW	GE	EASY to DIFF		RPI	PR	SS (68% BAND)
Cognitive Fluency	—	6.2	4.1	8.7	94/90	67	107 (104–109)
Exec Processes	—	5.8	3.4	9.5	92/90	62	105 (102–108)
Knowledge	—	9.4	7.1	12.9	99/90	96	126 (122–131)
Oral Language-Ext	—	6.6	3.8	11.0	94/90	70	108 (104–112)
Oral Expression	—	7.8	4.4	12.9	96/90	78	112 (107–117)
Listening Comp	—	5.5	3.4	9.5	92/90	56	102 (98–107)
Total Achievement	—	3.6	2.8	4.6	67/90	22	88 (87–90)
Broad Reading	—	2.8	2.4	3.3	24/90	8	79 (77–81)
Broad Math	—	6.6	5.0	8.8	96/90	84	115 (111–118)
Broad Written Lang	—	2.7	1.9	3.7	51/90	8	79 (76–82)
Basic Reading Skills	—	2.2	1.9	2.5	5/90	4	74 (71–76)
Reading Comp	—	3.9	2.8	5.8	82/90	34	94 (91–97)
Math Calc Skills	—	5.7	4.2	7.8	93/90	68	107 (102–112)
Math Reasoning	—	7.2	5.7	9.7	98/90	87	117 (113–121)
Basic Writing Skills	—	2.2	1.7	2.8	17/90	4	74 (70–77)
Written Expression	—	4.0	2.7	5.8	82/90	30	92 (88–97)

Cluster	RAW	GE	EASY to DIFF		RPI	PR	SS (68% BAND)
Academic Skills	—	2.7	2.3	3.2	19/90	4	74 (71–76)
Academic Fluency	—	3.9	3.0	5.0	75/90	27	91 (89–93)
Academic Apps	—	5.5	3.9	8.2	92/90	61	104 (100–109)
Academic Knowledge	—	9.3	7.3	12.5	99/90	95	125 (120–131)
Phon/Graph Know	—	1.8	1.5	2.3	29/90	7	78 (75–81)
Verbal Comprehension	—	8.2	5.9	11.1	98/90	87	117 (111–122)
Visual-Auditory Learning	33-E	1.2	K.1	2.7	63/90	3	73 (69–77)
Spatial Relations	72-D	12.6	4.9	>18.0	96/90	84	115 (109–120)
Sound Blending	12	K.4	<K.0	1.5	46/90	4	74 (68–81)
Concept Formation	26-E	5.1	3.4	8.2	90/90	51	100 (97–104)
Visual Matching	41–2	5.5	4.6	6.6	94/90	63	105 (99–110)
Numbers Reversed	7	1.5	K.9	2.2	20/90	7	78 (73–83)
Incomplete Words	13	<K.0	<K.0	2.5	63/90	5	76 (69–83)
Auditory Work Memory	11	2.2	1.2	3.5	54/90	14	84 (79–88)
General Information	—	9.5	7.0	12.9	99/90	94	124 (117–130)

(continued)

Table 7.1 (Continued)

Cluster	RAW	GE	EASY	to DIFF	RPI	PR	SS (68% BAND)
Retrieval Fluency	63	6.0	K.8	>18.0	91/90	61	104 (98–110)
Picture Recognition	53-D	>18.0	6.0	>18.0	97/90	87	117 (110–124)
Auditory Attention	33	2.1	K.6	9.6	83/90	30	92 (87–98)
Analysis-Synthesis	25-E	7.8	4.6	12.9	96/90	72	109 (103–115)
Decision Speed	29	5.4	4.0	7.1	92/90	56	102 (97–107)
Memory for Words	12	<K.0	<K.0	K.5	8/90	3	73 (67–78)
Rapid Picture Naming	112	6.9	5.5	8.4	97/90	69	107 (105–109)
Planning	—	5.7	<K.0	>18.0	90/90	54	102 (88–115)
Pair Cancellation	65	6.3	4.6	8.3	95/90	69	108 (105–110)
Form A of the following achievement tests was administered:							
Letter-Word Identification	36	2.4	2.2	2.7	2/90	3	72 (69–75)
Reading Fluency	29	3.1	2.6	3.6	27/90	17	86 (84–88)
Story Recall	—	5.9	1.1	>18.0	91/90	57	103 (94–111)
Understanding Directions	—	4.8	2.6	9.5	89/90	48	99 (94–104)
Calculation	19	5.3	4.2	6.7	92/90	56	102 (96–109)

Cluster	RAW	GE	EASY to DIFF		RPI	PR	SS (68% BAND)
Math Fluency	80	6.6	4.2	9.8	95/90	78	112 (109–114)
Spelling	20	1.7	1.3	2.1	5/90	2	69 (64–73)
Writing Fluency	14	4.2	3.3	5.3	80/90	35	94 (90–99)
Passage Comprehension	28	3.7	2.8	5.3	78/90	32	93 (89–97)
Applied Problems	43	8.1	6.4	11.1	99/90	88	118 (114–122)
Writing Samples	11-C	3.2	1.9	7.9	84/90	24	90 (81–98)
Word Attack	7	1.8	1.6	2.1	12/90	9	80 (76–83)
Picture Vocabulary	29	8.2	6.0	11.1	98/90	80	113 (108–118)
Oral Comprehension	21	6.0	4.0	9.5	93/90	60	104 (99–109)
Editing	7	2.9	2.3	3.6	45/90	14	84 (79–88)
Reading Vocabulary	—	4.3	2.9	6.1	85/90	41	97 (93–100)
Quantitative Concepts	—	6.4	5.0	8.5	96/90	77	111 (105–117)
Academic Knowledge	—	9.3	7.3	12.5	99/90	95	125 (120–131)
Spelling of Sounds	17	1.7	1.2	2.8	55/90	8	79 (75–84)
Sound Awareness	24	1.5	K.9	2.4	37/90	5	75 (71–78)
Punctuation & Capitals	15	3.6	2.7	5.0	75/90	25	90 (84–95)

(continued)

Table 7.1 (Continued)

Discrepancies	Standard Scores			Discrepancy		Significant at +/−1.50 SD (SEE)
	Actual	Predicted	Difference	PR	SD	
Intra-Individual						
Comp-Knowledge (Gc)	122	96	+26	99.6	+2.62	Yes
Long-term Retrieval (Glr)	77	100	−23	5	−1.62	Yes
Visual-Spatial Think (Gv)	120	98	+22	94	+1.53	Yes
Auditory Process (Ga)	79	100	−21	7	−1.50	Yes
Fluid Reasoning (Gf)	105	98	+7	72	+0.59	No
Process Speed (Gs)	104	98	+6	65	+0.40	No
Short-Term Mem (Gsm)	68	100	−32	1	−2.38	Yes
Phonemic Awareness	71	100	−29	2	−2.09	Yes
Working Memory	76	100	−24	2	−1.97	Yes
Basic Reading Skills	74	100	−26	0.3	−2.74	Yes
Reading Comp	94	98	−4	33	−0.45	No
Math Calc Skills	107	98	+9	77	+0.73	No
Math Reasoning	117	97	+20	97	+1.94	Yes
Basic Writing Skills	74	100	−26	1	−2.41	Yes
Written Expression	92	99	−7	30	−0.53	No
Oral Expression	112	98	+14	89	+1.20	No

Table 7.1

| Discrepancies | Standard Scores | | | Discrepancy | | Significant at |
	Actual	Predicted	Difference	PR	SD	+/−1.50 SD (SEE)
Listening Comp	102	98	+4	65	+0.39	No
Academic Knowledge	125	97	+28	99.6	+2.65	Yes
Intellectual Ability/Achievement Discrepancies*						
Broad Reading	79	99	−20	3	−1.89	Yes
Basic Reading Skills	74	99	−25	1	−2.20	Yes
Reading Comp	94	99	−5	31	−0.50	No
Broad Math	115	99	+16	93	+1.44	No
Math Calc Skills	107	99	+8	73	+0.61	No
Math Reasoning	117	99	+18	96	+1.71	Yes
Broad Written Lang	79	99	−20	3	−1.82	Yes
Basic Writing Skills	74	99	−25	1	−2.26	Yes
Written Expression	92	99	−7	27	−0.60	No
Oral Language-Extended	108	99	+9	77	+0.73	No
Oral Expression	112	99	+13	86	+1.09	No
Listening Comp	102	99	+3	60	+0.25	No
Academic Knowledge	125	99	+26	99	+2.48	Yes

*These discrepancies based on GIA (Ext) with ACH Broad, Basic, and Applied clusters.

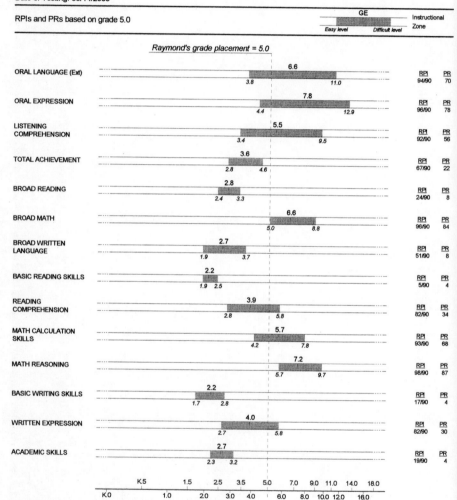

Figure 7.1 Profiles generated by WJ III Compuscore

WJ III Compuscore Version 1.1b - Standard Score/Percentile Rank Profiles   Page 2
S., Raymond
September 14, 2000

	SS	<40	40	50	60	70	80	90	100	110	120	130	140	150	160	>160
COGNITIVE FLUENCY	PR	<0.1		0.1	0.5 1	2	5 7 10 15 20	30 40 50 60 70	80 85 90 93 95	98	99 99.5	99.9				>99.9
EXECUTIVE PROCESSES	PR	<0.1		0.1	0.5 1	2	5 7 10 15 20	30 40 50 60 70	80 85 90 93 95	98	99 99.5	99.9				>99.9
KNOWLEDGE	PR	<0.1		0.1	0.5 1	2	5 7 10 15 20	30 40 50 60 70	80 85 90 93 95	98	99 99.5	99.9				>99.9
ORAL LANGUAGE (Ext)	PR	<0.1		0.1	0.5 1	2	5 7 10 15 20	30 40 50 60 70	80 85 90 93 95	98	99 99.5	99.9				>99.9
ORAL EXPRESSION	PR	<0.1		0.1	0.5 1	2	5 7 10 15 20	30 40 50 60 70	80 85 90 93 95	98	99 99.5	99.9				>99.9
LISTENING COMPREHENSION	PR	<0.1		0.1	0.5 1	2	5 7 10 15 20	30 40 50 60 70	80 85 90 93 95	98	99 99.5	99.9				>99.9
TOTAL ACHIEVEMENT	PR	<0.1		0.1	0.5 1	2	5 7 10 15 20	30 40 50 60 70	80 85 90 93 95	98	99 99.5	99.9				>99.9
BROAD READING	PR	<0.1		0.1	0.5 1	2	5 7 10 15 20	30 40 50 60 70	80 85 90 93 95	98	99 99.5	99.9				>99.9
BROAD MATH	PR	<0.1		0.1	0.5 1	2	5 7 10 15 20	30 40 50 60 70	80 85 90 93 95	98	99 99.5	99.9				>99.9
BROAD WRITTEN LANGUAGE	PR	<0.1		0.1	0.5 1	2	5 7 10 15 20	30 40 50 60 70	80 85 90 93 95	98	99 99.5	99.9				>99.9
BASIC READING SKILLS	PR	<0.1		0.1	0.5 1	2	5 7 10 15 20	30 40 50 60 70	80 85 90 93 95	98	99 99.5	99.9				>99.9
READING COMPREHENSION	PR	<0.1		0.1	0.5 1	2	5 7 10 15 20	30 40 50 60 70	80 85 90 93 95	98	99 99.5	99.9				>99.9
MATH CALCULATION SKILLS	PR	<0.1		0.1	0.5 1	2	5 7 10 15 20	30 40 50 60 70	80 85 90 93 95	98	99 99.5	99.9				>99.9
MATH REASONING	PR	<0.1		0.1	0.5 1	2	5 7 10 15 20	30 40 50 60 70	80 85 90 93 95	98	99 99.5	99.9				>99.9
BASIC WRITING SKILLS	PR	<0.1		0.1	0.5 1	2	5 7 10 15 20	30 40 50 60 70	80 85 90 93 95	98	99 99.5	99.9				>99.9
WRITTEN EXPRESSION	PR	<0.1		0.1	0.5 1	2	5 7 10 15 20	30 40 50 60 70	80 85 90 93 95	98	99 99.5	99.9				>99.9
ACADEMIC SKILLS	PR	<0.1		0.1	0.5 1	2	5 7 10 15 20	30 40 50 60 70	80 85 90 93 95	98	99 99.5	99.9				>99.9
ACADEMIC FLUENCY	PR	<0.1		0.1	0.5 1	2	5 7 10 15 20	30 40 50 60 70	80 85 90 93 95	98	99 99.5	99.9				>99.9

Figure 7.1 (Continued)

the superior range in comprehension-knowledge, the high-average range for visual-spatial thinking, the average range in fluid reasoning and processing speed, and in the low range to very low range in long-term retrieval, auditory processing, and short-term memory. His cognitive performance appears to be further influenced by his limited phonemic awareness, working memory, and attention.

Oral Language

Raymond's Relative Proficiency Index (RPI) on the Oral Language-Extended cluster of 94/90 suggests that when average grade-mates are having 90% success, Raymond will have 94% success. Although Raymond's oral language abilities are average when compared to others at his grade level, his performance on oral language tests involving the abilities of vocabulary and world knowledge (e.g., Verbal Comprehension, General Information, Academic Knowledge) is significantly higher than on tests involving both language comprehension and meaningful memory (e.g., Understanding Directions, Story Recall, and Oral Comprehension). This difference is most likely attributed to the memory component involved in these oral language tests. Raymond possesses a rich vocabulary and substantial knowledge, but his oral comprehension is compromised when tasks require listening and retention (e.g., Story Recall and Understanding Directions tests). On a longer passage of the Story Recall test, he commented that he had trouble remembering anything at all when lots of information was presented.

Academic Performance

Although Raymond's total achievement is in the low-average range, he has strengths in academic tasks that involve the application of acquired knowledge and reasoning and weaknesses in basic skill areas related to phonemic awareness and memory. When compared to others at his grade level, Raymond's academic knowledge and mathematics reasoning are in the high-average to superior range; his reading comprehension, math calculation, and written expression are in the average range; and his basic reading and writing skills and phoneme/grapheme knowledge are in the low range. In general, Raymond has more difficulty on tests involving basic skills (Academic Skills SS = 74 (71–76)) than on tests involving reasoning and problem solving (Academic Applications SS = 104 (100–109)).

Reading

Raymond's RPI on the Broad Reading cluster of 24/90 suggests that when average grade-mates are having 90% success, Raymond will have 24% (very limited) success (frustration level). Raymond's instructional zone in Basic Reading Skills ranges from end of first grade (easy) to mid-second grade (difficult). On the Reading Comprehension cluster, his instructional zone ranges from end of second grade (easy) to end of fifth grade (difficult).

Raymond's reading performance is affected by poor basic skills. He had difficulty pronouncing multisyllabic words on the Letter-Word Identification test and difficulty pronouncing nonwords on the Word Attack test. On an informal reading inventory, using a grade-level passage, his reading was characterized by a slow rate and numerous repetitions and hesitations. He mispronounced several high frequency words, including "her," "our," and "want." Miscues during reading and his low score on the Phoneme/Grapheme Knowledge cluster indicate that Raymond has not yet fully mastered sound-symbol correspondences. On several occasions, he mispronounced words containing the digraph /sh/ as "ch" and misread medial vowel sounds, pronouncing "give" as "gave" and "run" as "ran." Although his pronunciations shared letter patterns in common with the stimulus words, he did not appear to attend to all of the letters in the word. For example, he pronounced "young" as "you," "built" as "belt," and "next" as "exit." Presently, Raymond's lack of automaticity in word recognition is affecting his ability to read fluently and, therefore, to comprehend words.

Mathematics

Raymond's RPI on the Broad Math cluster of 96/90 suggests that when average grade-mates are having 90% success, Raymond will have 96% success (independent level). On the WJ III Math Calculation Skills cluster, Raymond's instructional zone ranges from beginning fourth grade (easy) to end of seventh grade (difficult). On the Math Reasoning cluster, scores range from mid-fifth grade (easy) to mid-ninth grade (difficult). Raymond was able to compute correctly problems involving the four operations. He was able to solve calculations involving fractions. In problem solving, he was able to tell time, make change, and solve questions involving fractions. Raymond commented that math was his favorite subject in school but that it had taken him a long time to memorize his math facts.

Written Language

Raymond's RPI on the Broad Written Language cluster of 51/90 suggests that when average grade-mates are having 90% success, Raymond will have 51% success (frustration level). On the WJ III Basic Writing Skills cluster, Raymond's instructional zone ranges from end of first (easy) to end of second grade (difficult). His instructional zone on the Written Expression cluster ranges from end of second grade (easy) to end of fifth grade (difficult). Although Raymond was able to express his ideas clearly on the Writing Samples test, his extreme difficulties with both spelling and handwriting were apparent.

Raymond's instructional zone on the Phoneme/Grapheme Knowledge cluster illustrates his difficulty with word pronunciation and spelling, with his scores ranging from mid-first grade (easy) to beginning second grade (difficult). Similar to the errors he made in reading, when spelling, Raymond confused vowel sounds and had trouble sequencing sounds. Weaknesses were noted in both phonology (poor sequencing and confusion of sounds) and in orthography (reversing and transposing letters and misspelling common letter strings). During the evaluation, Raymond commented on how difficult writing was for him and that he really disliked having to write. At one point when writing, he asked, "Can I just tell you the rest of the answers?"

Academic Knowledge

Raymond's RPI of 99/90 suggests that when average grade-mates are having 90% success on similar tasks, Raymond will have 99% success and perform the tasks very easily. The instructional zone for Raymond's Academic Knowledge cluster ranges from beginning 7th to mid 12th grade. He responded quickly and accurately to a wide range of questions involving science, social studies, literature, art, and music. The quality of his responses indicated advanced factual knowledge and vocabulary.

Discrepancies

The WJ III has two types of discrepancies, intra-ability (used to document strengths and weaknesses) and ability/achievement (used for prediction). Raymond had statistically significant discrepancies within both types.

Intra-Ability Discrepancies

When comparing all of Raymond's cognitive and academic abilities, Raymond has significant strengths in comprehension/knowledge, visual-spatial thinking, math reasoning, and academic knowledge. Raymond will be highly successful on tasks involving vocabulary, knowledge, thinking with designs and patterns, and math problem solving. In contrast, Raymond had significant weaknesses in long-term retrieval, auditory processing, short-term and working memory, phonemic awareness, and basic reading and writing skills. Raymond's weaknesses in abilities related to memory, phonemic awareness, and attention appear to have contributed to his difficulty acquiring the phoneme/grapheme knowledge essential for basic reading and writing skills. Raymond will struggle with grade-level tasks involving memory, phonological awareness, and basic reading and writing skills.

Ability/Achievement Discrepancies

When Raymond's GIA-Extended score is compared to his achievement clusters, his performance is significantly lower in Broad Reading, Basic Reading Skills, Broad Written Language, and Basic Writing Skills. These discrepancies suggest that Raymond is not performing academically as well as one would predict from his general intellectual competence. Raymond's performance is significantly higher than predicted in the areas of math reasoning and knowledge. Given his advanced performance on tests involving vocabulary and world knowledge and his good problem-solving skills, one would predict that Raymond is capable of making significant gains in academic areas with systematic, intensive instruction.

Recommendations

Educational Programming

1. The multidisciplinary team should review Raymond's continued eligibility for LD services. Significant ability/achievement discrepancies exist, as well as significant discrepancies among his abilities. In addition, Raymond has a documented history of learning disabilities.
2. Presently, Raymond needs intensive instruction in basic reading and writing skills.

Accommodations

1. Because of his present difficulties with basic reading and writing skills, Raymond will require oral testing or oral clarifications on exams requiring extensive reading or writing.

2. Raymond will need to have extended time or shortened reading and writing assignments.
3. Do not penalize Raymond for misspellings on initial drafts or on class assignments.
4. Based upon poor word identification abilities and a slow reading rate, Raymond will need taped textbooks for all content areas. Based upon his good vocabulary and knowledge, he should be able to understand passages if he follows along with the actual text.
5. Provide Raymond with keyboarding instruction so that he can learn to write his papers using a word processor. Use of a spelling checker will help him correct some of his errors and contribute to improved spelling performance.
6. So as not to impede his progress in tasks involving mathematical reasoning, permit Raymond to use a calculator when necessary for solving mathematical problems.
7. During the first or second month of the school year, carefully monitor Raymond's behavior to ensure that he is able to listen to and profit from classroom group instruction. If problems persist, encourage the parents to reopen the discussion of medical therapies with their pediatrician.
8. Have Raymond sit in a location near to the teacher so that he or she can easily monitor his attention.

Instruction

1. Provide opportunities for Raymond to develop his extensive acquired knowledge. Encourage oral discussions, cooperative learning activities, and class activities that integrate speaking, reading, and writing.
2. Provide direct instruction to increase phoneme/grapheme knowledge. Raymond would benefit from a structured multisensory phonics program (such as the Wilson Reading System) that provides systematic, controlled instruction. (Wilson Language Training, 175 West Main Street, Millbury, MA 01527-1441, (800) 899-8454, www.WilsonLanguage.com)
3. Once Raymond is able to pronounce multisyllabic words, begin a method to build rate and fluency, such as repeated readings or *Great*

Leaps in Reading (Great Leaps Reading Program, Campbell, K.U.,
Diarmuid, Inc., P.O. Box 138, Micanopy, FL 32667, (352) 466-3878,
www.greatleaps.com.).

4. Recognize that classroom tasks involving memorization will be particularly difficult for Raymond. Teach Raymond various strategies to
use in situations where he is required to memorize information.

PSYCHO-EDUCATIONAL EVALUATION FOR STANLEY G.

Name: Stanley G.	Referred by: Mr. Todd Dumont
Birthdate: 10/27/87	School: Rural Middle School
Chronological Age: 13–0	Examiner: Adapted from Barbara G. Read, Ed.M.
Grade: 7.2	Test Dates: 10/31, 11/07, 11/15/00

Reason for Referral

Stanley was referred for an evaluation by his parents to determine his specific
learning strengths and weaknesses. Stanley's parents were primarily concerned
about his organizational skills and his difficulties with tasks involving written
language. Mr. Todd Dumont, the special education teacher at Rural Middle
School, made the formal request for this evaluation.

Background Information

The following information was obtained from a review of the referral information, including the Evaluation Referral Form completed by Stanley's teachers, his school records, and interviews with school staff working with Stanley.
Stanley resides with his family in Rural Town, VT. His family situation is considered to be stable and supportive. Stanley's mother is a substitute teacher
within the school system and Stanley's father is a mechanic. Stanley also has an
older sister and younger brother. Stanley's parents are actively involved in his
education and support and reinforce educational pursuits.

Stanley's general health is reported as good and his school attendance is
regular. No concerns have been noted regarding Stanley's hearing or visual
acuity. Stanley was diagnosed with Attention-deficit Hyperactivity Disorder

(ADHD) in elementary school and took Ritalin for a period of time. He stopped taking medication in fifth grade. School records indicate that the Evaluation and Planning Team at the Rural Town Elementary School developed a plan for him, under section 504, specifying accommodations and modifications related to his ADHD. This plan did not provide for any specific instructional interventions. Current school and parental concerns involve ongoing difficulties with Stanley's ability to organize, produce, and complete written academic assignments. Stanley's teachers also report that he experiences difficulties with on-task behavior at times within his classes.

Tests and Evaluation

Woodcock-Johnson III (WJ III)
   Tests of Cognitive Abilities (WJ III COG)
   Tests of Achievement (WJ III ACH)
Test of Written Language-Third Edition (TOWL-3)
Informal Assessment
File Review & Staff Consultation

Observations During Testing

Testing was conducted over several sessions at the Rural Middle School. Stanley came readily to all sessions, was cooperative, and worked diligently. During the first session, the testing room was adjacent to a busy corridor and across from the band practice room. This setting provided an opportunity to observe Stanley's attentional resources when background noise was present. Although he became distracted momentarily by talking in the hallway, he was able to redirect himself back to task. Because of the concern regarding Stanley's attention difficulties, tests involving listening were not administered during the first session. The second session was conducted in a different, quiet testing room. Stanley's attention and concentration were more consistent within this setting. The current results are considered to be valid and reasonable estimates of Stanley's present performance levels.

Test Results

The WJ III COG is a comprehensive battery of individually administered tests measuring different intellectual/cognitive abilities. The WJ III presents a number of scores for the purpose of interpreting a subject's performance. The following descriptions are presented to help the reader understand the various scores that appear within the tables of data in this report.

- The Age Equivalent (AE) band scores show Stanley's current developmental age along with range from which he would find similar tasks easy to where he would be likely to experience frustration or to find them difficult.
- The RPI score describes Stanley's Relative Proficiency Index. It is a ratio score that presents Stanley's percent of success compared to that at which his age-mates would typically show a 90% level of success. Thus a 90/90 would represent an equivalent level of success as compared to his peers. An average range of success is considered within 75/90 to 96/90. Scores approaching the level of 75/90 or lower are considered to be at a level that would cause difficulty or frustration for Stanley.
- Standard Scores (SS) reported have a mean of 100 and standard deviation of 15 points. The range (SEM values) around each standard score illustrates error measurement, or the amount of statistical imprecision occurring in that score.

The WJ III GENERAL INTELLECTUAL ABILITY-EXTENDED SCALE (GIA Ext.) includes 14 tests. It provides a broad-based measure of intellectual/cognitive ability based on two measures for each of seven cognitive factors represented in the WJ III COG: Comprehension/Knowledge, Long-term Retrieval, Visual-Spatial Thinking, Auditory Processing, Fluid Reasoning, Processing Speed, and Short-term Memory (see Table 7.2). The following are brief descriptions of these different abilities:

- *Comprehension/Knowledge (Gc)* is the breadth and depth of an individual's declarative (factual) and procedural knowledge and the effective application of it (verbal reasoning), including language comprehension. This cluster contains the Verbal Comprehension and General Information tests.
- *Long-Term Storage/Retrieval (Glr)* is defined as a thinking ability to learn new information and to store and retrieve that information effectively through association over a period of extended time. This cluster contains the Visual-Auditory Learning and Retrieval

Table 7.2 Table of Scores

Cluster/test	AE	EASY to DIFF		RPI	PR	SS (±SEM BAND)
GIA-Extended	19	14–6	>24	98/90	94	124 (121–127)
Comp-Knowledge	16–10	13–10	20	97/90	84	115 (111–119)
Verbal Comprehension	14–9	12–4	17–8	95/90	69	107 (102–113)
General Information	20	15–10	29	99/90	91	120 (115–126)
L-T Retrieval	>22	9–7	>22	94/90	84	115 (108–121)
Visual-Auditory Learning	>19	12–9	>19	96/90	84	115 (107–122)
Retrieval Fluency	16–0	6–7	>30	91/90	68	107 (101–113)
Visual-Spatial Thinking	>25	10–4	>25	95/90	75	110 (105–116)
Spatial Relations	>25	11–8	>25	96/90	77	111 (106–117)
Picture Recognition	16–9	9–4	>25	93/90	62	104 (99–110)
Auditory Process	20	10–9	>25	94/90	74	110 (104–115)
Sound Blending	>26	14–7	>26	97/90	80	112 (107–118)
Auditory Attention	11–9	7–6	>20	89/90	44	98 (91–104)
Fluid Reasoning	>21	18–4	>21	99/90	96	126 (119–133)
Concept Formation	>21	>21	>21	100/90	97	129 (120–138)
Analysis-Synthesis	>20	14–0	>20	97/90	83	114 (107–121)

Cluster/test	AE	EASY to DIFF		RPI	PR	SS (±SEM BAND)
Processing Speed	11–2	10–1	12–6	68/90	22	88 (85–92)
Visual Matching	10–6	9–9	11–5	41/90	12	83 (78–87)
Decision Speed	12–4	10–8	14–6	86/90	42	97 (92–102)
Short-Term Memory	>22	>22	>22	100/90	99.5	138 (134–143)
Numbers Reversed	>22	>22	>22	100/90	99.7	141 (136–145)
Memory for Words	>23	>23	>23	100/90	97	128 (121–135)
Clinical Clusters						
Working Memory	>22	18–7	>22	99/90	96	125 (122–129)
Numbers Reversed	>22	>22	>22	100/90	99.7	141 (136–145)
Auditory Work Memory	12–5	10–4	15–6	87/90	44	98 (94–102)
Cognitive Fluency	11–2	9–3	13–9	80/90	29	92 (89–94)
Retrieval Fluency	16–0	6–7	>30	91/90	68	107 (101–113)
Decision Speed	12–4	10–8	14–6	86/90	42	97 (92–102)
Rapid Picture Naming	9–9	8–7	11–2	49/90	22	89 (87–91)
Cog Efficiency (Ext)	19	14–10	>21	98/90	90	119 (115–123)
Visual Matching	10–6	9–9	11–5	41/90	12	83 (78–87)
Numbers Reversed	>22	>22	>22	100/90	99.7	141 (136–145)
Decision Speed	12–4	10–8	14–6	86/90	42	97 (92–102)
Memory for Words	>23	>23	>23	100/90	97	128 (121–135)

Fluency tests, which measure associative memory and ideational fluency.

- *Visual-Spatial Thinking (Gv)* is the ability required to perceive nonlinguistic visual patterns, spatial configurations, visual details, and visual memory. It contains the Spatial Relations and Picture Recognition tests.

- *Auditory Processing (Ga)* is defined as a thinking ability relating to auditory information and to the ability to analyze and synthesize sounds within words. This cluster contains the Sound Blending and Auditory Attention tests.

- *Fluid Reasoning (Gf)* is defined as a thinking ability to reason, form concepts, and solve problems that include unfamiliar information or novel situations. It contains the Concept Formation and Analysis-Synthesis tests, which measure inductive and deductive reasoning.

- *Processing Speed (Gs)* is the ability to maintain speed and accuracy on activities requiring sustained attention for a period of time. It is also described as the fluency and speed with which an individual can "cycle" or integrate all types of information. This is an area that is related to cognitive fluency and is considered to be an important "automatic process" for academic fluency. This cluster contains the Visual Matching and Decision Speed tests.

- *Short-Term Memory (Gsm)* is described as the ability to retain information and use that information within a short period of time. This area is considered to be another critical automatic process. The short-term memory cluster contains the Numbers Reversed and Memory for Words tests.

Additional tests were administered to obtain the following clinical clusters:

- *Broad Attention:* Numbers Reversed (attentional capacity), Auditory Attention (selective attention), Auditory Working Memory (divided attention), Pair Cancellation (sustained attention).

- *Cognitive Fluency:* Retrieval Fluency (speed of retrieval for stored information), Decision Speed (speed of forming simple concepts), Rapid Picture Naming (lexical speed and access of vocabulary).

- *Working Memory:* Numbers Reversed (storage and performance of a cognitive operation on information), Auditory Working Memory (division of attention and management of the limited capacity of short-term memory).

Intra-cognitive Discrepancies

These scores present a "statistical picture" of the variability among Stanley's abilities.

Discrepancies	Standard Scores			Discrepancy	
	Actual	Predicted	Difference	PR	SD
Comprehension Knowledge	115	113	+2	57	+0.19
Long-term Retrieval	115	114	+1	52	+0.06
Visual-Spatial Thinking	110	110	0	51	+0.03
Auditory Processing	110	112	–2	44	–0.16
Fluid Reasoning	126	112	+14	89	+1.24
Processing Speed	88	113	–25	4	–1.81
Short-term Memory	138	108	+30	99	+2.45
Working Memory	125	109	+16	91	+1.34

Discussion of Cognitive Testing

Stanley's scores indicate superior overall cognitive/intellectual ability. Within his cognitive profile, however, he demonstrates significant variability. Stanley demonstrates a strong and well-developed fund of knowledge and verbal knowledge. When asked specific questions, he demonstrated a superior level of general information. Stanley was most capable with conceptual-level tasks that required problem solving. He enjoyed the challenge of these types of activities. Stanley demonstrated that he is most comfortable when tasks require him to work in the abstract, conceptual realm. His cognitive style was precise, yet reflective and flexible. He showed a keen ability to shift strategies effectively in response to the changing demands of tasks and was open and receptive to instructional feedback. Stanley's auditory memory abilities are also in the high-average range.

In contrast, Stanley demonstrated considerable difficulties processing symbols rapidly. His slow speed impacted heavily on all timed tasks involving fluency, lexical access, and rapid decision-making. Stanley's slow speed of processing affected his overall efficiency when he was required to work with accuracy and speed. When speed and fluency were not essential features of an activity, Stanley demonstrated remarkable memory and conceptual problem-solving capabilities (see Short-term Memory and Fluid Reasoning clusters). The contrast between Stanley's superior knowledge and higher-order thinking abilities and his more limited cognitive fluency are likely to be quite puzzling and frustrating to him. It is difficult to perceive oneself as "smart" while experiencing significant problems with the speed of production.

Achievement Battery

The WJ III ACH is a comprehensive battery of individually administered tests measuring the academic achievement areas of reading, oral language, mathematics, written language, and general knowledge. Similar to the AE scores, GE scores show the instructional level that Stanley has obtained. The Instructional Zone depicts the grade level of work likely to be easy or difficult for him. Table 7.3 shows Stanley's levels of functioning in each academic area.

Test of Written Language-Third Edition (TOWL-3)

In addition to the WJ III, Stanley was also administered the spontaneous writing portion of the Test of Written Language-Third Edition (TOWL-3). This section of the TOWL-3 was presented in order to examine Stanley's ability to organize his language and ideas for expressive writing. The spontaneous writing section of the TOWL-3 presents Stanley with a stimulus picture about which he needs to create a story. The body of Stanley's composition is used to generate three separate subtest scores:

- *Contextual Conventions* measures Stanley's ability to apply spelling and knowledge of the rules that govern the conventions of punctuation, capitalization, and grammar.
- *Contextual Language* measures Stanley's facility with vocabulary, the complexity of his sentence constructions, and his general use of various parts of speech (e.g. phrases, subject-verb agreement, embedded clauses, etc.).
- *Story Construction* measures Stanley's ability to write in a logical, organized manner and to develop a theme or plot that is coherent and interesting to the reader.

Table 7.3 Table of Scores

Cluster/Test	GE	EASY to DIFF		RPI	PR	SS (±SEM BAND)
Broad Reading	7.1	5.8	8.7	86/90	45	98 (96–100)
Letter-Word Id	8.5	6.8	10.9	95/90	64	105 (101–110)
Reading Fluency	5.4	4.6	6.3	36/90	25	90 (88–92)
Passage Comp	11.3	7.5	>18.0	96/90	73	109 (104–115)
Broad Math	7.2	5.5	9.8	88/90	46	99 (96–101)
Calculation	7.3	5.7	9.8	90/90	49	100 (95–104)
Math Fluency	5.1	3.0	7.8	76/90	13	83 (80–86)
Applied Problems	11.3	7.5	>18.0	94/90	59	103 (100–107)
Broad Written Lang	6.9	5.0	10.0	88/90	45	98 (95–101)
Spelling	10.9	7.7	13.0	98/90	80	113 (108–117)
Writing Fluency	5.3	4.2	6.7	62/90	19	87 (82–92)
Writing Samples	5.6	2.5	12.9	86/90	32	93 (85–102)
Math Calc Skills	6.4	4.7	8.9	84/90	34	94 (90–97)
Calculation	7.3	5.7	9.8	90/90	49	100 (95–104)
Math Fluency	5.1	3.0	7.8	76/90	13	83 (80–86)
Basic Writing Skills	8.9	6.5	12.2	93/90	58	103 (100–106)
Spelling	10.9	7.7	13.0	98/90	80	113 (108–117)
Editing	7.5	5.4	10.0	80/90	37	95 (91–99)
Written Expression	5.3	3.7	7.8	76/90	22	88 (84–93)
Writing Fluency	5.3	4.2	6.7	62/90	19	87 (82–92)
Writing Samples	5.6	2.5	12.9	86/90	32	93 (85–102)
Academic Skills	8.6	6.6	11.8	95/90	70	108 (104–111)
Letter-Word Id	8.5	6.8	10.9	95/90	64	105 (101–110)
Calculation	7.3	5.7	9.8	90/90	49	100 (95–104)
Spelling	10.9	7.7	13.0	98/90	80	113 (108–117)
Academic Fluency	5.3	4.2	6.6	59/90	19	87 (85–89)
Reading Fluency	5.4	4.6	6.3	36/90	25	90 (88–92)
Math Fluency	5.1	3.0	7.8	76/90	13	83 (80–86)
Writing Fluency	5.3	4.2	6.7	62/90	19	87 (82–92)
Academic Apps	8.9	6.0	13.0	93/90	62	105 (101–108)
Passage Comp	11.3	7.5	>18.0	96/90	73	109 (104–115)
Applied Problems	11.3	7.5	>18.0	94/90	59	103 (100–107)
Writing Samples	5.6	2.5	12.9	86/90	32	93 (85–102)

Stanley obtained the following scores for the administered subtest and composites.

	Scaled Score (M = 10/SD = 3)	Standard Score (M = 100/SD = 15)
Subtests		
Contextual Conventions	5	75
Contextual Language	6	80
Story Construction	3	65
Composite		
Spontaneous Writing Quotient		66

Stanley had trouble planning a story on the TOWL-3. On the writing prompt, Stanley listened to the explanation of the task (i.e., to write a story about the picture), and then said, "But I'm just not sure what I'm supposed to do." After looking at the picture, he only produced a few loosely connected sentences that concretely described what he saw in the picture.

Discussion of Achievement Testing

A review of Stanley's performance across the various scores from the different test batteries, as well as his response patterns within tasks, shows a number of important and interesting patterns. Stanley is generally most competent on tasks that simply require him to demonstrate his knowledge and reasoning in an untimed format (see WJ III ACH cluster groupings of Academic Skills, Academic Applications, and Academic Fluency).

Stanley's writing abilities at the "skill" level are within the average range. His spelling and knowledge of conventions are instructionally appropriate for his grade placement; however Stanley is not effective at applying those skills to actual spontaneous writing. He expends a great deal of energy trying to organize and produce his ideas (see TOWL-3, Contextual Conventions).

Stanley finds it difficult to organize and present his thoughts in writing. Even when the conceptual demands were very simple (e.g., the Writing Fluency test) Stanley often could only come up with sentence fragments or needed to skip over items because he was unable to think of a sentence that used three specific words. For example, when Stanley was presented with the three words "the, foot, little" he did not recognize that he simply needed to add the word "is" in order to produce a logical sentence. Instead Stanley wrote a sentence fragment "the little foot."

Stanley's organizational difficulties are not limited to timed activities, nor are they specific only to writing. Stanley also showed similar confusions (although to a milder extent) with grammatical organization on listening and reading comprehension tasks. Stanley's listening skills are compromised when competing noise is present in the environment, as observations of him during listening tasks showed.

Stanley's reading, writing, and math scores are discrepant to his overall intellectual functioning and below his superior level of oral language as well. Stanley has average levels in basic skills and applications, but has low academic fluency. These findings suggest that he may benefit from specific accommodations, modifications, and assistance in these areas.

Ability/Achievement Discrepancies

Discrepancies	Standard Scores			Discrepancy	
	Actual	Pred	Diff	PR	SD
*Intellectual Ability/Achievement Discrepancies**					
Broad Reading	98	117	–19	3	–1.81
Broad Math	99	116	–17	4	–1.71
Math Calc Skills	94	114	–20	6	–1.52
Broad Written Lang	98	117	–19	4	–1.71
Basic Writing Skills	103	115	–12	14	–1.07
Written Expression	88	116	–28	1	–2.38

*These discrepancies are based on GIA (Ext) with ACH Broad, Basic, and Applied clusters.

The Ability/Achievement Discrepancy Profiles indicate that virtually all of Stanley's academic skills are below his high-average predicted levels. However, only his writing skills meet a standard that is considered by state guidelines to indicate "adverse effect" in terms of his ability to function within an appropriate instructional range for age and grade. Stanley's needs in written expression skills warrant systematic instructional intervention of a type that extends beyond the conventional seventh grade language arts curriculum.

Summary and Recommendations

Stanley is a bright and personable student who has been experiencing difficulties with organizational writing skills. Stanley's background history indicates that he was diagnosed with an attention disorder when he was attending elementary school in Rural Town, VT. School records further indicate that his educational program was managed through an accommodation plan under Section 504. Stanley reportedly did not receive specific instructional intervention in any academic area under this accommodation plan.

The current evaluation indicates that Stanley possesses superior cognitive/intellectual abilities but demonstrates some difficulties with tasks involving automatic processing speed and has difficulties organizing linguistic information effectively. Stanley's difficulty with automaticity is both statistically noteworthy (i.e., well below his other abilities) and of qualitative significance (i.e., frustrating for him and below a developmental norm for his age). From a clinical perspective, regardless of "eligibility" issues, these difficulties constitute a process-based learning disability.

Stanley's academic profile is consistent with his cognitive profile. He demonstrates considerable difficulty with tasks that require fluency, organization, and automaticity. These difficulties are observable within all areas (reading, writing, and math) but have the greatest impact upon his abilities to compose and produce writing.

Accommodations

Stanley will need accommodations and modifications to assist him within his general education classes. The following six suggestions are accommodations/modifications to ensure that Stanley can successfully take part and benefit from his classroom instruction. Additional strategies and accommodations developed by Stanley's teachers or parents should also be implemented.

1. Set aside periodic opportunities to check the accuracy of his notes or to determine that he obtained all the details, instructions, and assignments that were presented.
2. Whenever possible, provide Stanley with a visual outline or other visual cues to help anchor his attention when an oral presentation or lecture is being presented.

3. Be sensitive to the fact that Stanley will most likely need modifications in testing procedures for timed tests or those that require the recall of information through open-prompt formats. Stanley will likely need information presented or asked "in context" and presented with specificity in structured formats in order to ensure that he can recall/retrieve, formulate, and produce his responses effectively.

4. When possible provide Stanley the time needed to respond to a question or point. Allow Stanley to indicate when he is ready to respond.

5. Provide accommodations for timed assignments in his general education classes. When evaluating his work, place the emphasis on accuracy rather than speed.

6. Help Stanley organize steps for extended assignments such as research papers. Help him develop his own personal outline of what he needs to do and when.

Written Language

Stanley needs to receive systematic help for the development of written expression. The goal for instruction is to help Stanley be able to recognize *independently* how and when to integrate different types of organizational styles when composing complex writing (e.g., research papers).

The following are examples of the types of intervention that would be effective.

1. Teach Stanley how to write formula paragraphs so that he is able to respond to various writing demands (e.g., descriptive, opinion, compare/contrast).

2. Review and provide practice using joining words (cohesive ties) that denote the relationships among ideas. Show him how cohesive ties are used by teaching a variety of listening and reading activities and then providing opportunities to apply these words in his own writing.

3. Teach Stanley how to use graphic organizers to assist in generating and organizing paragraphs, essays, and reports.

The results of this evaluation will be shared with Stanley's parents and the members of the Rural Middle School multidisciplinary team.

EDUCATIONAL EVALUATION FOR ALISON W.

Name: Alison W.   Examiner: N. Mather, Ph.D
Birthdate: 12/2/83   School: Santa Ana High School
Chronological Age: 18–10   Test Dates: 9/19, 9/23/01.
Grade: 12.5

Reason for Referral

Alison's parents requested a private educational evaluation to help determine their daughter's present performance in mathematics. Throughout school, Alison has had a difficult time in math courses. Alison's parents are planning her postsecondary education and are concerned that Alison will not succeed in math courses and, as a result, be unsuccessful in college. They wondered whether she had a specific math disability, and if so, whether she would qualify for modified entrance requirements to the state university or would be eligible for the program for students with LD. They requested an academic assessment as a basis for considering whether additional intellectual/cognitive testing would be necessary or beneficial.

Background Information and Previous Test Results

Currently, Alison is in the middle of her senior year in a private religious school. She is an only child. Her mother is a pediatrician with a successful private practice and her father owns a small business that sells computer accessories. Alison reports that she would like to go to college and become an elementary school teacher. During her last summer vacation, she volunteered at the church preschool program. She noted that she really enjoyed interacting with the children and their families.

Her mother recalls that Alison passed all developmental milestones within normal limits. In the first grade, Alison was retained because she was having trouble reading and seemed unable to learn math facts. Her 1st-grade teacher felt that another year would help her catch up. In the following year, Alison quickly advanced in reading but continued to struggle with math. These difficulties persisted throughout elementary school. Alison recalls struggling to learn to count to 100. She commented that even the page numbers on books were confusing to her as she could never find the right place. She remembered feeling that the number system just did not make sense. She commented that she has never been able to memorize the multiplication tables. Alison received resource services from third to sixth grade. She was discontinued from special education services when she entered middle school and has received no additional support services since that time.

Throughout high school, she has struggled in both science and math classes. In her sophomore year, Alison failed Algebra I once, withdrew during her second attempt, and then passed the course in summer school with a grade of D. She commented that the only reason she thought she passed was that the summer school teacher just felt sorry for her.

In her senior year, her chemistry teacher stated that Alison had particular difficulty with the math involved in chemistry. Her Algebra II teacher also stated that Alison lacked flexibility in solving problems and in understanding abstract concepts. Alison explained that in math and the math-related sciences, she memorizes formulas and patterns but cannot understand the logic. When the application changes, she cannot figure out how to solve the problems.

Alison commented that math is different from other subject areas because it builds on itself. When she begins to lose the logic or does not learn certain facts, she becomes lost as new topics are introduced. Alison thinks that her difficulties with chemistry and biology are largely related to their mathematical aspects (e.g., formulas, genetic probabilities, equations). Alison also acknowledged that math tests make her feel very anxious and the second that she comes to a problem she does not understand, her concentration is affected for the rest of the test and she can rarely complete the exam.

Tests Administered

Woodcock-Johnson III
  Tests of Achievement (Form A): Tests 1–11, 14–16, 18, 19

Behavioral Observations

During testing, Alison was consistently personable, cooperative, and attentive. Midway through the first session, Alison made up a credible story about having to leave, and did so, when she learned that the next test involved math. With her mother's insistence, another brief session was scheduled.

Test Results

The tests of the WJ III were scored according to grade norms. When no difference was found between the two component tests of a factor or cluster, only the factor or cluster score is discussed. The Compuscore printouts are appended to this report (see Table 7.4).

Academic Achievement

Alison's Total Achievement score is in the average range. Performance in mathematics, however, was significantly lower than other areas of academic functioning.

Reading

The results of the WJ III Broad Reading cluster indicate that Alison's reading ability is in the high-average range. Alison pronounced both real words and nonwords with relative ease. She remarked that she always likes to have a good book to read.

Written Language

Results of the WJ III Written Language cluster indicate that Alison's overall written language skills are in the high-average range. Basic writing skills were relatively lower than written expression skills, with most of her errors in spelling. Alison's ability to express her ideas in writing was in the superior range. A writing sample from her English class was analyzed for a more in-depth analysis of written expression. Alison's ideas were well-sequenced, had clear transitions, and were clearly organized around a central theme. She made good use of examples, details, and description to add interest. Within the essay, she had several minor spelling, usage, and punctuation errors.

Mathematics

Alison's greatest weakness is within quantitative ability, a broad, but distinct area of intelligence. This ability requires competence in comprehending quantitative concepts and relationships and in manipulating numerical symbols. It

Table 7.4 Table of Scores: Woodcock-Johnson III Tests of Achievement (Compuscore Version 1.1b Score Report) Norms based on grade 12.6

Cluster	RAW	GE	EASY	DIFF	RPI	PR	SS (68% BAND)
Oral Language-Ext	—	15.4	10.5	>18.0	95/90	74	109 (105–114)
Oral Expression	—	13.7	8.4	>18.0	92/90	59	103 (98–109)
Listening Comprehension	—	17.3	12.7	>18.0	97/90	78	111 (106–117)
Total Achievement	—	14.6	12.0	>18.0	96/90	72	109 (107–111)
Broad Reading	—	>18.0	>18.0	>18.0	100/90	91	120 (118–122)
Broad Math	—	6.6	5.0	8.8	52/90	11	81 (79–84)
Broad Written Language	—	15.5	11.5	>18.0	96/90	78	111 (107–116)
Math Calc Skills	—	6.5	4.7	9.0	54/90	8	79 (76–82)
Math Reasoning	—	6.7	5.3	8.8	51/90	18	87 (84–89)
Basic Writing Skills	—	10.5	7.7	13.0	83/90	39	96 (93–98)
Written Expression	—	>18.0	>18.0	>18.0	98/90	96	127 (121–133)
Academic Skills	—	11.1	8.3	13.4	86/90	42	97 (94–100)
Academic Fluency	—	>18.0	17.3	>18.0	99/90	84	115 (113–117)
Academic Apps	—	13.2	9.8	>18.0	94/90	63	105 (101–109)
Academic Knowledge	—	13.5	9.9	18.0	92/90	55	102 (97–107)

(continued)

Table 7.4 (Continued)

Test	RAW	GE	EASY	DIFF	RPI	PR	SS (68% BAND)
	Form A of the following achievement tests was administered:						
Letter-Word Identification	74	>18.0	>18.0	>18.0	99/90	91	120 (114–126)
Reading Fluency	95	>18.0	>18.0	>18.0	100/90	87	117 (115–118)
Story Recall	—	12.9	2.5	>18.0	91/90	53	101 (94–109)
Understanding Directions	—	>18.0	12.3	>18.0	96/90	80	113 (103–122)
Calculation	20	5.7	4.5	7.4	32/90	6	76 (72–81)
Math Fluency	92	7.9	5.2	12.2	74/90	16	85 (83–87)
Spelling	42	9.0	6.7	12.9	78/90	32	93 (89–97)
Writing Fluency	33	>18.0	>18.0	>18.0	99/90	92	121 (115–126)
Passage Comprehension	44	>18.0	>18.0	>18.0	99/90	94	124 (116–131)
Applied Problems	40	6.8	5.5	8.6	48/90	19	87 (84–90)
Writing Samples	20-E	>18.0	16.2	>18.0	97/90	98	131 (118–144)
Picture Vocabulary	34	14.7	10.6	>18.0	93/90	59	104 (98–109)
Oral Comprehension	29	16.7	12.9	>18.0	97/90	72	109 (104–113)
Editing	22	11.7	8.9	15.0	87/90	46	98 (95–102)
Quantitative Concepts	—	6.7	5.2	8.9	54/90	19	87 (83–91)
Academic Knowledge	—	13.5	9.9	18.0	92/90	55	102 (97–107)

Table 7.4 (Continued)

Discrepancies	Standard Scores			Discrepancy		Significant at ±1.50 SD (SEE)
	Actual	Predicted	Difference	PR	SD	
Intra-Achievement						
Broad Reading	120	101	+19	98	+1.97	Yes
Broad Math	81	111	−30	0.4	−2.67	Yes
Broad Written Language	111	103	+8	79	+0.82	No
Oral Language	110	103	+7	73	+0.62	No
*Oral Language/Achievement Discrepancies**						
Broad Reading	120	104	+16	89	+1.23	No
Broad Math	81	105	−24	2	−2.00	Yes
Math Calc Skills	79	104	−25	2	−1.96	Yes
Math Reasoning	87	106	−19	5	−1.69	Yes
Broad Written Language	111	105	+6	69	+0.50	No
Basic Writing Skills	96	104	−8	28	−0.59	No
Written Expression	127	104	+23	96	+1.81	Yes
Academic Knowledge	102	107	−5	33	−0.43	No

*These discrepancies based on Oral Language (Ext) with ACH Broad, Basic, and Applied clusters.

includes mathematical problem solving and the logical-mathematical knowledge that is necessary for deciding which of previously learned facts, algorithms, methods, and theorems are useful in solving a specific problem. The WJ III measures this cognitive ability as mathematical achievement in the areas of computation, fluency, application, and concepts.

Alison scored in the low-average range in Broad Mathematics and Math

Reasoning and in the low range in Math Calculation Skills. Her score on the Calculation test was in the low range and her scores on the Math Fluency, Applied Problems, and Quantitative Concepts tests were in the low-average range. Alison took more than 20 minutes to complete the Calculation test. She studied problems and often made numerous changes to her answers before moving onto the next question. Analysis of her errors on these tests indicates that Alison has difficulty with problems involving division with three-digit divisors, division of fractions, calculation of percent, conversion of fractions to percents, place value with numbers having decimals, adding and subtracting with negative numbers, and applying measurement concepts. On the Math Fluency test, which involves the computation of simple addition, subtraction, and multiplication problems, Alison paused for a moment on several multiplication facts and "skip-counted" to get the solution.

When asked how many inches were in a foot, Alison shrugged her shoulders and said, "I know I should know that but I don't." In contrast, Alison solved three algebraic equations correctly, suggesting that she had more success doing problems she has encountered more recently.

Throughout the math tests, Alison made comments reflecting her perceived incompetence in this area. As examples, she stated, "I'm just no good at this." "I've never really understood this stuff." "I don't know why this is so hard for me." When she reached the first computation involving fractions, she exclaimed, "Oh, no! Not fractions!"

Oral Language/Knowledge

Results of the Oral Language and Knowledge clusters, as well as informal conversation with Alison, indicate that her oral language abilities and general knowledge of science, social studies, and humanities are in the average range. She was able to identify pictured objects, follow directions, and listen to and recall stories. She answered questions regarding curricular knowledge with relative ease. On several items on the Science subtest, she was quick to respond, "Don't know that one, but I probably should."

Discrepancies

When Alison's oral language abilities, measured by the Oral Language-Extended cluster, are compared to her performance in mathematics (Broad

Mathematics cluster), a significant discrepancy exists. Only 2 out of 100 individuals would obtain a math score the same or lower. In addition, Alison's math achievement is significantly lower than predicted based on the average of her other achievement cluster scores. When her predicted SS of 111 is compared to her actual SS of 81, only 4 out of 1000 people would have a score the same or lower. Clearly, abilities related to language are a relative strength for Alison, whereas abilities related to mathematics are a significant weakness.

Conclusions

Test results and educational history indicate that Alison has difficulty learning and retaining mathematical skills and concepts. Math is highly visual and spatial; Alison appears to have significant difficulty with abstract reasoning using visual patterns. Comprehension of mathematical patterns and numerical problems also requires adequate mastery of basic skills. Alison's retention of mathematical procedures and her processing of basic math facts are significantly slower than average grade-peers. When new math skills are presented in class, she might not have enough time to comprehend the current information before the teacher moves on to new information. Alison's self-description and behavior during testing suggest that she has developed a level of math anxiety that is further contributing to her math difficulties. Based on the current testing, Alison appears to have the motivation and literacy abilities to succeed in college. She is likely, however, to need tutorial support in classes related to mathematics.

Recommendations

1. Conduct further intellectual/cognitive assessment to help determine the specific factors that are inhibiting math development and performance. Administer measures of reasoning ability, working memory, and visual-spatial thinking to determine if any of these abilities are affecting mathematical performance. These findings should be integrated with results from the present assessment.
2. Schedule a multidisciplinary conference to consider Alison's eligibility for Special Education services for math remediation and support

for the remainder of the school year. Do informal testing to determine relevant instructional goals.

3. Based on the findings of the more comprehensive report, Alison and her parents should explore modified entrance requirements to the state university, as well as procedures for applying to the program for students with learning disabilities.

4. As part of math instruction, review procedures involved in computations with fractions, percents, and decimals. Specifically teach strategies for translating word problems into computation. Help Alison learn to visualize what is happening in the problem. When possible, review math skills using independent living skills: balancing the checkbook, figuring interest on a car loan, budgeting her salary, measuring for cooking, adjusting a recipe, using map skills (e.g., rate × time = distance).

5. Consider requesting accommodations for extended time on math-related exams.

6. Consider the possibility of a math waiver, a course substitution, or an adapted or self-paced math class at the state university.

✎ TEST YOURSELF ✎

1. Write a descriptive statement about Raymond's intra-individual discrepancy PR of .3 on Basic Reading Skills.

2. Using Raymond's Grade Profile, determine his independent level (easy), his instructional level, and his frustrational (difficult) level on Broad Reading.

3. Using Raymond's Grade Profile, identify the academic area that illustrates the most rapid growth at this point in time.

4. Using Raymond's SS/PR Profile, determine if a statistically significant difference exists between his performance on Broad Reading and Broad Mathematics.

5. Using Stanley's scores from the ability/achievement discrepancies, write a descriptive statement about his performance in Written Expression.

6. Write a statement to describe Stanley's Written Expression RPI of 76/90.

7. Describe Alison's instructional range for the Broad Math cluster.

8. When oral language is used as the ability score to predict achievement, what are Alison's significant discrepancies? (strengths and weaknesses)

Answers: 1. Only 3 out of 1,000 of Raymond's grade-mates with the same predicted score would have a score as low or lower on Basic Reading. 2. Raymond's independent reading level on Broad Reading cluster is mid-second grade (2.4), his instructional level is end of second grade (2.8), and his frustrational level is beginning third grade (3.3). 3. Basic Reading Skills. 4. Yes, a statistically significant difference exists. 5. Stanley has a significant ability/achievement discrepancy in Written Expression. Only 1 in 100 of his grade-mates with a GIA of 124 would have obtained a score of 88 on Written Expression. 6. Compared to average seventh graders with 90% proficiency on written expression tasks, Stanley would only have 76% proficiency. 7. Alison's instructional zone on Broad Math ranges from an independent level (easy) of beginning fifth grade to a difficult (frustration) level of mid- to end-eighth grade. 8. Alison has significant weaknesses in Broad Math, Math Calculation Skills, and Math Reasoning. She has a significant strength in Written Expression.

Appendix A

Fine Points of WJ III ACH Administration

Test 1: Letter-Word Identification *(Reading-Writing Grw)*
1. Know *exact* pronunciation of each word.
2. Use Suggested Starting Points.
3. Basal: six lowest-numbered items correct, or Item 1.
4. Ceiling: six highest-numbered items incorrect, or last test item.
5. Do not penalize an examinee for mispronunciations due to articulation errors, dialect variations, or regional speech patterns.
6. If you do not hear a response, have the examinee reread all the items on the page, *not* just the one in question. Score only the item in question. Do not rescore the other items.
7. Do not tell the examinee any letters or words during the test.
8. If the examinee pronounces the word phoneme by phoneme or syllable by syllable say, "First read the word silently and then say the word smoothly." This reminder may only be given *once* during the test.
9. Test by complete pages.
10. Count items below the basal as correct.

Test 2: Reading Fluency *(Reading-Writing Grw)* (Timed) (SRB)
1. Timed test: 3-minute time limit.
2. A stopwatch is preferred. If not using a stopwatch, record exact starting and stopping times.
3. Use the SRB.
4. All subjects begin with Sample Items and then Item 1.
5. If subject has fewer than three correct on Practice Exercises C through F, discontinue testing and record a score of 0 in the Number Correct box.
6. If subject appears to be answering items without reading, remind him or her to read each sentence.

7. Do not tell the subject any letters or words.

8. If subject stops at the bottom of a page or column, remind him or her to continue at the top of the next column or page.

9. If finishing time is not exactly 3 minutes, record exact finishing time in minutes and seconds on the Test Record. Software program will make an adjustment.

10. Use the scoring overlay for easy scoring

11. Count the number of correct responses *and* the number of errors. Do not include items that were not attempted during the time limit as errors. When using the software program, enter both the number correct and the number incorrect.

12. To obtain estimated AE/GE, subtract the number of errors from the number correct to obtain the total. If the result is a negative number, use 0 when consulting the scoring table.

13. This test may be administered to a small group of two to three examinees.

Test 3: Story Recall *(Comprehension-Knowledge Gc)* (Taped)

1. Follow taped test procedures. Locate the appropriate starting point prior to testing.

2. On the Test Record, record date and time of administration if Test 10 will be administered.

3. Use Suggested Starting Points.

4. Follow the Continuation Instructions in the Test Book to determine which stories to administer and when to discontinue testing.

5. Pause or stop the recording after each story to allow response time.

6. Do not repeat or replay any stories.

7. Do not penalize a subject for mispronunciations due to articulation errors, dialect variations, or regional speech patterns.

8. In the Test Record, place a check mark over each element recalled correctly (separated by /).

9. Score 1 for each correctly recalled.

10. Words that are **bold** must be recalled exactly. Non-bold elements may be paraphrased in any way that preserves the meaning.

11. If necessary, present the stories orally.

12. When using the software, an entry must be made for each group of two stories. For groups of stories administered, enter the number of points. For groups not administered, enter an "X."

Test 4: Understanding Directions *(Comprehension-Knowledge Gc)* (Taped)

1. Follow taped test procedures. Locate the appropriate starting point prior to testing.
2. Use Suggested Starting Points.
3. Allow subject to review the picture for approximately 10 seconds before administering the items.
4. Pause or stop the recording after the last item for each picture.
5. Do not repeat or replay any item unless an obvious noise (e.g., bell ringing) interferes. In this case, finish the picture and then read-minister the specific item only.
6. Subject must complete all steps contained in the direction to receive a 1.
7. If the direction does not specify the sequence, the subject can point in any order.
8. If necessary, present the items orally.
9. When using the software, an entry must be made for each picture. Enter the number of points for each picture administered. Enter an "X" for each picture not administered.

Test 5: Calculation *(Mathematics Gq)* (SRB)

1. Use the SRB.
2. Use Suggested Starting Points.
3. Basal: six lowest-numbered items correct, or Item 1.
4. Ceiling: six highest-numbered items incorrect, or last test item.
5. If subject responds incorrectly to both Sample Items, you may discontinue testing and record a score of 0.
6. Accept poorly formed or reversed numbers.
7. Score transposed numbers (e.g., 14 for 41) 0.
8. Score items skipped by the subject 0.
9. Complete any queries as listed in the Test Book.
10. Do not point out the "signs" to the subject.
11. Count items below the basal as correct.

Test 6: Math Fluency *(Mathematics Gq)* (Timed) (SRB)
1. Timed test: 3-minute time limit.
2. A stopwatch is preferred. If not using a stopwatch, record exact starting and stopping times.
3. Use the SRB.
4. All subjects begin with Item 1.
5. If subject has three or fewer correct after 1 minute, discontinue testing. Record a time of 1 minute in the Test Record as well as the number correct (0 to 3).
6. Do not point out signs or remind the subject to pay attention to signs once testing begins.
7. Do not penalize for poorly formed or reversed numbers.
8. Remind subject to proceed across the page from left to right, row by row, if he or she starts skipping around.
9. If finishing time is not exactly 3 minutes, record exact finishing time in minutes and seconds on the Test Record. Software program will make an adjustment.
10. Score skipped items as incorrect.
11. Use the scoring overlay provided for easy scoring.
12. This test may be administered to a small group of two to three examinees.

Test 7: Spelling *(Reading-Writing Grw)* (SRB)
1. Use SRB.
2. Use Suggested Starting Points.
3. Basal: six lowest-numbered items correct, or Item 1.
4. Ceiling: six highest-numbered items incorrect, or last test item.
5. Know the correct pronunciation of each item.
6. Do not penalize for poor handwriting or reversed letters as long as the letter does not become a new letter (e.g., a reversed "b" becomes a "d" so it would be an error).
7. Printed (manuscript) responses are requested but cursive responses are acceptable.
8. Accept upper- or lower-case responses unless case is specified.
9. Count items below the basal as correct.

Test 8: Writing Fluency *(Reading-Writing Grw)* (Timed) (SRB)

1. Timed test: 7-minute time limit.
2. A stopwatch is preferred. If not using a stopwatch, record exact starting and stopping times.
3. Use SRB.
4. Start with Sample Items for all subjects.
5. If the subject gets a 0 on Samples B through D, discontinue testing. Record a score of 0 in the Number Correct box.
6. If the subject has three or less correct after 2 minutes have elapsed, discontinue testing. Record a time of 2 minutes and the number correct (0–3) in the Test Record.
7. If finishing time is not exactly 7 minutes, record the exact finishing time in minutes and seconds in the Test Record. The software program makes an adjustment.
8. You may read any stimulus words to the subject upon request.
9. Responses must be complete and reasonable sentences that use all target words to receive credit. Target words may not be changed in any way (e.g., verb tense or nouns changed from singular to plural).
10. Do not penalize for spelling, punctuation, or capitalization errors.
11. Do not penalize for poor handwriting unless the response is illegible.
12. Score skipped items as 0.
13. Score responses that omit critical words as 0.
14. Score responses that omit less meaningful words (e.g., "the," "a") as correct if all other criteria are met.
15. Accept abbreviations (e.g., "w/" for "with") or symbols (e.g., "&" for "and") if all other criteria are met.
16. This test may be administered to a small group of two to three examinees.

Test 9: Passage Comprehension *(Reading-Writing Grw)*

1. Begin with Introduction for subjects at a preschool or kindergarten level.
2. Begin with Item 5 for all subjects at a Grade 1 level.
3. Begin with Sample Item B for all other subjects. Then select appropriate starting point.

4. Basal: six lowest-numbered items correct, or Item 1.
5. Ceiling: six highest-numbered items incorrect, or last test item.
6. Do not penalize for mispronunciations due to articulation errors, dialect variations, or regional speech patterns.
7. The subject should read the passages silently. If the subject persists in reading aloud even after you have asked him or her to read silently, do not insist on silent reading.
8. Do not tell the subject any words.
9. Unless noted, only one-word responses are acceptable.
10. The subject must provide only the word that goes in the blank. It is not correct if the word is supplied in context when reading aloud. In these cases say, "Tell me the one word that should go in the blank." Score the response as incorrect if the word is not provided.
11. Responses that differ in verb tense or number are accepted as correct unless otherwise specified.
12. Responses that substitute different parts of speech are incorrect.
13. Test by complete pages.
14. Count items below the basal as correct.

Test 10: Applied Problems *(Mathematics Gq)* (SRB)

1. Use SRB.
2. Use Suggested Starting Points.
3. Basal: six lowest-numbered items correct, or Item 1.
4. Ceiling: six highest-numbered items incorrect, or last test item.
5. Read all items to the subject.
6. Provide SRB and pencil at any time if the subject requests it or appears to need it (e.g., uses finger to write on table or in air).
7. Give the subject a pencil and the SRB at Item 30.
8. Repeat any questions if requested by subject.
9. Test by complete pages.
10. Count items below the basal as correct.

Test 11: Writing Samples *(Reading-Writing Grw)* (SRB)

1. Use SRB.
2. Use Suggested Starting Points.
3. Administer the prescribed block of items.
4. Read any words upon request from the subject.

5. Do not penalize for spelling, punctuation, capitalization, or usage errors unless otherwise noted in guide.
6. Ask subject to write as neatly as possible if it appears responses are illegible or difficult to read.
7. If items appear too easy or too difficult for subject, administer additional items as directed in test record.
8. Use the Scoring Guide in Appendix B of the *Examiner's Manual* to score items *after* testing.
9. Score items as 2, 1.5, 1, .5, or 0 points.
10. Score illegible items as 0.
11. Do not ask subject to read his or her response for the purpose of scoring the item.
12. If the subject misinterprets the picture but provides a correct sentence based on that perception, score it as correct.
13. If subject writes more than one sentence for an item, select and score the one sentence that best satisfies the task demands.
14. Severe grammatical or usage errors reduce the score of an item by 1 point.
15. Minor grammatical or usage errors are not penalized.
16. Use only *one* of the specified blocks of items when calculating the number correct.
17. If examinee's score falls in a shaded area of the scoring table, administer the additional items noted in the Adjusted Item Block chart in the Test Record. Use the most appropriate block for scoring.
18. Scores that end in .50 exactly should be rounded to the nearest *even* number.
19. This test may be administered to a small group of two to three participants.
20. On the Test Record, check the box for the block of items administered. Software program requires this information.

Test 12: Story Recall-Delayed *(Long-Term Retrieval Glr)*
1. Administer 30 minutes to 8 days after administering Test 3 Story Recall.
2. Record the date and time on the Test Record before testing.

3. Administer the same group of items that were presented on Test 3 Story Recall.
4. Check stories to be administered on the Test Record before testing.
5. Place a check mark over each part of the story recalled accurately.
6. Do not score prompts that are used to initiate recall.
7. Record the number of points for each story in the space provided.
8. Sum each group of two stories as indicated on the Test Record.
9. When using the software program, an entry must be made for each group of stories. Enter the number of points for the groups administered. Enter an "X" for each group not administered.

Test 13: Word Attack *(Reading-Writing Grw)*
1. Use Suggested Starting Points.
2. Basal: six lowest-numbered items correct, or Item 1.
3. Ceiling: six highest-numbered items incorrect, or last item.
4. Know correct pronunciation of each item.
5. Do not penalize for mispronunciations due to articulation errors, dialect variations, or regional speech patterns.
6. Examinees must pronounce the last response fluently to receive credit.
7. If the subject pronounces the pseudo-word phoneme by phoneme or syllable by syllable say, "First read the word silently and then say the word smoothly." This reminder may be given only *once* during the test.
8. If you do not hear a response, complete the page and then ask the subject to repeat all the words on that page. Rescore only the item in question.
9. Do not tell the subject any letters or words.
10. Test by complete pages.
11. Count all items below the basal as correct.
12. Record errors for further analysis.

Test 14: Picture Vocabulary *(Comprehension-Knowledge Gc)*
1. Use Suggested Starting Points.
2. Basal: six lowest-numbered items correct, or Item 1.
3. Ceiling: six highest-numbered items incorrect, or last item.

4. Point to the appropriate picture or picture part as directed.
5. Complete any queries listed in Test Book.
6. Test by complete pages.
7. Count all items below the basal as correct.
8. Record errors for further analysis.

Test 15: Oral Comprehension *(Comprehension-Knowledge Gc)* (Taped)
1. Follow taped test procedures. Locate Sample C on the tape prior to testing.
2. Begin with Sample A and B for all subjects. Present orally.
3. After samples, use Suggested Starting Points.
4. Basal: six lowest-numbered items correct, or Item 1.
5. Ceiling: six highest-numbered items incorrect, or last item.
6. Present Samples C and D and all test items from the recording.
7. Pause or stop the recording if the subject needs more time to respond.
8. Unless noted, only one-word answers are acceptable. Ask for a one-word answer if subject provides a two-word or longer response.
9. Accept responses that differ in tense or number unless otherwise indicated.
10. Responses that substitute a different part of speech are incorrect unless otherwise indicated.
11. Do not penalize for mispronunciations due to articulation errors, dialect variations, or regional speech patterns.
12. Count all items below the basal as correct.
13. If necessary, present items orally.

Test 16: Editing
1. Begin with Samples A through D for all subjects.
2. Discontinue testing if subject has a score of 0 on four sample items, or Items 1 through 4. Record a score of 0.
3. After samples, use Suggested Starting Points.
4. Basal: six lowest-numbered items correct, or Item 1.
5. Ceiling: six highest-numbered items incorrect, or last item.
6. Subject must clearly indicate where the error is *and* how to correct it to receive credit.

7. Upon request, tell subject individual words. Do not read an entire item.
8. If the subject reads an item aloud and inadvertently corrects the error in context say, "Tell me how to correct the error."
9. If the subject indicates the error without explaining how to correct it say, "How would you correct that mistake?"
10. Test by complete pages.
11. Count all items below the basal as correct.

Test 17: Reading Vocabulary *(Reading-Writing Grw)*

1. Administer all three subtests (17A Synonyms, 17B Antonyms, 17C Analogies) to obtain a score.
2. Start with Sample Items for all subjects on each subtest.
3. After samples, use Suggested Starting Points for each subtest.
4. Basal for each subtest: four lowest-numbered items correct, or Item 1.
5. Ceiling for each subtest: four highest-numbered items incorrect, or last item.
6. Know correct pronunciation of all items.
7. After the samples, do not read any words or items to the subject.
8. Only one-word responses are acceptable, unless noted. If subject gives a two-word or longer response, ask for a one-word answer.
9. Responses that differ in verb tense or number are correct.
10. Responses that substitute a different part of speech are incorrect.
11. Test by complete pages.
12. Count all items below the basal on each subtest as correct.
13. Record errors for further analysis.
14. Record the number correct for each subtest. Use these numbers when entering data in the software program. Add the three numbers to obtain estimated AE/GE scores from the scoring table in the Test Record.

Test 18: Quantitative Concepts *(Mathematics Gq)* (SRB)

1. Use the SRB.
2. Administer both subtests (18A: Concepts, 18B: Number Series) to obtain a score.
3. Use Suggested Starting Points for each subtest.

4. Administer Sample A from 18B: Number Series to all subjects.
5. Basal for 18A: Concepts: four lowest-numbered items correct, or Item 1.
6. Ceiling for 18A: Concepts: four highest-numbered items incorrect, or last item.
7. Basal for 18B: Number Series: three lowest-numbered items correct, or Item 1.
8. Ceiling for 18B: Number Series: three highest-numbered items incorrect, or last item.
9. Repeat any item upon request.
10. Give 1-minute to respond to each item in 18B: Number Series.
11. The examinee must give all parts of an answer to receive credit.
12. Test by complete pages.
13. Count all items below the basal on each subtest as correct.
14. Record the number correct for each subtest. Use these numbers when entering data in the software program. Add the two numbers to obtain estimated AE/GE scores from the scoring table in the Test Record.

Test 19: Academic Knowledge *(Comprehension-Knowledge Gc)*
1. Administer all three subtests (19A: Science, 19B: Social Studies, 19C: Humanities) to obtain a score.
2. Use Suggested Starting Points for each subtest.
3. Basal for each subtest: three lowest-numbered items correct, or Item 1.
4. Ceiling for each subtest: three highest-numbered items incorrect, or last test item.
5. Know the correct pronunciation of all words.
6. Repeat any item upon request.
7. Do not penalize for mispronunciations due to articulation errors, dialect variations, or regional speech patterns.
8. Test by complete pages.
9. Count all items below the basal on each subtest as correct.
10. Record the number correct for each subtest. Use these numbers when entering data in the software program. Add the three numbers to obtain estimated AE/GE scores from the scoring table in the Test Record.

Test 20: Spelling of Sounds *(Auditory Processing Ga)* (Taped) (SRB)
1. Follow taped test procedures. Locate Item 6 before testing.
2. Use the SRB.
3. Use the Suggested Starting Points.
4. Present Samples A through D and Items 1 through 5 orally. Use audio recording for all other items.
5. When letters are printed within slashes, such as /m/, say the most common sound (phoneme) of the letter *not the letter name.*
6. Basal: four lowest-numbered items correct, or Item 1.
7. Ceiling: four highest-numbered items incorrect, or last item.
8. Discontinue testing if subject has a score of 0 on Items 1 through 5. Record a 0 for the test.
9. Responses listed in the Test Book are the *only* correct answers.
10. Do not penalize for reversed letters as long as the letter does not become a new letter.
11. First 5 items require a single letter response and are scored 1 point each.
12. Items 6 to 12 are multi-point items, with one point for each correctly written and sequenced letter or word part. Points are only awarded if the grapheme or word part is in the proper sequence *and* spelled using the most frequent orthographic pattern. For example, 3-point item "gat," response = gate. Score is 2 points. One point for the "g" and one for the "t." No point for the "a" because the "e" at the end changes the vowel sound. See *Examiner's Manual* for scoring guidelines.
13. General principle for scoring: points are deducted for sounds that are not present, sounds that have been altered by extra letters, or sounds out of sequence.
14. Pause or stop audio recording if subject requires additional response time.
15. Replay items upon request.
16. If necessary, present items orally.
17. Count all items below the basal as correct.

Test 21: Sound Awareness *(Auditory Processing Ga)* (Taped)
1. Follow taped test procedures. Locate Sample B for 21B: Deletion before testing.

2. Administer all four subtests (21A: Rhyming, 21B: Deletion, 21C: Substitution, 21D: Reversal) to obtain a score.
3. Administer Sample Items on each subtest to all subjects.
4. Say the most common sound of letters printed with slashes, such as /s/, not the letter name.
5. Begin with Item 1 for all subjects on each subtest.
6. Ceiling for 21A: Rhyming and 21B: Deletion: four highest-numbered items incorrect, or last item.
7. Ceiling for 21C: Substitution & 21D: Reversal: three highest-numbered items incorrect, or last item.
8. Do not penalize for mispronunciations due to articulation errors, dialect variations, or regional speech patterns.
9. Responses must be real words.
10. Administer 21A: Rhyming orally.
11. Administer 21B: Deletion Sample A orally and all other items using the audio recording.
12. Administer 21C: Substitution Samples A and B and Items 1 to 3 orally and all remaining samples and items using the audio recording.
13. Administer 21D: Reversal Sample A and Items 1 to 9 orally and Sample B from the audio recording.
14. Pause or stop the audio recording if the subject requires additional response time.
15. Repeat items upon request by the subject.
16. If necessary, administer items orally.
17. Record errors for further analysis.
18. Record the number correct for each subtest. Use these numbers when entering data in the software program. Add the four numbers to obtain estimated AE/GE scores from the scoring table in the Test Record.

Test 22: Punctuation and Capitalization *(Reading-Writing Grw)* (SRB)
1. Use the SRB.
2. Use Suggested Starting Points.
3. Basal: six lowest-numbered items correct, or Item 1.
4. Ceiling: six highest-numbered items incorrect, or last item.

5. Know pronunciation of all items.
6. Do not penalize for poorly formed or reversed letters as long as the letter does not become a new letter.
7. Items marked with a "P" are punctuation items. Items marked with a "C" are capitalization items.
8. Request printing, but cursive is acceptable.
9. Count all items below the basal as correct.

Writing Evaluation

Handwriting Legibility Scale

1. Use Handwriting Legibility Scale in Appendix C of *Examiner's Manual* to obtain a standardized evaluation of handwriting.
2. Scale ranges from 0 to 100 in 10-point increments, with 0 being illegible and 100 being artistic.
3. Select a representative sample of examinee's handwriting from Test 11 Writing Samples or from other sources.
4. Match appearance of examinee's writing to samples on the scale in Appendix C. Examples are shown for the 10, 30, 50, 70, and 90 ratings.
5. Consider legibility and general appearance when scoring.
6. If the examinee's writing is judged to be between two illustrated levels, assign the value halfway between. For example, if the writing falls between 30 and 50, assign 40. If the writing is closer to 50, then assign 45.
7. Record the rating in the box on the appropriate page in the Test Record.

Handwriting Elements Checklist

1. Use the Handwriting Elements Checklist located in the Test Record to obtain an informal evaluation of handwriting.
2. Select a representative sample of subject's handwriting from Test 11 Writing Samples or from other sources.
3. When evaluating the six elements that affect handwriting quality, identify specific areas of need and record comments relevant to instructional planning.
4. Note any specific errors that detract from legibility.

Writing Evaluation Scale (WES)

1. Use the reproducible WES in Appendix D of the *Examiner's Manual* to evaluate longer, more complex passages of an individual's writing.
2. Select one or more samples of the subject's work, such as a story or essay written in class.
3. Follow the steps in the *Examiner's Manual* for direction in completing the WES.
4. Use the WES as an initial assessment or to monitor progress.

Appendix B

Frequently Asked Questions about the WJ III ACH

This section provides a summary of commonly asked questions and answers. These questions are organized into the categories of general administration, specific test administration and scoring, technical issues, and interpretation.

GENERAL ADMINISTRATION ISSUES

Selective Testing
Question:
Do I need to administer all the tests in the battery?

Answer:
No, the WJ III uses the principle of "selective testing." The WJ III provides a comprehensive set of tests, but it is not intended that all tests be administered to all examinees. Examiners need to determine which tests to administer based on the referral questions or the information they are trying to obtain. A Selective Testing Table, designed to facilitate this process, is located in each Test Easel Book and *Examiner Manual.*

Articulation Errors
Question:
How do I score responses that appear to be errors due to mispronunciation?

Answer:
Do not penalize an examinee for errors resulting from articulation problems or regional or dialectical speech differences. It is important for examiners to be familiar with the speech patterns of the individuals they evaluate.

Timed Tests
Question:
If the examinee finishes before the time limit on timed tests (i.e., Reading Fluency, Math Fluency, Writing Fluency), are they allowed to use the remaining time to check and correct their work?

247

Answer:

Yes. If this behavior is initiated by the examinee, the examiner should allow him or her to continue working until the time limit is reached. Examiners should not "suggest" nor "discourage" this behavior. Early finishers do receive bonus points. However, the examinee does not know this and the examiner should not give this information. The behavior should be noted as qualitative information.

Basals
Question:

If an individual doesn't attain a basal, can the examiner use the raw score or is that test unusable?

Answer:

When the examinee does not obtain a basal, the examiner must test backward until either the basal is established or Item 1 has been administered. Item 1 is then the basal. Unless otherwise specified by the test directions (e.g., cutoff or discontinue rules), the test result is usable. Any points earned by the examinee are counted as the raw score. If the raw score is a zero, then the examiner must determine the usability of that score (see "Zero Raw Scores" question).

False Basals/False Ceilings
Question:

What if the examinee appears to have two basals or two ceilings? Is the first one considered "false" and, therefore, the examiner should ignore it?

Answer:

The concept of "false" basals or ceilings does not apply on the WJ III. In the event of two apparent basals, examiners are directed to use the lowest-numbered one as the true basal. In the event of two apparent ceilings, examiners are directed to use the highest-numbered one as the true ceiling.

Zero Raw Scores
Question:

Can a zero raw score be used?

Answer:

It depends on several factors (e.g., age of the examinee, task required, developmental appropriateness). Examiners must make a determination about the usability of zero raw scores. The *Examiner Manual* gives the following guidance:

> "When a subject receives a score of 0 on any test, one needs to judge whether that score is a true assessment of ability or is a reflection of the subject's inability to perform the task. If the latter is the case, it may be more appropriate to assume that the subject has no score for the test rather than using the score of 0 in further calculation and interpretation. For example, if a third-grade student had a score of 0 on the Editing test, the score may be an accurate representation of the child's ability. However, if a kindergarten student obtained a 0 on the Editing test, the score may indicate that the child has not yet learned to read." (p. 72)

Question:
Why don't I get any standard scores for tests that have a zero raw score?

Answer:
When an individual obtains a zero raw score, derived scores, other than AEs or GEs, are not available. A decision was made not to assign standard scores when an individual is unable to get at least one item correct. However, if the test with a zero raw score contributes to a cluster, all derived scores for the cluster are reported.

Hand-scoring
Question:
Because a scoring program comes with the test kit, does this mean I must use it to get scores? Is there any hand-scoring option?

Answer:
The software program must be used to produce all derived scores. Examiners can obtain estimated AEs and GEs for all tests except Story Recall-Delayed by using the scoring tables in the Test Record. This is the only hand-scoring option available.

Intra-Achievement Discrepancies
Question:
Exactly what clusters must be administered to generate an intra-achievement discrepancy?

Answer:

There are two options. Using just the ACH-STD you can generate intra-achievement discrepancy calculations by administering the Broad Reading, Broad Math, Broad Written Language, and Oral Language-Std. clusters. (This requires administration of Tests 1–11.)

The other option requires administration of tests from the ACH-STD and ACH-EXT batteries: Tests 1 through 11 from the Standard Battery and Tests 13 through 19 from the Extended Battery. This intra-achievement discrepancy calculation is based on nine areas of academic performance: Basic Reading Skills, Reading Comprehension, Math Calculation Skills, Math Reasoning, Basic Writing Skills, Written Expression, Oral Expression, Listening Comprehension, and Academic Knowledge.

Table 4.7 in Chapter 4 of this book, Table 5.6 on page 90 of the *Examiner's Manual,* and Table 1.8 on page 6 of the *Technical Manual* all list the clusters necessary for intra-achievement discrepancy calculations.

Practice Effect
Question:

Many districts routinely administer the Woodcock Language Proficiency Battery (WLPB) and occasionally the Bilingual Verbal Ability Test (BVAT) for initial Speech and Language assessments. Because some of these items are also in the Picture Vocabulary test, isn't there the danger of practice effect?

Answer:

Generally, on *Gc*-type tests there would not be a practice effect. The exception would be if the examinee consulted a dictionary after testing (highly unlikely) or if the examiner inappropriately indicated the correct answers.

However, practice effect is something to consider when administering the BVAT. Because the BVAT requires that any items that the examinee missed in English be readministered in the examinee's first language, this would provide additional information that may be used when the BVAT is administered again in English. It is generally recommended that tests not be readministered for a month or two.

Cognitive Academic Language Proficiency (CALP)
Question:

It appears from page 74 of the *Examiner's Manual* that a CALP score can be derived for Academic Knowledge and some of the oral and written language tests and clusters. Is that true? If so, which tests and clusters yield a CALP score?

Answer:

A CALP level can be obtained for Academic Knowledge and several other clusters including Oral Language-Standard, Oral Language-Extended, Listening Comprehension, Broad Reading, Reading Comprehension, Broad Written Language, and Written Expression.

To display these levels you must select CALP as the additional score in the Program Options section of the software program. The CALP level will appear in the last column of the score report for any of the above clusters that were administered.

If using the CALP level as an indicator of proficiency, any of these clusters can be helpful. However, if trying to use the CALP level as an eligibility score (entrance/exit criteria) then it is recommended that examiners use the broadest clusters available:

- CALP for oral language use Oral Language-Extended
- CALP for reading use Broad Reading
- CALP for written language use Broad Written Language

TEST ADMINISTRATION & SCORING

Test 1: Letter-Word Identification, Form A or Form B
Question:

If the examinee "sounds out" the word first and then pronounces it as the correct, complete word, would that be scored as a 1 or a 0?

Answer:

Because examiners score the last response given, this would be scored a 1. As long as the examinee pronounces the stimulus word as a complete, blended word, it can be scored a 1. However, if an examinee reads the word syllable by syllable or sound by sound and does not pronounce the word as a whole on the last response, it would be scored a 0.

At the first occurrence of a "sounded" out response that is not pronounced as a complete word by the examinee, the examiner should remind the examinee to "first read the word silently and then say the word smoothly." The examiner may only do this once during the entire test.

However, this is not a test of automaticity. Many readers need to use decoding strategies and should not be penalized for sounding out responses prior to pronouncing the complete word. An example is Item 39, Form A-"island." If the examinee first reads "is-land" and then says, "Oh that's 'island'" (pronounced correctly), the examiner scores that a 1. However, if the examinee reads "is-land" and never pronounces it correctly, it is scored a 0.

Question:

I've been told that some examiners mark a response as incorrect if the examinee hasn't given any response or a correct response within a 5-second period. Is that how we should be handling this? Does the examinee only have 5 seconds to respond to each item, or do I have some discretion as an examiner if the examinee appears to need more time?

Answer:

Generally speaking, 5 seconds is enough time for most individuals to respond. However, this is a guideline, not a rule. Examiners must use their judgment. If the examinee has made "no response" after 5 seconds, typically examiners would move on to the next item. However, if the examinee has attempted a response or is working through a decoding strategy, more time can be allowed. Examiners should be reasonable about extending the time and should encourage a response to keep testing moving.

Test 2: Reading Fluency
Question:

Can I let the examinee skip around when taking the test?

Answer:

No, do not allow the examinee to skip around. Examinees may skip an item they don't know, but they should work in sequence. This is important because the scoring is based on "number correct" and "number incorrect" *within the range of attempted items*. Items that fall beyond the last item attempted are not factored into the score. If an examinee skips around, it would be difficult to tell where the range of attempted items begins and ends.

Question:

Why is the score based on "number correct minus number incorrect?" Isn't that unfair to the examinee?

Answer:

This method of scoring is used to reduce the influence of "guessing." Because Reading Fluency requires the individual to mark "yes" or "no" for each item, there is a 50% chance the individual will get each item correct even if he or she doesn't read the item. Therefore, evaluating correct and incorrect responses within the range of attempted items is preferable. The norms are based on this procedure (number correct – number incorrect), so the examinee is not being punished. Remember, examiners need to observe examinees during testing and remind them to read each item and to continue working in sequence if it appears they are randomly circling or skipping around.

Test 3: Story Recall

Question:

Can examinees earn a point for either bolded or paraphrased information? For example, on Story 7 the element is/she saw a **turtle** swimming/. Can a point be earned if the examinee simply recalls "turtle" because that is bolded? Can a point be earned if the examinee does not say "turtle" but does say a paraphrase of the element, such as "she saw something swimming"?

Answer:

If there is bolded information within an element, the only way a point is earned is if the bolded information is recalled exactly. On your example, recall of "turtle" earns a point. Recall of "she saw something swimming" does not earn a point. The only leeway on bolded elements is the use of a very close synonym or derivative, such as "Billy" for "Bill." These would be counted as correct.

Test 4: Understanding Directions

Question:

Can the recording be stopped to allow for extended processing time after each item within a set?

Answer:

Any taped test in the WJ III ACH may be stopped between items if the examinee requires more response time.

Test 5: Calculation

Question:

Can I point out the signs to the examinee if it appears he or she is doing the wrong operation?

Answer:

No, examiners may not point out the signs.

Test 6: Math Fluency

Question:

How should I present the SRB to the examinee? Should I present it folded so that only one page is exposed, or should I present it open to both pages?

Answer:

Although this is not specified in the test materials, it is preferable to present one page at a time. This is how the subject response materials were presented during the standardization.

Test 8: Writing Fluency

Question:

May I read any of these words to the examinee?

Answer:

Yes, you may read any words upon request.

Question:

Do I score the sentence a zero if the examinee misspells one of the stimulus words? It says the stimulus words cannot be changed in any way. Does spelling count?

Answer:

Misspelling or incorrectly copying the stimulus words does not affect the scoring. As long as the examinee does not change the stimulus word to a different part of speech, tense, or number, a misspelling is accepted.

Question:

If the examinee's handwriting is so poor that I cannot decipher the response, may I ask him to read the response to me for scoring purposes?

Answer:

No, examiners may not ask the examinee to read the response aloud for scoring purposes. During the test, examiners should remind the examinee to write more neatly if the writing seems illegible.

Test 9: Passage Comprehension
Question:

On Item 42 of Passage Comprehension-Form A, how would you score the response "instinct"?

Answer:

That response would be scored as correct (1). It was scored as correct in the norming.

Question:

On Item 45 of Passage Comprehension-Form A, how would you score the response "thereby"?

Answer:

That response would be scored as incorrect (0). It was scored as incorrect in the norming. "Therefore" was also scored as incorrect in the norming.

Test 11: Writing Samples
Question:

Should I penalize a response for poor spelling?

Answer:

Spelling errors are not penalized, with two exceptions. First, if spelling is part of the criteria for scoring that item, then examiners would score as directed. Second, if the misspelling makes the word unreadable, then examiners would score the response and omit that word. If the word is critical to the sentence, then points need to be reduced. However, if the word is a minor word, points do not need to be reduced. In Writing Samples, this test primarily scores the quality of the written idea. Other tests measure skills such as spelling.

Question:

How do I score a run-on sentence?

Answer:

Run-on sentences can be scored by selecting the part of the run-on sentence that best meets the task demands and then scoring that part. The rest should be ignored.

Question:

What if the examinee writes several sentences in response to an item? How do I score that?

Answer:

As with run-on sentences, the examiner should select the one sentence that best meets the task demands and score that one sentence. Other sentences should be ignored.

Question:

Can I ask the examinee to read aloud what he or she wrote if I'm having trouble deciphering the writing?

Answer:

No, examiners may not ask examinees to read their responses for the purpose of scoring. If the response is illegible, it must be scored a zero. This test helps examiners evaluate how well the examinee can communicate ideas in writing. It is not a test of oral language. Examiners should remember the ultimate criterion for scoring: if an adult without knowledge of the item content cannot read the response, it should be scored as a zero.

Test 12: Story Recall-Delayed
Question:

When I'm giving Test 3: Story Recall, may I warn the examinees that I will be asking them about these stories later?

Answer:

No, examinees may not be warned. Examiners should be sure to record the date and time they administered Test 3 and Test 12. This information is needed to calculate the delay interval.

Test 13: Word Attack
Question:

How do I score a response that includes all the correct sounds but is not pronounced as a complete word?

Answer:

Responses that are not blended together and pronounced as a complete word are scored as incorrect. On the first occasion that the examinee "sounds out" the word but does not blend it together, the examiner provides a reminder, "First read the word silently and then say the word smoothly." This reminder may be given only once during the entire Word Attack test. Just as in Letter-Word Identification, examiners score the last response the examinee provides.

Test 14: Picture Vocabulary
Question:

What if the examinee provides a response that demonstrates knowledge of the item, but does not ever say the correct answer? For example, for the picture of the whistle, the response is "you blow it." How do I score that?

Answer:

Typically, when an examinee demonstrates knowledge of an item by describing an attribute or function but cannot retrieve the specific word, it is indicative of a word-finding difficulty. They have the knowledge but cannot retrieve it on demand. In these cases, examiners could repeat the question, providing additional response time to retrieve the word. If the correct response is still not retrieved, examiners should score the item 0 and record the incorrect responses for error analysis. The goal is to determine if the errors are due to lack of knowledge or the inability to retrieve that knowledge.

Test 17: Reading Vocabulary
Question:

If the examinee has difficulty reading the stimulus word, may I read it for them and see if they know the synonym or antonym?

Answer:

No, examiners may not read any words for examinees when administering a reading test. This test is measuring the examinee's reading abilities, not the examiner's reading abilities. It is a good idea to evaluate the examinee's oral language abilities, but examiners do not use the reading test for this purpose. They should administer Test 1: Verbal Comprehension from the WJ III COG if they wish to compare oral performance on synonyms, antonyms, and analogies to reading performance on those tasks.

Question:

On 17A: Synonyms, what if the examinee misreads the stimulus word but provides a response that is a correct synonym for the misread word? For example, the stimulus word is "pal" but the examinee misreads it as "pail" and then gives the synonym "bucket." May I score that as correct?

Answer:

No, it would be scored a 0. This is a reading test, not an oral language measure. The examinee's misreading of the stimulus word does not effect scoring. This test only scores the synonym that is supposed to be provided. Examiners should record all errors for analysis.

Test 18B: *Quantitative Concepts-Number Series, Form A*
Question:

How do you solve items 21, 22, and 23 in the Number Series subtest?

Answer:

Just like Analysis-Synthesis in the WJ III COG, examiners don't need to know how to solve the problems. The answers in the Test Book are correct, and examinees will employ various strategies for solving problems. To preserve the integrity of the items, the solutions cannot be revealed here.

Test 20: *Spelling of Sounds*
Question:

To get examinees in my region of the country to spell the nonsense words correctly, I would have to pronounce them as they "sound" here. May I present the items orally, incorporating the regional dialect?

Answer:

No. The tape presents the nonsense words using "standard" English pronunciation that we are all exposed to on radio, television, movies, and so forth. The task is not just to spell the nonsense word as it "sounds," but to spell it using the most common orthographic patterns for that sound. The standard English pronunciations lead to the common orthographic spelling patterns, which is essentially what this test is measuring. Dialect is an "oral language" issue. Spelling of Sounds is a written test requiring "standard" English spellings.

Question:

Do the multi-point items (6–12) have to be scored 0 to count toward the ceiling, or just not receive full value? In other words, if the examinee had zeros on Items 3, 4, and 5 and then got a 1 on Item 6 (1 of 3 possible points), is that a ceiling because four consecutive items are incorrect?

Answer:

No, that would not be a ceiling. The four consecutive items have to be scored 0 to establish the ceiling. The multi-point items (6–12) must be scored 0 to count toward the ceiling. Partial credit means the item is partially correct.

Test 21: Sound Awareness
Question:

Is something wrong with my audiotape on Test 21D: Reversal? Nothing is on it after Sample B, not even any of the test items.

Answer:

Nothing is wrong with your audiotape. The only portion of Test 21D: Sound Awareness-Reversal that is on the tape is Sample B. The instructions in Sample B require the pronunciation of phonemes as the reversal task is explained. Some examiners may have difficulty with this task so Sample B is on tape. However, the items are pronounced as whole words, can easily be pronounced by the examiner, and, therefore, are not on the tape.

TECHNICAL ISSUES

Special Education Students in the Norm Sample
Question:

Are special education students represented in the WJ III norm sample?

Answer:

Special education students are included in the WJ III norm sample to the same extent to which they are represented in the typical classrooms in the nation. Via random sampling of general education classroom rosters, a percentage of special education students that approximates the percent of those special education students who spend the majority of their time in general education classes was obtained.

A number of studies have found that it really doesn't make much difference in the norms if a sample includes or excludes students in special education. One study calculated norms with special education students included and then recalculated the norms with special education students excluded. The parameters used for norm generation (means and standard deviations) hardly changed a fraction of a point. The real value of including exceptional groups in a norm sample is to ensure that the materials work with a large range of students.

Predicted Scores
Question:

Regarding the use of the Oral Language-Extended cluster to do ability/achievement discrepancy analysis, I was surprised to see the predicted score vary with each achievement area. Why doesn't the predicted score based on Oral Language-Extended remain constant?

Answer:

The predicted score is a function of the Oral Language-Extended score and the correlation between it and each specific achievement cluster at that age or grade level. This is true for the other ability score options in the WJ III COG: GIA or Predicted Achievement (aptitude). The predicted scores vary because the correlation varies between the aptitude score and each achievement cluster. Stated differently, oral language correlates differently with different achievement clusters at a given age or grade. Because the correlation is the foundation for the predicted score, the predicted scores will, therefore, vary.

The Oral Language-Extended score does not change, but the predicted score may vary depending on the correlation between oral language and the achievement domain at that particular age or grade. If the correlation were perfect, the predicted score would be identical to the oral language score. For example, if the Oral Language score was 70 and the correlation is 1.00, then the predicted achievement score would be 70.

If the correlation is not perfect, then the predicted achievement score will fall closer to the mean (regression to the mean). For example, if the correlation is .70, the predicted score will be 70% of the distance away from the mean toward the aptitude score. In this case, if the oral language score is 70 the predicted score will be 79.

There are two primary causes for confusion about variation among WJ III predicted scores: (a) Examiners who do not correct for regression use the "ability" score as the predicted score, so they appear to be the same; or (b) examiners who do correct for regression use the same correlation for all areas at all ages or grades and get predicted scores that appear to be unchanging. (Note: Correlations are *not* the same across curriculum areas at the same age or grade.)

INTERPRETATION

Z Scores
Question:

What is a z score and how do I interpret it?

Answer:

A z score is an SS with a mean of 0 and an SD of 1. A z score indicates how far above or below the mean the individual's score falls. A z score of +2.0 indicates the individual scored 2 standard deviations above the mean. A z score of −2.0 indicates the individual scored 2 standard deviations below the mean. In many cases, ±1.5 SD is used as a cut point. The z score is very helpful in these instances because a z of + or −1.5 represents this criterion. Appendix C of this book presents a table that converts z scores to PR and SS ($M = 100, SD = 15$).

Interpretation of the z Score for Test 12: Story Recall-Delayed
Question:

Am I correct in thinking that the Story Recall-Delayed score is a z score reflecting the difference between the immediate and the delayed recall scores rather than an absolute measure of the delayed recall?

Answer:

The z score reported is a discrepancy score—between the expected delayed recall (DR) performance and the actual DR performance. The z scores can be interpreted just like the *SD* scores for the other types of WJ III discrepancies.

A person's DR performance is compared to others with (a) the same age or grade, (b) the same delay interval, and, (c) the same initial score. An "expected" level of performance on a DR test is generated (based on examinee's initial score, age or grade, and delay interval). The person's actual DR performance is then compared to the "expected" DR performance. This is much like an ability/achievement discrepancy.

The objective of the z score on this test is to determine whether the examinee's DR score is within normal limits given age or grade, initial score, and delay interval.

RPI Scores
Question:
What is an RPI and how do I interpret it?

Answer:
An RPI (Relative Proficiency Index) is a criterion-referenced score that predicts level of success on a task and describes functionality. It is expressed as a fraction with the denominator fixed at 90. The denominator represents 90% proficiency, or mastery, by average age- or grade-mates. The numerator changes based on the examinee's performance and ranges from 0 to 100. For example, if a 7th-grade boy obtains an RPI of 45/90 on Letter-Word Identification, this is interpreted to mean that when average seventh graders have 90% proficiency with this type of task, this examinee has only 45% proficiency. In other words, on this task he is half as proficient as "average" grade-mates. Conversely, if the examinee has an RPI of 99/90, it means this examinee is more proficient on the task than average grade-mates.

Comparing WJ-R Scores to WJ III Scores
Question:
How do WJ-R scores compare to WJ III scores?

Answer:
The WJ III test materials do not report correlations between WJ-R and WJ III. Test and cluster composition is different between the batteries, making it impractical to compare scores directly.

Using Batería-R and WJ III
Question:

Can I use Batería-R results with WJ III results?

Answer:

This depends on the purpose for testing. If the examiner is conducting a bilingual evaluation for cognitive ability or oral language, then he or she should not use the Batería-R with the WJ III. When testing cognitive abilities or oral language abilities in two languages, it is important to use parallel tasks, as presented in the Batería-R and the WJ-R. The oral language tasks are not parallel in the Batería-R and the WJ III. However, if the examiner is conducting a monolingual evaluation for an English-dominant individual, then the WJ III can be used.

The WJ III ACH can be used as the achievement measure in a bilingual or monolingual evaluation as parallelism not as critical here. Other factors, such as educational opportunity, must be considered when interpreting achievement results in each language.

Appendix C

Table for Converting z-scores (z) to Percentile Ranks (PR) or Standard Scores (SS)

Table 1. Table for Converting z-scores (z) to Percentile Ranks (PR) or Standard Scores (SS)

Z	PR	SS	Z	PR	SS
+2.33	99	135	0.00	50	100
+2.05	98	131	− .02	49	100
+1.88	97	128	− .05	48	99
+1.75	96	126	− .08	47	99
+1.64	95	125	− .10	46	98
+1.56	94	123	− .13	45	98
+1.48	93	122	− .15	44	98
+1.40	92	121	− .18	43	97
+1.34	91	120	− .20	42	97
+1.28	90	119	− .23	41	97
+1.23	89	118	− .25	40	96
+1.18	88	118	− .28	39	96
+1.13	87	117	− .31	38	95
+1.08	86	116	− .33	37	95
+1.04	85	116	− .36	36	95
+1.00	84	115	− .39	35	94
+ .95	83	114	− .41	34	94
+ .92	82	114	− .44	33	93
+ .88	81	113	− .47	32	93
+ .84	80	113	− .50	31	92
+ .81	79	112	− .52	30	92

Table I. (Continued)

Z	PR	SS	Z	PR	SS
+ .77	78	112	− .55	29	92
+ .74	77	111	− .58	28	91
+ .71	76	111	− .61	27	91
+ .68	75	110	− .64	26	90
+ .64	74	110	− .68	25	90
+ .61	73	109	− .71	24	89
+ .58	72	109	− .74	23	89
+ .55	71	108	− .77	22	88
+ .52	70	108	− .81	21	88
+ .50	69	108	− .84	20	87
+ .47	68	107	− .88	19	87
+ .44	67	107	− .92	18	86
+ .41	66	106	− .95	17	86
+ .39	65	106	−1.00	16	85
+ .36	64	105	−1.04	15	84
+ .33	63	105	−1.08	14	84
+ .31	62	105	−1.13	13	83
+ .28	61	104	−1.18	12	82
+ .25	60	104	−1.23	11	82
+ .23	59	103	−1.28	10	81
+ .20	58	103	−1.34	9	80
+ .18	57	103	−1.40	8	79
+ .15	56	102	−1.48	7	78
+ .13	55	102	−1.56	6	77
+ .10	54	102	−1.64	5	75
+ .08	53	101	−1.75	4	74
+ .05	52	101	−1.88	3	72
+ .02	51	100	−2.05	2	69
0.00	50	100	−2.33	1	65

References

American Educational Research Association (AERA), American Psychological Association (APA), & National Council on Measurement in Education (NCME). (1999). *Standards for educational and psychological testing.* Washington, DC: AERA.

Berninger, V. W. (1990). Multiple orthographic codes: Key to alternative instructional methodologies for developing the orthographic-phonological connections underlying word identification. *School Psychology Review, 19,* 518–533.

Bradley, L., & Bryant, P. E. (1985). *Rhyme and reason in reading and spelling.* Ann Arbor: University of Michigan Press.

Carroll, J. B. (1993). *Human cognitive abilities: A survey of factor-analytic studies.* Cambridge, England: Cambridge University Press.

Cattell, R. B. (1963). Theory for fluid and crystallized intelligence: A critical experiment. *Journal of Educational Psychology, 54,* 1–22.

Cawley, J. F. (1985, February). *Arithmetical word problems and the learning disabled.* Paper presented at the Association for Children with Learning Disabilities, International Conference, San Francisco, CA.

Chall, J. (1983). *Stages of reading development.* New York: McGraw-Hill.

Cruickshank, W. M. (1977). Least-restrictive placement: Administrative wishful thinking. *Journal of Learning Disabilities, 10,* 193–194.

Cummins, J. (1984). *Bilingualism and special education: Issues in assessment and pedagogy.* Austin, TX: PRO-ED.

Diederich, P. B. (1974). *Measuring growth in English.* Urbana, IL: National Council of Teachers of English.

Fleischner, J. E., Garnett, K., & Shepherd, M. J. (1982). Proficiency in arithmetic basic fact computation of learning disabled and nondisabled children. *Focus on Learning Problems in Mathematics 4,* 47–55.

Fletcher, J. M., Francis, D. J., Rourke, B. P., Shaywitz, S. E., & Shaywitz, B. E. (1993). Classification of learning disabilities: Relationships with other childhood disorders. In G. R. Lyon, D. B. Gray, J. F. Kavanagh, & N. A. Krasnegor, (Eds.), *Better understanding learning disabilities: New views from research and their implications for education and public policies* (pp. 27–55). Baltimore: Paul H. Brookes.

Fletcher, J. M., Francis, D. J., Shaywitz, S. E., Lyon, G. R., Foorman, B. R., Stuebing, K. K., & Shaywitz, B. A. (1998). Intelligent testing and the discrepancy model for children with learning disabilities. *Learning Disabilities Research and Practice, 13,* 186–203.

Gerber, M. M., & Hall, R. J. (1987). Information processing approaches to studying spelling deficiencies. *Journal of Learning Disabilities, 20,* 34–42.

Gregg, N. (2001). Written expression disorders. In L. Bailet, A. Bain, & L. Moats (Eds.), *Written language disorders* (2nd ed., pp. 65–98). Austin, TX: PRO-ED.

Gregory, R. J. (1996). *Psychological Testing: History, principles, and applications.* Needham Heights, MA: Allyn & Bacon.

Hasselbring, T. S., Goin L. I., & Bransford, J. D. (1987). Developing automaticity. *Teaching Exceptional Children, 19*(3), 30–33.

Horn, J. L. (1988). Thinking about human abilities. In J. R. Nesselroade & R. B. Cattell (Eds.), *Handbook of multivariate psychology* (2nd ed., pp. 645–865). New York: Academic Press.

Horn, J. L. (1991). Measurement of intellectual capabilities: A review of theory. In K. S. McGrew, J. K. Werder, & R. W. Woodcock (Eds.), *WJ-R technical manual* (pp. 197–232). Itasca, IL: Riverside Publishing.

Horn, J. L., & Cattell, R. B. (1966). Refinement and test of the theory of fluid and crystallized intelligence. *Journal of Educational Psychology, 57,* 253–270.

Huot, B. (1990). The literature of direct writing assessment: Major concerns and prevailing trends. *Review of Educational Research, 60,* 237–263.

Juel, C., Griffith, P. L., & Gough, P. B. (1986). Acquisition of literacy: A longitudinal study of children in first and second grade. *Journal of Educational Psychology, 78,* 243–255.

Kaufman, A. S., & Lichtenberger, E. O. (1999). *Essentials of WAIS-III Assessment.* New York: John Wiley & Sons.

Kirby, J. R., & Becker, L. D. (1988). Cognitive components of learning problems in arithmetic. *Remedial and Special Education, 9*(5), 7–16.

Litowitz, B. E. (1981). Developmental issues in written language. *Topics in Language Disorders, 1*(2), 73–89.

Lyon, G. R. (1996). State of Research. In S. Cramer & W. Ellis (Eds.), *Learning disabilities: Lifelong issues* (pp. 3–61). Baltimore: Brooks Publishing.

Lyon, G. R. (1998). Why reading is not natural. *Educational Leadership, 3,* 14–18.

Mather, N. (1991). *An instructional guide to the Woodcock-Johnson Psycho-Educational Battery-Revised.* New York: John Wiley & Sons.

Mather, N., & Healey, W. C. (1990). Deposing aptitude-achievement discrepancy as the imperial criterion for learning disabilities. *Learning Disabilities: A Multidisciplinary Journal, 1,* 40–48.

Mather, N., & Jaffe, L. (in press). *Woodcock-Johnson III: Recommendations and reports.* New York: John Wiley & Sons.

Mather, N., & Woodcock, R. W. (2001). Examiner's Manual. *Woodcock-Johnson III Tests of Achievement.* Itasca, IL: Riverside Publishing.

McGrew, K. S., & Flanagan, D. P. (1998). *The intelligence test desk reference (ITDR): Gf-Gc Cross-Battery Assessment.* Boston: Allyn & Bacon.

McGrew, K. S. & Woodcock, R. W. (2001). Technical Manual. *Woodcock-Johnson III.* Itasca, IL: Riverside Publishing.

McGrew, K. S., & Hessler, G. L. (1995). The relationship between the WJ-R Gf-Gc cognitive clusters and mathematics achievement across the life-span. *Journal of Psychoeducational Assessment, 13,* 21–38.

Meltzer, L. J. (1994). Assessment of learning disabilities: The challenge of evaluating cognitive strategies and processes underlying learning. In G. R. Lyon (Ed.), *Frames of reference for the assessment of learning disabilities: New views on measurement issues* (pp. 571–606). Baltimore: Paul H. Brookes.

Novick, B. Z., & Arnold, M. M. (1988). *Fundamentals of clinical child neuropsychology.* Philadelphia: Grune & Stratton.

Perfetti, C. (1985). *Reading ability.* New York: Oxford University Press.

Rack, J. P., Snowling, M., & Olson, R. (1992). The nonword reading deficit in developmental dyslexia: A review. *Reading Research Quarterly, 27,* 28–53.

Rasch, G. (1960). *Probablistic models for some intelligence and attainment tests.* Copenhagen, Denmark: Danish Institute for Educational Research.

Schrank, F. A., Flanagan, D. P., Woodcock, R. W., & Mascolo, J. (in press). *Essentials of the WJ III Tests of Cognitive Abilities Assessment.* New York: John Wiley & Sons.

Schrank, F. A., & Woodcock, R. W. (2001). *WJ III Compuscore and Profiles Program* [Computer software]. Itasca, IL: Riverside Publishing.

Siegel, L. S. (1989). IQ is irrelevant to the definition of learning disabilities. *Journal of Learning Disabilities, 22,* 469–479.

Stanovich, K. E. (1982). Individual differences in the cognitive processes of reading: I. Word decoding. *Journal of Learning Disabilities, 15,* 485–493.

Stanovich, K. E. (1986). Matthew effects in reading: Some consequences of individual differences in the acquisition of literacy. *Reading Research Quarterly, 21,* 360–406.

Stanovich, K. E. (1988). Explaining the differences between the dyslexic and the garden-variety poor reader: The phonological-core-variable-difference model. *Journal of Learning Disabilities, 21,* 590–604, 612.

Stanovich, K. E. (1991a). Conceptual and empirical problems with discrepancy definitions of reading disability. *Learning Disability Quarterly, 14,* 269–280.

Stanovich, K. E. (1991b). Discrepancy definitions of reading disability: Has intelligence led us astray? *Reading Research Quarterly, 26,* 7–29.

Stanovich, K. E. (1994). Are discrepancy-based definitions of dyslexia empirically defensible? In K. P. van den Bos, L. S. Siegel, D. J. Bakker, & D. L. Share (Eds.), *Current directions in dyslexia research* (pp. 15–30). Alblasserdam, Holland: Swets & Zeitlinger.

Swanson, H. L., & Hoskyn, M. (1998). Experimental intervention research on students with learning disabilities: A meta-analysis of treatment outcomes. *Review of Educational Research, 68,* 277–321.

Steeves, K. J. (1983). Memory as a factor in the computational efficiency of dyslexic children with high abstract reasoning ability. Annals of Dyslexia, 33, 141–152. Baltimore: International Dyslexia Association.

Vygotsky, L. S. (1978). *Mind in society: The development of higher psychological processes.* Cambridge, MA: Harvard University Press.

Wagner, R. K., & Torgesen, J. K. (1987). The nature of phonological processing and its causal role in the acquisition of reading skills. *Psychological Bulletins, 101,*(2), 192–212.

Wendling, B. J., & Mather, N. (2001). *WJ III Tests of Achievement Examiner Training Workbook.* Itasca, IL: Riverside Publishing.

Wiig, E., & Semel, E. (1984). *Language assessment and intervention for the learning disabled.* Columbus, OH: Charles E. Merrill.

Wise, B. W., & Olson, R. K. (1991). Remediating reading disabilities. In J. E. Obrzut & G. W. Hynd (Eds.), *Neuropsychological foundations of learning disabilities: A handbook of issues, methods, and practice* (pp. 631–658). San Diego, CA: Academic Press.

Wolf, M. (1991). Naming-speed and reading: The contribution of the cognitive neurosciences. *Reading Research Quarterly, 26*(2), 123–141.

Woodcock, R. W. (1978). *Development and standardization of the Woodcock-Johnson Psycho-Educational Battery.* Itasca, IL: Riverside Publishing.

Woodcock, R. W. (1987). *Woodcock Reading Mastery Tests-Revised.* Circle Pines, MN: American Guidance Service.

Woodcock, R. W. (1990). Theoretical foundations of the WJ-R measures of cognitive ability. *Journal of Psychoeducational Assessment, 8,* 231–258.

Woodcock, R. W., & Dahl, M. N. (1971). *A common scale for the measurement of person ability and test item difficulty.* (AGS Paper No. 10). Circle Pines, MN: American Guidance Service.

Woodcock, R. W., & Johnson, M. B. (1977). *Woodcock-Johnson Psycho-Educational Battery.* Itasca, IL: Riverside Publishing.

Woodcock, R. W., & Johnson, M. B. (1989). *Woodcock-Johnson Psycho-Educational Battery-Revised.* Itasca, IL: Riverside Publishing.

Woodcock, R. W., McGrew, K. S., & Mather, N. (2001a). *Woodcock-Johnson III.* Itasca, IL: Riverside Publishing.

Woodcock, R. W., McGrew, K. S., & Mather, N. (2001b). *Woodcock-Johnson III Tests of Achievement.* Itasca, IL: Riverside Publishing.

Woodcock, R. W., McGrew, K. S., & Mather, N. (2001c). *Woodcock-Johnson III Tests of Cognitive Abilities.* Itasca, IL: Riverside Publishing.

Woodcock, R. W., & Muñoz-Sandoval, A. F. (1996). *Batería Woodcock-Muñoz: Pruebas de aprovechamiento-Revisada.* Itasca, IL: Riverside Publishing.

Wright, B. D., & Stone, M. H. (1979). *Best test design.* Chicago: MESA Press.

Annotated Bibliography

Carroll, J. B. (1993). *Human cognitive abilities: A survey of factor-analytic studies*. Cambridge, England: Cambridge University Press.

This seminal work had a significant impact on the design of the WJ III. It reviews about 1,500 references covering the last 50 to 60 years of factor analytic research. Carroll used exploratory methods, letting the data emerge. This work resulted in Carroll's Three-Stratum Theory of Intelligence. Carroll's work was combined with the work of Raymond Cattell and John Horn to form the CHC theory, which underlies the WJ III.

Flanagan, D. P., Ortiz, S. O., Alfonso, V. C., & Mascolo, J. T. (in press). *The Achievement Test Desk Reference (ATDR): A comprehensive framework for LD determination*. Boston: Allyn & Bacon.

The ATDR provides psychometric, qualitative, and theoretical information for over 50 recent achievement tests and batteries. In addition, the authors of the ATDR present an operational definition of learning disability (LD) and demonstrate how to use both achievement and cognitive ability tests within a comprehensive framework for LD determination based on this definition. Numerous tables, charts, summary sheets, and worksheets organized around the CHC theory and the seven academic areas of LD listed under the federal definition facilitate comprehensive and selective assessment.

Mather, N. (1991). *An instructional guide to the Woodcock-Johnson Psycho-Educational Battery-Revised*. New York: John Wiley & Sons.

Although based on the WJ-R, this book provides a wealth of information about instructional strategies and approaches for the academic areas covered in the test. Because the WJ III covers the same broad academic areas, the information is still applicable. Various instructional approaches for remediating each academic area are explained. Sample psychoeducational reports are included in the Appendix. The intent of the book is to help examiners who use the WJ-R translate test results into meaningful information for program development. While the cognitive tests are included, the primary focus is on the achievement tests.

Mather, N., & Jaffe, L. (in press). *Woodcock-Johnson III: Recommendations and reports*. New York: John Wiley & Sons.

This book is intended to serve as a resource for evaluators using the WJ III in educational and clinical settings. Its purpose is to assist examiners in preparing and writing psychoeducational reports for individuals of all ages. It covers both the cognitive and achievement batteries.

Mather, N., & Woodcock, R. W. (2001). Examiner's Manual. *Woodcock-Johnson III Tests of Achievement.* Itasca, IL: Riverside Publishing.

The manual comes as part of the WJ III ACH test kit. It provides a description of the tests and clusters in the WJ III ACH, as well as information about administering, scoring, and interpreting the test. The Scoring Guide for Writing Samples, the Handwriting Legibility Scale, and the reproducible Writing Evaluation Scale are included in the Appendixes.

McGrew, K. S. & Woodcock, R. W. (2001). Technical Manual. *Woodcock-Johnson III.* Itasca, IL: Riverside Publishing.

This manual comes as part of the WJ III ACH test kit. It provides information about the design criteria for the complete WJ III, development of the norms, and the standardization procedures. This manual presents reliability and validity studies and covers both the cognitive and achievement batteries. Numerous statistical tables are included for clinicians and researchers.

Schrank, F. A., Flanagan, D. P., Woodcock, R. W., & Mascolo, J. (in press). *Essentials of the WJ III Tests of Cognitive Abilities Assessment.* New York: John Wiley & Sons.

This is a companion book covering the administration, scoring, and interpretation of the WJ III COG. For those professionals using the cognitive battery with the WJ III ACH, this book will provide additional insights for interpretation.

INDEX

Basic Reading Skills cluster, 120–121
Basic Writing Skills cluster, 138
Behavior disorder. *See* Accommodations, behavioral/attention disorders
Bilingualism. *See* English language learners
Broad Mathematics cluster, 133
Broad Reading cluster, 120
Broad Written Language cluster, 137

Calculation test:
  administration, 50–51
  fine points, 234
  interpretation, 128–130
  scoring, 92
CALP. *See* Cognitive Academic Language Proficiency (CALP)
Carroll, John. *See* CHC theory
Case report, format of, 191–192
  background information, 192–193, 209–210, 222–223
  behavioral observations, 194, 210, 223–224
  previous evaluations, 193–194
  reason for referral, 192, 209, 222
  recommendations, 207–209, 220–222, 229–230
  test results and interpretation, 194–207, 210–219, 224–229
Case studies:
  Alison (math disability), 222–230
  Raymond (reading disability), 192–209
  Stanley (written language disability), 209–222
Cattell, Raymond. *See* CHC theory
Cattell-Horn-Carroll theory of cognitive abilities. *See* CHC theory
Ceilings, 36–40. *See also individual tests*
CHC theory, 15, 17–19, 111, 113. *See also specific abilities*
Clinical applications, 166–189
  and generalized low/high performance, 181–183

and learning disabilities, 166–169, 178–179
  math, 176–178
  oral language, 179–181
  reading, 169–173
  written language, 173–176
Clusters. *See specific clusters*
Cognitive Academic Language Proficiency (CALP), 105–106, 110
Comprehension-Knowledge *(Gc)*, 113, 122, 124–125, 127–128, 130, 134, 139. *See also* CHC theory
Computer scoring. *See* WJ III Compuscore and Profiles Program
Confidence bands, 107–108, 144–146
Co-norming, 3, 22, 159
  best practice, 22
Content, of tests and clusters, 5–8, 11–13. *See also individual tests and clusters*
Cross-academic clusters, 139–141
Crystallized Intelligence. *See* Comprehension-Knowledge *(Gc)*

Delayed recall, 124
Developmental delay. *See* Performances generalized low/high
Disabilities:
  diagnostic indicators of, 187–188
  learning, 33, 117, 166–169, 178–179
  See also specific disabilities
Discrepancies:
  ability/achievement (*see* Ability/achievement discrepancy)
  interpretation of, 147–155, 183–187
  intra-ability, 148–152
  intra-achievement, 149–152, 183–185
  oral language/achievement, 153–154, 185–187
  significance of, 147–148
Dyscalculia, 176. *See also* Mathematics
Dysgraphia, 174–175, 193. *See also* Written Language
Dyslexia, 141, 171–173. *See also* Reading

Acknowledgments

We would like to express our appreciation to several individuals who have contributed to or assisted in the preparation of this book.

Our appreciation is extended to our friend and colleague, Barbara Read, for her contribution of the Stanley case study.

Since its publication, examiners trying to learn the WJ III have asked numerous questions. We are thankful for those asking questions as this has helped us learn ourselves and shape information presented in this book.

Finally, the contributions of Tracey Belmont and the rest of the staff at John Wiley are gratefully acknowledged.